# Contemporary Japan

## Contemporary States and Societies

This series provides lively and accessible introductions to key countries and regions of the world, conceived and designed to meet the needs of today's students. The authors are all experts with specialist knowledge of the country or region concerned and have been chosen also for their ability to communicate clearly to a non-specialist readership. Each text has been specially commissioned for the series and is structured according to a common format.

*Published*

**Contemporary India**
Katharine Adeney
and Andrew Wyatt

**Contemporary Russia** (2nd edition)
Edwin Bacon

**Contemporary South Africa** (2nd edition)
Anthony Butler

**Contemporary France**
Helen Drake

**Contemporary America** (3rd edition)
Russell Duncan
and Joseph Goddard

**Contemporary Japan** (3rd edition)
Duncan McCargo

**Contemporary Britain** (3rd edition)
John McCormick

**Contemporary Latin America** (3rd edition)
Ronaldo Munck

**Contemporary Ireland**
Eoin O'Malley

*Forthcoming*

**Contemporary Spain**
Paul Kennedy

**Contemporary Asia**
John McKay

**Contemporary China**
Kerry Brown

*Also planned*

**Contemporary Africa**
**Contemporary Europe**
**Contemporary Germany**

Contemporary States and Societies
Series Standing Order
ISBN 978–0–333–75402–3 hardcover
ISBN 978–0–333–80319–6 paperback
(outside North America only)

You can receive future titles in this series as they are published by placing a standing order. Please contact your bookseller or, in the case of difficulty, write to us at the address below with your name and address, the title of the series and one of the ISBNs quoted above.

Customer Services Department, Palgrave Ltd
Houndmills, Basingstoke, Hampshire RG21 6XS, England, UK

# Contemporary Japan

**Third Edition**

Duncan McCargo

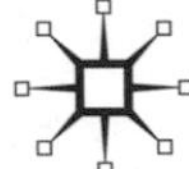



First edition 2000
Second edition 2004
Third edition 2013

Published by
PALGRAVE MACMILLAN

Palgrave Macmillan in the UK is an imprint of Macmillan Publishers Limited, registered in England, company number 785998, of Houndmills, Basingstoke, Hampshire RG21 6XS.

Palgrave Macmillan in the US is a division of St Martin's Press LLC, 175 Fifth Avenue, New York, NY 10010.

Palgrave Macmillan is the global academic imprint of the above companies and has companies and representatives throughout the world.



ISBN 978-0-230-24868-7 hardback
ISBN 978-0-230-24869-4 paperback

This book is printed on paper suitable for recycling and made from fully managed and sustained forest sources. Logging, pulping and manufacturing processes are expected to conform to the environmental regulations of the country of origin.

A catalogue record for this book is available from the British Library.

A catalog record for this book is available from the Library of Congress.

10 9 8 7 6 5 4 3 2 1
22 21 20 19 18 17 16 15 14 13

Printed in China

# Contents

# List of Illustrative Materials

## Figures



## Tables



## Boxes

**Maps**



**Illustrations**

# Preface and Acknowledgements

I am an Asia specialist, but a Japan generalist; I have spent three years living and teaching in Japan, but I have no academically useful knowledge of Japanese. This book is largely a synthesis of English-language secondary sources, drawing on many years of teaching Japanese politics to undergraduates at the University of Leeds. With a non-specialist readership in mind, I have taken a couple of contentious editorial decisions. Macrons (used to indicate vowel length) have been omitted from Japanese words, and Japanese names have been written in the western style, with the family name second (for example, Ichiro Ozawa, rather than Ozawa Ichiro).

I should like to repeat the thanks I have offered in previous editions to all of my friends and former colleagues in Japan, especially Wayne Wilson, and to everyone else who has supported my work. Stephanie Winters helped me to see Japan through fresh eyes during our visit in 2009. Special thanks are due to my research assistants, Kanako Hiraoka, Jacqueline Hicks, and Chunyao Yi, for earlier editions. While preparing this third edition, I benefited greatly from my discussions with Gerald Curtis, Reto Hoffmann, Hisahiro Kondoh, Aiko Mizumori, Haruka Matsumoto and Paul Waley, among others. Interviews cited in Chapter 6 were originally conducted by Lee Hyon-suk for a previous joint publication (McCargo and Lee, 2010). This time I was very ably assisted by Saya Kurita and by Yoshimi Onishi, who created all the tables. It was my privilege to finalize the manuscript at the Weatherhead East Asian Institute, Columbia University: warm thanks are due to my hosts there, especially Myron Cohen, Carol Gluck, Waichi Ho, and Andrew Nathan. Many thanks to Keith Povey for his editorial work on all three editions, and to Anthony Horton for preparing the index.

Steven Kennedy has been a very supportive publisher since he originally commissioned the first edition of this book more than fifteen years ago. Helen Caunce has been a great help with the third edition. As before, the mistakes are all mine.

*New York* DUNCAN MCCARGO

# List of Abbreviations

| | |
|---|---|
| APEC | Asia Pacific Economic Cooperation |
| ASEAN | Association of Southeast Asian Nations |
| ASEM | Asia-Europe Summit Meeting |
| CM | Citizens' Movement |
| DLP | Democratic Liberal Party |
| DP | Democratic Party |
| DSP | Democratic Socialist Party |
| EAEC | East Asian Economic Caucus |
| EU | European Union |
| GATT | General Agreement on Tariffs and Trade |
| GDP | Gross Domestic Product |
| GNP | Gross National Product |
| IMF | International Monetary Fund |
| JCP | Japan Communist Party |
| JDP | Japan Democratic Party |
| JET | Japan Exchange and Teaching programme |
| JLP | Japan Liberal Party |
| JNP | Japan New Party |
| JRP | Japan Renewal Party |
| JSP | Japan Socialist Party |
| LDC | Less Developed Country |
| LLDC | Least among Less-Developed Countries |
| LNG | Liquefied Natural Gas |
| LDP | Liberal Democratic Party |
| LP | Liberal Party |
| MITI | Ministry of International Trade and Industry |
| MTDPE | Mid-Term Defence Programme Estimate |
| NAFTA | North American Free Trade Association |
| NDP | National Defence Programme outline |
| NFP | New Frontier Party |
| NGOs | Non-Governmental Organizations |
| NHK | Japan's semi-governmental broadcasting agency |

| | |
|---|---|
| NIC | Newly Industrialized Country |
| ODA | Overseas Development Aid |
| OECD | Organisation for Economic Co-operation and Development |
| PISA | Programme for International Student Assessment |
| PKO | Peace-Keeping Operation |
| SCAP | Supreme Commander for the Allied Powers |
| SDF | Self-Defence Forces |
| SDP(J) | Social Democratic Party (of Japan) |
| TEPCO | Tokyo Electric Power Company |
| TPP | Trans-Pacific Partnership |

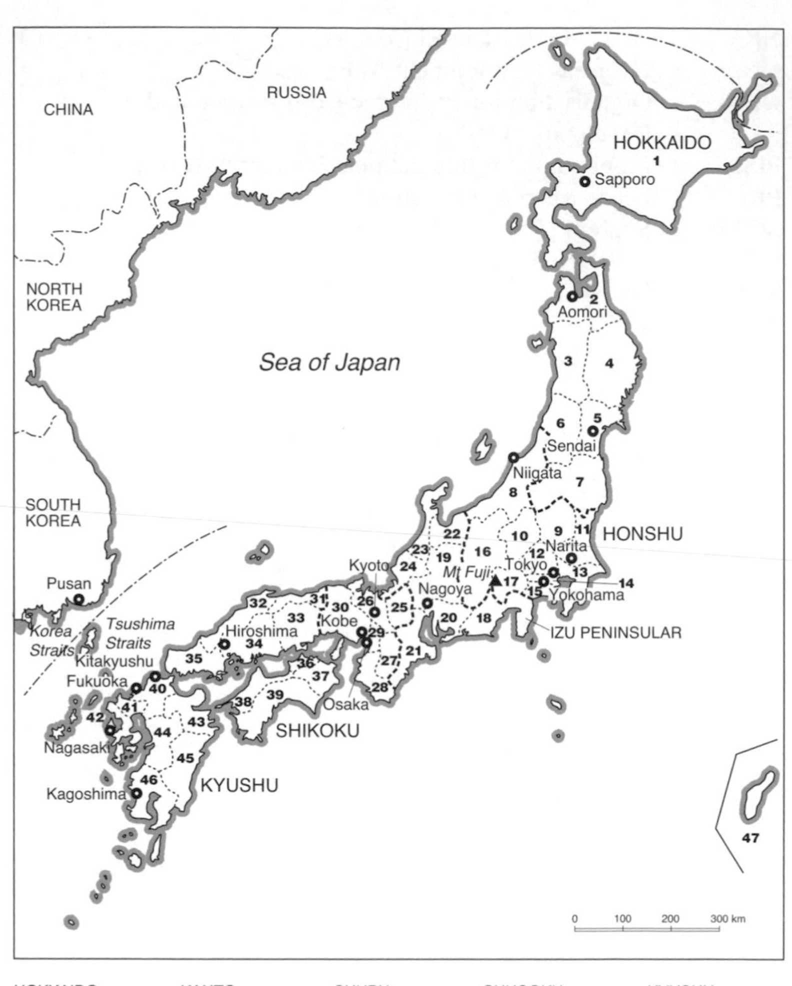


HOKKAIDO
1 Hokkaido

TOHOKU
2 Aomori
3 Akita
4 Iwate
5 Miyagi
6 Yamagata
7 Fukushima

KANTO KOSHINETSU
8 Niigata
9 Tochigi
10 Gunma
11 Ibaraki
12 Saitma
13 Chiba
14 Tokyo
15 Kanagawa
16 Nagano
17 Yamanashi

CHUBU
18 Shizuoka
19 Gifu
20 Aichi
21 Mie
22 Toyama
23 Ishikawa
24 Fukui

KINKI
25 Shiga
26 Kyoto
27 Nara
28 Wakayama
29 Osaka
30 Hyogo

CHUGOKU
31 Tottori
32 Shimane
33 Okayama
34 Hiroshima
35 Yamaguchi

SHIKOKU
36 Kagawa
37 Tokushima
38 Ehime
39 Kochi

KYUSHU
40 Fukuoka
41 Saga
42 Nagasaki
43 Oita
44 Kumamoto
45 Miyazaki
46 Kagoshima

47 Okinawa

**Map of Japan**

# 1

# Introduction: Themes and Debates

You are now entering contested territory. The nature of contemporary Japan is hotly debated by specialists and observers, both inside and outside Japan. Whether the topic is Japan's domestic politics, international relations or economic order, apparently simple questions such as 'Is Japan a liberal democracy?', 'Is Japan a superpower?', or 'Does Japan have a free market economy?' will provoke radically different answers from different scholars and analysts. Facts about Japan are often buried under different interpretations and perspectives. When reading books or articles about contemporary Japan, we need to be constantly alert to the biases and preferences of their authors. This book starts from the assumption that in order to understand much about contemporary Japan, we need to understand the alternative perspectives to be found in the literature on Japan.

Accordingly, this book will invite you to view Japan from three alternative perspectives, which will be referred to regularly in each chapter: mainstream, revisionist and culturalist. In reality, of course, there is a much wider range of perspectives, which can be used to explain and to understand contemporary Japan, and many individual students of Japanese society and politics draw on elements of more than one. The three approaches presented here, however, provide a clear indication of the extent of debate and its range and character.

Japan is currently in the throes of a new wave of national soul-searching, brought on by the terrible events of 11 March 2011: a huge earthquake, a terrible tsunami, and then the worst nuclear crisis since Chernobyl. These events have so far left nearly 20,000 people dead or missing, have shaken popular faith in bureaucrats, business leaders and politicians, and clearly demand a renewed sense of collective purpose. So far, the verdict remains out on whether post-tsunami Japan is responding effectively to the challenges created by the triple disasters of March 2011. To a large extent, opinions on this issue vary based on the perspective of the commentator.

## The mainstream perspective

The first approach might best be described as the 'mainstream' perspective, and is generally the most common perspective to be found in the literature about Japan. Using methods derived from the sub-discipline of comparative politics, the mainstream perspective emphasizes points of comparison between Japan and other societies. Indeed, some books written from this perspective explicitly compare Japan with one or more other countries, often including the USA. More commonly, however, the comparisons are implicit rather than explicit. Japan is treated as having economic, political and social systems that are broadly similar to those of other developed countries. Typically, Japan is seen by mainstream scholars as a fully functioning liberal democracy with a free market economy (albeit with minor variations).

Many scholars who adopt this perspective are based in the USA. This is unsurprising on one level, since the United States contains the largest concentration of Japan specialists outside Japan itself. At the same time, the American Occupation of Japan at the end of the Second World War was an immensely important factor in shaping the course of Japanese history. The United States attempted to reshape Japan into something more closely resembling its own image, and American officials and scholars have consistently sought to emphasize the success of the Occupation project and the extent to which its goals have been realized. The mainstream perspective on contemporary Japan is partly a continuation of the philosophy and objectives of the US occupation. At the same time, the enormous differences between Japan and the United States raise serious questions about the utility of comparing the two countries.

There are strong arguments for comparing Japan with various European countries (which share such features as constitutional monarchies, parliamentary systems, multi-party systems, centralized education systems, capital-city dominance, and economic interventionism by the state). Even more salient arguments exist for comparing Japan with other Asian territories such as South Korea and Taiwan (economies characterized by state-led development), or Thailand and the Philippines (political orders characterized by factionalism and structural corruption).

The scholars most closely identified with the mainstream approach have been affiliated with Harvard University. One of their gurus was the historian and former US Ambassador to Japan, Edwin O. Reischauer, author of numerous books including *The Japanese* and *The Japanese Today*. Reischauer promoted a positive image of Japanese society, politics and culture, and played an important role in maintaining the strong relationship between the two countries which persists to this day. He argued that although there were many differences between the Japanese political system and the politics of western countries, Japan 'appears to measure up quite well as an effective system of democratic rule' (Reischauer, 1977: 327). In *Japan as Number One*, his colleague Ezra Vogel (1979) sought to present Japan, not simply as a successful imitator of American values and systems, but as a state which was succeeding in displacing the USA from a position of industrial and political dominance.

Many American political scientists (for example, Ellis Krauss, Bradley Richardson, Scott Flanagan, Gerald Curtis and John Creighton Campbell) have adopted a broadly positive view of Japan which could well be described as mainstream, and the themes of their work are shared by well-known Japanese counterparts such as Takashi Inoguchi. They see Japanese politics as pluralistic, characterized by free elections, genuine political parties and open public debate. Japanese society is typically depicted as meritocratic, stable and characterized by limited class conflict. Vogel and others have even argued that other countries need to 'learn from Japan' in order to increase their levels of economic productivity, to limit social inequalities, and reduce problems such as drug abuse and crime. The mainstream approach reached its zenith of popularity during the 1980s, when Japan's extraordinary economic growth seemed to pose a real challenge to the global hegemony of the West, and especially the position of the United States. However, some mainstream analysts have been guilty of exaggerating the successes of Japan, glossing over the shortcomings of the Japanese system.

## The revisionist approach

The late Chalmers Johnson – a leading 'revisionist' – argued that the majority of American Japan experts:

> spend their time not studying the Japanese state itself but looking for candidates within the Japanese political system who, they hope, might one day assume political direction over the activities of the state. If they could find such a person or group, this would help confirm the American proposition that democratic politics inevitably conforms to the pluralist paradigm. (Johnson, 1995: 14)

If the mainstream perspective sometimes fails to see the darker side of Japan, the revisionist perspective often concentrates on little else. Revisionists typically see Japan as a different sort of country altogther from western liberal democracies. They view Japan as operating according to distinctive principles of its own: typically, they regard it as undemocratic, and as characterized by a deeply flawed political system that features a considerable degree of structural corruption. They view Japan's economic system as far more state-led and far less open to outside competition than mainstream analysts typically acknowledge. Some revisionists go so far as to see Japan as a kind of 'soft authoritarian' state, characterized by repressive elements of social and political conformity. Revisionists typically view Japan's relations with the rest of the world with a sceptical eye, arguing that Japan cynically manipulates its trade, aid and defence policies for its own advantage. Indeed, the revisionist view of Japan became popular during the intense trade frictions between Japan and the USA in the 1980s. Pro-Japan commentators labelled revisionist scholars and analysts 'Japan-bashers', and some revisionist themes were taken up by American politicians who sought to play to domestic electorates (such as the congressman who put a sledgehammer to various Japanese appliances).

Nevertheless, most revisionists themselves reject the 'Japan-basher' label, and it is difficult to generalize about the perspectives of so-called revisionists, who constitute a heterogeneous group with divergent views. They range from Chalmers Johnson, a political economist and Asia specialist, to Karel van Wolferen, a Dutch journalist, former US trade negotiator Clyde Prestowitz, and James Fallows, an American journalist. They also include scholars who have arrived at similarly critical views of Japanese society from a Marxist-influenced perspective, including Gavan McCormack and Yoshio Sugimoto. Stockwin lumps these (and other) critical scholars together under the catch-all category of 'controversial approaches' (Stockwin, 2008: 34–5, 260).

A common feature of the revisionists is their collective exasperation with what they see as the successful public relations of the Japanese government, and the unduly sympathetic line on Japan adopted by mainstream writers and academics. Partly because of their sense of adopting a minority position that challenges academic orthodoxies, the revisionists have sometimes been unnecessarily combative and provocative in their writings. At the same time, writers such as Johnson and van Wolferen produce books and articles which are far more readable than the relatively turgid output of some mainstream scholars, and their work is often highly persuasive, not to say seductive.

## The culturalist perspective

To paraphrase L. P. Hartley: 'Japan is a foreign country: they do things differently there.' To study Japanese politics (or, indeed, the politics of any Asian country) it is necessary to understand that what people raised in a western society take to be the normal rules of social behaviour do not necessarily apply. Adherents of the culturalist perspective typically seek to explain the nature of Japanese politics, economy and society primarily by reference to cultural differences. Many of the originators of this perspective were American anthropologists (such as Ruth Benedict and John Embree); however, their arguments have been elaborated and developed by numerous Japanese scholars, giving rise to a vast literature on 'Japaneseness' which typically accentuated the supposedly distinctive and even unique character of Japan. Dale has strongly criticized this approach, which he reduces to three core assumptions: a belief that the Japanese possess 'a culturally and socially homogeneous racial identity' which has not changed since prehistoric times; that the Japanese are entirely different from other peoples; and that they proceed from an intensely nationalistic basis which is hostile to non-Japanese sources (Dale, 1986: i). This approach is more difficult to grasp than either the mainstream or the revisionist approaches. At the core of the culturalist perspective is a stress on the Japanese as 'groupist' rather than individualist, an approach often referred to as the 'group model' of Japanese society.

A problem with the so-called 'group model' is that it can suggest a simplistic image of a harmonious, virtually conflict-free Japanese society. Many works by Japanese scholars – a genre known as '*nihon(jin)ron* literature' – emphasize the supposedly 'unique' nature of the Japanese 'miracle'. Among the most notorious is Tadanobu Tsunoda's *The Japanese Brain: Uniqueness and Universality,* which argues that Japanese brains function differently from those of non-Japanese (Tsunoda, 1985). Other books 'explain' Japaneseness by reference to characteristics such as the Japanese 'non-carnivorous' diet, and (a very widely believed argument) the rice agriculture theory of Japanese society. Although these examples of *nihon(jin)ron* literature differ in their answers to the enigma of Japaneseness, they belong to the same strain of popular scholarship, a scholarship of admiration for Japan.

The assumptions behind this 'group model' literature need to be teased out and questioned. Harumi Befu has argued that Japanese groups are not nearly so internally harmonious as has been suggested. In particular, Japanese education is ruthlessly competitive, especially at senior high-school level when pupils prepare to take entrance examinations for the prestigious universities (Befu, 1980). Befu also challenges the idea that there is no class conflict in Japan, arguing that the Japanese have their own 'native concepts' of social classes, which testify to the existence of horizontal strata in Japanese society.

Mainstream and revisionist scholars may themselves make use of culturalist arguments: some mainstream scholars refer to Japanese culture as one of the sources of Japan's political, social and economic virtues. Revisionist scholars are typically more critical of culturalist interpretations. Yoshio Sugimoto has argued that what he calls the 'learn from Japan' school has a built-in elite bias, concentrating on examples from government and big business while neglecting less impressive areas of the Japanese order. Sugimoto questions whether Japan really is a consensual society, asking firstly 'Who defines the content of consensus?', and secondly 'In whose interests is consensus formed?' He suggests that:

> Groupism is itself an explicit ideology directly communicated to subordinate groups in an attempt to routinise the obedience of individuals to the so-called needs of the company, school, or state. (Sugimoto, 1986: 68)

Whilst such criticisms of the group model challenge over-idealistic views of Japan, the existence of a potential for competition and conflict between individual Japanese, between employees and employers, and between different social classes, offers the possibility of more dynamic interpretations of Japanese politics. Instead of a static, harmonious and self-sustaining system, Japanese politics is seen as a system of competing interests.

At the same time, some revisionists have flirted with cultural explanations in their analyses of contemporary Japan: Karel van Wolferen, for all his criticisms of the Japanese order and his emphasis on the political origins of culture, appears to regard Japan as a unique country, distinctively characterized by a multi-tentacled 'System', rather than a conventional state. Although it is possible to differentiate between mainstream, revisionist and culturalist approaches, there are numerous points of intersection, overlap, and crossover between these three perspectives.

## The country and its people

What is Japan? Our images of other countries are shaped by a variety of sources, including popular culture, consumer goods, art, music, literature, and our (often hazy) understandings or misunderstandings of history. Japan is often seen as remote and rather mysterious. Picturesque scenes of *geisha* and Mount Fuji are typically mixed up with high-tech images of robot-like factory workers, and bullet trains. Whilst these images contain elements of truth, they are also stereotypes. Westerners frequently view the disparate facets of Japan as highly bizarre and contradictory: a favourite image is the salesman in the electronics store, totting up a customer's bill on a wooden abacus. Japan is seen as a place where tradition and novelty, the ancient and the modern, the very simple and the highly sophisticated, exist side-by-side in a kind of profound contradiction, which the Japanese are uniquely able to create and to comprehend. Bemused western visitors are always writing books and articles about the deep paradoxes of Japan, writings that often tell you more about the deep ignorance of their authors than anything else. Serious students of Japan need to pass quickly through this phase of initial bafflement and awe. To see Japan primarily in terms of 'otherness' and to be preoccupied by its difference from the West exemplifies what Edward Said calls 'orientalism' – a tendency to make essentialist and patronizing generalizations about non-western societies.

**Illustration 1.1 Tokyo skyline**

It is important to remember that Japanese people are not defined by their Japaneseness: they are human first, and Japanese second, not the other way around. A European country such as Britain, with its ancient monarchy, often fusty traditions and its long history, displays many of the same discrepancies and overlaps between the new and the old which are evident in Japan. A comparison of Japan with other Asian countries such as India, Thailand or Singapore quickly reveals that there is nothing at all unusual about mixing the ancient and the modern in a single country.

The origins of the Japanese people are obscure and controversial. Reischauer argues that there was 'a broad flow of peoples from Northeastern Asia through the Korean peninsula into Japan, especially during the first seven centuries of the Christian era' (1977: 35). However, other accounts emphasize the continuities between prehistoric settlements and modern Japan, implying that the Japanese have existed in some form for many thousands of years. Certainly, many Japanese people are resistant to the idea that they might be of Chinese or Korean origin.

Japan is an island nation, perhaps in more ways than one. Japan's island identity has significant psychological and political implications. Although non-Japanese think of Japan primarily as one country in Asia, the Japanese for the most part tend to feel that they are a

**Box 1.1 Key facts about Japan**

| | |
|---|---|
| Government type | Constitutional monarchy |
| Capital | Tokyo |
| Currency | Yen |
| Highest point | Mount Fuji, 3776 metres |
| Population | 127,078,679 (July 2010 est.) |
| Population growth rate | -0.191% (2010 est.) |
| Urban population as a % | 66% (2008) |
| of total population | 127.51 million (2009) |
| Total area | 377,915 sq km (2010) (Nearly 1.5 times the land area of the United Kingdom or slightly less than that of California) |
| Land use | Agriculture Land 12.5% |
| | Forest and Fields 66.4% |
| | Others 21.1% (2010) |
| Nature resources | Negligible mineral resources, fish |
| Labour force | 65.93 million (2009 est.) |
| Unemployment rate | 5.2% (July, 2010) |
| GDP | $4.15 trillion (PPP, 2009 est.) |
| GDP per capital | $32,700 (PPP, 2009 est.) |
| GDP composition by secto | Agriculture: 1.6% r<br>Industry: 21.9%<br>Services: 76.5% (2009 est.) |
| Major cities (in population) | Tokyo (8.41m), Yokohama (3.58m), Osaka (2.51m), Nagoya (2.16m), Sapporo (1.88m), Kobe (1.5m), Kyoto (1.38m), Fukuoka (1.37m), Kawasaki (1.34m) (2008) |

*Sources*: Statistics Bureau, Ministry of Public Management, Home Affairs, Posts and Telecommunications, Japan, *Japan Statistical Yearbook 2010;* CIA (2010), *The World Factbook 2010*.

distinct civilization in their own right. There is an obvious comparison here with Britain's ambiguous relationship with the rest of Europe. Japan is a very sizeable country in population terms, with around 127 million people in 2010: the population is concentrated in urban areas, since many parts of Japan are mountainous and largely uninhabitable. Japan's population density in comparison to other countries is shown in Figure 1.1.

Less than a fifth of Japan's land area is sufficiently level for agriculture or other economic activity, and apart from the tiny city-states of Singapore and Hong Kong, Japan has the world's highest population density per square mile of habitable land. Japan's mountains are steep, but not especially high. Japan consists largely of 'long stretches of forest-covered hills interlaced with narrow valleys that form slim strips of agriculture and habitation' (Reischauer, 1977: 5). Central Honshu contains several ranges of mountains known as the Japan Alps, which reach heights of 3,195 metres. Mount Fuji, at 3,776 metres, is Japan's highest mountain. The only sizeable plains area in Japan is the Kanto area, around Tokyo. Before the construction of modern roads and railways, sea transportation was widely used to move goods and people around different parts of the country. Japan's difficult terrain probably contributed to the emergence of a medieval feudal order, long controlled by local warlords. Apart from an abundance of water, Japan is singularly lacking in natural resources, and very reliant upon imported raw materials (though there

*Figure* 1.1 Population density ((pop. per km$^2$) 2010)

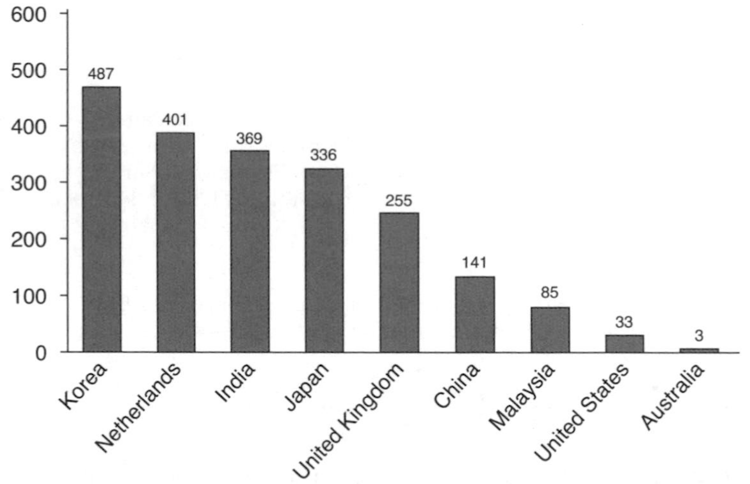


*Source*: United Nations, Population Database, *World Population Prospects*, http://esa.un.org/unpp/.

is a significant domestic timber industry). All in all, Japanese topography is singularly unsuitable for the task of building a powerful and centrally managed industrial economy.

The relationship between Japanese people and nature is a complex one. On the one hand, the Japanese have been very destructive of the natural environment in their quest for rapid industrialization; yet at the same time they retain a close affinity with the idea of nature, and constantly celebrate nature's transient beauties. The Japanese are extremely aware of the changing seasons: there are numerous special foods, festivals and social rituals marking seasonal changes. Certain places are renowned as beauty spots at particular times of the year, and may receive hundreds of thousands of visitors within a given two-week period. Japan has four seasons, roughly corresponding to the climate of the east coast of the United States: a hot, humid summer, a beautiful autumn, a winter which can be surprisingly severe (especially on the Japan Sea coast of Honshu, where snow-filled winds blow in from Siberia), and a short, spectacular spring (symbolized by the famous *sakura,* or cherry blossoms), which is over almost as soon as it has begun. Some observers argue that Japan has five seasons, since June and July typically see intense spells of heavy rain, followed by a wave of typhoons in late summer and early autumn. The Tohoku earthquake and tsunami of March 2011 was just the latest in a series of terrible disasters to strike Japan, including the 1923 Tokyo and 1995 Kobe earthquakes. Such events are an accepted fact of life for the Japanese, who often see themselves pitted in a sort of cosmic struggle with potentially hostile natural forces.

Japan's four main islands comprise: the central island of Honshu – by far the most important – which contains the great cities of Tokyo, Osaka and Nagoya, the ancient capital of Kyoto, and the three largest urban regions (Kanto, Kansai and Tokai); Kyushu, to the south, home to Nagasaki, Kagoshima and Fukuoka; Shikoku, the smallest of the main islands, to the east of southern Honshu; and Hokkaido (Japan's equivalent of Scotland), a far less densely populated island to the north. In terms of size of population and economic importance, Japan is dominated by the three main urban regions along the Pacific Coast of Honshu: Kanto (greater Tokyo), Tokai (greater Nagoya), and Kansai (greater Osaka). These regions include the ancient capitals of Kyoto and Nara, and Tokyo's huge siblings, Yokohama and Kawasaki. The country is divided into 47 prefectures for administrative purposes. Politically, Tokyo rules supreme (see Illustration 1.1): despite the existence of elected politicians at prefectural, city and municipal level, purse strings are controlled largely by ministries in the capital. There are big disparities in income between urban and rural areas.

Traditionally, most Japanese people lived from farming (especially rice farming) and fishing. Some argue that the cooperative efforts involved in rice production and harvesting fostered a group culture among the Japanese (Reischauer 1977: 17), an argument which revisionists find far-fetched. Nevertheless, the Japanese have an emotional attachment to the idea of themselves as an agricultural people and, during the post-war period, farmers have been the recipients of considerable government largesse. The word for rice (*gohan*) is synonymous with the word for meal. The Japanese like to claim that they eat everything produced by the sea, from whalemeat, fish and shrimps to shellfish and seaweed. A typical Japanese meal consists of rice, vegetables and fish. Unlike most other Asian foods, Japanese food is not spicy, but is served with side dishes of sauces and pickles. Great importance is attached to the visual impact of a meal, which is often exquisitely presented and typically served in lacquered containers or ceramic dishes. Noodle dishes are a staple local fast food. In recent decades, the Japanese diet has changed greatly; people now eat far more meat than before and young Japanese people are often considerably taller than their parents. International cuisines – ranging from Italian to Indian, Thai and Vietnamese – are now extremely popular and widely available.

### *Culture*

Japan is singularly rich in terms of culture. The Japanese passion for detail is revealed in innumerable wonderful artworks, such as the many wooden carved Buddhist images to be found in temples, beautifully painted scrolls and screens from various periods, and very fine ceramics. Outside Japan, Edo-period *ukiyoe* prints showing famous landscapes, beauties and actors are widely appreciated and collected, though for most Japanese these prints are ephemeral works rather than high art. Japan has an outstanding literary tradition, as evidenced in genres such as *haiku* poetry, and in the novels of internationally renowned twentieth-century writers such as Soseki Natsume, Yasunari Kawabata and Yukio Mishima. Recently, novelists such as Banana Yoshimoto and Haruki Murakami have gained world-wide audiences for their highly contemporary modes of storytelling. The Japanese are avid readers of everything from serious non-fiction to comic books, especially on long commuter rides between home and work. Traditional Japanese drama, such as *kabuki* and *noh*, continues to be widely performed, and is generating increasing interest outside Japan.

Other important aspects of Japanese culture are the traditional cultural pursuits favoured by many women: the tea ceremony with its combination of the simple and elaborate, *ikebana* or Japanese flower-arranging, and playing musical instruments such as the harp-like *koto*. Previously, mastery of these feminine arts was a prerequisite for finding a good husband. Many people are fascinated by western classical music, and the popularity of the 'Suzuki method' reflects the large number of Japanese children learning to play instruments. In contrast with many other societies, cultural matters are taken very seriously in Japan, and attract considerable attention. Special exhibitions of western painting (often at department stores) or some rarely displayed Japanese screens (usually at a temple, shrine or museum) can draw huge crowds. Certain objects of historical or artistic significance are designated 'national treasures', while outstanding artists may be given the status of 'living national treasures'.

Since the 1990s, traditional sources of Japanese pride have been declining: the economy has been in the doldrums, and questions have been asked about the successes of Japan in areas such as education and crime. Yet at the same time, popular culture in Japan has enjoyed unparalleled growth, and the influence of Japanese comics, computer games, fashions, pop music and mobile phone technologies have transformed the lives of young people. This influence has not been confined to Japan itself, but has greatly affected the rest of Asia and much of the western world. Treat argues of Japan's popular culture that: 'A failure to engage it seriously will mean a failure to take Japan seriously' (Treat, 1996: 30).

In fact, a fashion for things Japanese is not a new phenomenon: 'Japonisme' was all the rage in late nineteenth-century Europe, manifesting itself in everything from clothes to furnishings. But the new wave of Japanese fashion designers who achieved world-wide fame in the 1980s were seen as collectively representing an exotic, stylish and distinctive 'Japaneseness', as foreigners 'orientalized' the designs of Rei Kawakubo, Yohji Yamamoto and Issey Miyake (Skov 1996: 137–40). Japanese pop idols like Rie Miyazawa became household names in the new tiger economies of South Korea, Taiwan, Singapore and Hong Kong; and to a slightly lesser extent in south-east Asian countries such as Thailand and the Philippines (Ching,

1996: 170). The huge popularity of karaoke in Asia was another example of this trend towards cultural Japanization. Karaoke may reflect the continuation of a long-established 'performance tradition' in Japan, which is adapted in differing ways when the activity is exported to other cultures (Kelly, 1998: 84–5).

Despite the immense strategic importance of the USA in Asia, young people in much of the region have been increasingly consuming Japanese cultural products. Cartoons have become one of Japan's most important cultural exports in the twenty-first century, ranging from Robotech to Doraemon, Sailor Moon and Dragon Ball. Spin-off marketing sees cartoon images reproduced on everything from stationery to t-shirts. *Manga* comics are now widely translated, and enjoy global distribution (Craig, 2000: 4–5). Tsutsui argues that *manga* and other forms of Japanese popular culture are dominated by four main themes: 'an apocalyptic imagination, fascination with the monstrous, soft spot for the cute, and mecha fantasies' (Tsutsui 2010: 21). Fashions in cities such as Bangkok and Hong Kong take their cue from the latest trends in Tokyo, as anyone who travels regularly between Thailand and Japan can testify. Asian pop stars produce imitations of Japanese originals, and Nintendo, Pokemon and Hello Kitty can be found all over the world.

### *Youth cultures*

Young people in Japan are often strongly drawn to popular sub-cultures involving specific forms of fashion, music and behaviour that are closely linked to gender and imagery drawn from *manga*. Although adherents of these *zoku* (tribal sub-cultures) may appear rebellious or deviant compared with more conventional youths, they often follow very strict internal codes of dress and demeanour. Such codes somewhat resemble western sub-cultures – such as punks or Goths – but tend to take on more extreme forms. Because fashions change very rapidly, it is hard to make fixed classifications of these sub-cultures, and there are numerous variations within each category. but the following 'types' have been especially evident in recent years: *Harajuku* girls; *Shibuya gal/garu oh*; *Yamanba*; and *Akiba kei/otaku*. A related trend is the rise of *soushoku-kei danshi* (herbivorous/grass-eating boys), and their female antithesis, *nikshoku-kei* (carnivorous/meat-eating) girls.

*Akiba kei/otaku* are obsessive fans of animations (anime), video games, comic books and idols, who spend much of their time online or playing with computers. Many of them collect animation-related items. Garcia lists seven main types of *otaku*: *manga otaku*, *anime otaku*, *figure otaku* (fixated on plastic figurines from their favourite series), *pasokon* (personal computer) *otaku* (obsessed with personal computers), *wota* (otaku who love pop idols), *gemu* (game) *otaku*, and *densha* (train) *otaku* (Garcia 2010: 86). In practice many *otaku* combine elements of these different types. Although Tokyo's Akihabara area, famous for computer and electronic goods, is the best known *seichi* (holy place) for *otaku*, other major cities in Japan have their own equivalents, such as Nihonbashi in Osaka, and Centre Plaza in Kobe. *Otaku* also gather at annual events such as the Tokyo Game Show and '*Comike(t)*' (the world largest manga festival). Most *otaku* are young and middle-aged men from their twenties to forties, with 'geeky' tendencies, many of whom have trouble forming normal friendships, and especially healthy relationships with women. Okada Toshio – known as *otaku no kyouso/ karisuma* (the founder/master of *otaku*) – points out that many frequent visitors of Akihabara prefer to avoid the trials and tribulations of real-life romantic relationships. Rather than dating and marrying normal women from mainstream Japanese society, many *otaku* fall in love with idol groups such as the incredibly popular AKB 48, or become obsessed with maids in *meido kissa,* coffee shops where girls dressed up as maids serve food and provide entertainment such as singing and game shows. Some young people go as far to engage in *cosplay* (or *kospre,* 'dressing up'), becoming look-a-likes of popular animation, game, and comic book characters. Cosplayers take part in competitions at clubs and conventions, and take part in elaborately posed photo-shoots for amateur photographers known as *cameko* (Garcia 2010: 95).

*Harajuku* girls are groups of girls who wear costumes inspired by Goth, Lolita, and 'Visual-*kei*' bands ('a sub-category of musicians who are 'visually oriented'', often described as the combinations of 'feminine appearance with new and attractive images of young men' (Iida, 2005:59)). These bands include X Japan and Luna Sea, which became popular during the 1980s and 1990s. *Harajuku* girls are so known because many of them gather in the central Tokyo area of Harajuku on Sunday afternoons, when the main street, Omotesando, is temporarily closed to traffic. The *Harajuku* phenomenon is extremely ritualized and time-limited; at 6.00 pm precisely, Omotesando re-opens and the girls rapidly disperse.

Shibuya *gal* (female) and *garu oh* (male) are a youth sub-culture with dyed hair, fake tan, heavy make-up, and colourful, often revealing clothing. Liu (2005) points out the influence of hip-hop culture in understanding this trend. Many of them also imitate celebrity singers such as Namie Amuro and Ayumi Hamasaki. According to Iida *kogyaru* (literally meaning 'small gals') first appeared in 1993, and can be described as a 'young female type, who displays herself in a very short school girl's kilt, white knee socks, and brown or blonde dyed hair' (Iida 2005: 65). In the late 1990s, a more extreme type of gal emerged called *yamanba* (meaning 'evil old woman') 'who displays an aesthetically displeasing style of make-up called *ganguro* – 'black faces' – with their artificially darkened faces and overtly exaggerated features, such as huge threatening eyes and white painted lips' (Iida 2005: 65). Some young women become *lolitas*, donning sexualized parodies of girls' clothing that assume various styles (Garcia 2010: 94). Members of all these youth cultures also invent their own 'in-group' vocabulary, making it difficult for other people to follow what they are talking about.

Japanese television is populated by various kinds of stars – known as *geinojin* – ranging from *aidoru* (idols, glamorous young women who serve little function other than to add sex appeal to a programme) to *geinin* (comedians), *haiu-joyu* ('drama' actors and actresses), *tarento* (talents – TV personalities with no obvious talent), *kashu* (singers who also host programmes) and the ubiquitous *anaunsaa* (newcasters or hosts) (Garcia 2010: 120–1). Television in Japan offers amazing insights into popular culture and behaviour; to the western eye, much of the programming seems pretty absurd, while the advertising is often completely ludicrous.

In recent years, however, Korean soap operas and entertainment have become increasingly popular in Japan. *Winter Sonata*, a Korean drama series, became the most popular television drama in Japan. In August 2011, there were some nationalist protests in Tokyo against the rise of Korean programming on Japanese television. K-Pop – Korean pop music – has a tougher, more edgy image than its Japanese counterpart J-Pop, which typically emphasizes the *kawaii* (cute) above all else, and is dominated by young female singers. The rise of Korean television dramas and the 'Korean wave' in Japan shows that Japanese people are now more open to other Asian cultures; at the same time. Japanese popular culture now has considerable appeal both across and beyond Asia. Douglas McGray has called this 'a mighty engine of national cool' which Japan could deploy as a major resource of soft power internationally (cited in Tsutsui 2010: 59).

Here is an ironic contrast to the problems faced by other Japanese industries, and challenges claims that Japan's education system has produced a society lacking in innovation and creativity. Japan's popular culture industries have continued long-established traditions of craftsmanship and high quality, channelling such cultural strengths into new outlets such as television commercials. Foreign images and ideas are often 'borrowed' before being reconceptualized, then turned into something quite new (Craig, 2000: 7–8). Many of the worlds invoked in Japanese pop culture have dark and disturbing elements quite absent from their American counterparts, and yet also feature an incredibly dreamy idealism which beguiles young audiences. From a mainstream perspective, Japan's thriving popular and youth culture is evidence of a dynamic society; revisionists, however, are concerned by the rise of *otaku* and *zoku,* seeing them as evidence of an inward-looking cultural turn with disturbing and unhealthy overtones.

## Conclusion

Contemporary Japan is one of the world's most fascinating, important and complex nations. Understanding Japan is an important task for everyone who studies modern economic, social and political systems, yet gaining an accurate understanding is often hindered by the extensive debates and disagreements among Japan scholars themselves, disagreements which permeate most of the available published literature. When reading and studying about Japan, it is very important to be aware of being constantly in disputed territory, caught in the crossfire between mainstream analysts, revisionists and culturalists. To start to understand Japan, we need to begin by adopting a critical, sceptical and questioning attitude to everything we hear and read – including, of course, this book.

# 2

# Historical Background

After a long period of relative isolation from the beginning of the seventeenth century, in the late 1800s, Japan began a process of extraordinarily rapid industrialization and social change, making the transition from an essentially feudal society to a modern nation-state within a couple of decades. Following its successful defeat of a western power in the Russo-Japanese War, Japan increasingly turned towards imperialism, and eventually to the militarism which culminated in the disastrous Pacific War. After the humiliating surrender of August 1945, Japan again recreated itself, this time as an economic giant. By the 1980s, Japan was challenging even the United States in trade and manufacturing. Yet, by the second decade of the twenty-first century, Japan faced new challenges, as its political and economic systems appeared to be losing direction. Many aspects of this history are highly contentious.

## The Tokugawa period (1603–1868)

During the Tokugawa period, Japan was unified following the period of the warring states, a long spell of civil conflict. By defeating their rivals militarily, the Tokugawa family gained control over the country, bringing under their jurisdiction the numerous local feudal lords. During this Edo (an earlier name for Tokyo) or Tokugawa period, Japan was relatively removed from foreign influences. Under the policy of national isolation, the Tokugawa *shogun* expelled all Europeans from Japan, with the exception of a small Dutch trading community that was confined to an island in the port of Nagasaki. Christianity was outlawed. It was only with the arrival of the famous 'black ships' – an American fleet commanded by Commodore Matthew Perry – in 1853 that Japan was compelled to re-open to western trade.

However, the image of Japan as a 'closed country' has been somewhat exaggerated, and the distinctiveness and uniqueness of Japanese culture has been over-emphasized (Pyle, 1996b: 57–9). In practice, there was substantial foreign trade throughout this period, especially with China and Korea, and through the Ryukyu Islands (now better known as Okinawa), which provided a staging post for trade with China and Southeast Asia. Dutch traders were presented to the *shogun* in Edo, western books other than Christian tracts were allowed to circulate in Japan after 1720, and Japanese experts in 'Dutch studies' (knowledge about the West) were engaged in translating and assimilating information from abroad, especially material relating to advances in science and technology.

During the 265 years when Japan was relatively insulated from the outside world, real political power lay in the hands of the Edo *shogun* (or 'generalissimo'), while the emperor lived in seclusion in Kyoto. Although notionally subordinate to the Emperor, the *shogun* was effectively a ruler to whom other lords swore allegiance. The country was tightly regimented: firm action was taken against subversive elements, and even members of the elite were subject to considerable control. The *shogun* directly controlled around a quarter of all lands, while the remaining three-quarters were administered by the 260 or so *daimyo,* or great land-owning aristocrats. Although Edo Japan is often loosely termed 'feudal', a combination of central military power and local devolution to the *daimyo* amounted to a 'feudal–central hybrid'. The *shogun* could rearrange or reassign the domains of *daimyo* at will – and during the first century of Tokugawa rule often did so, in order to establish their own power and control. The *daimyo* were also forced to divide their time between Edo and their domains through a system of 'alternate residence' (see Waswo, 1996: 9–17). Maintaining two lavish residences encouraged many *daimyo* to live beyond their means, engaging in patterns of conspicuous consumption which concealed growing indebtedness: under these conditions, the merchant class was able to amass considerable wealth. This gradually had the effect of shifting power away from the *samurai* (retainers of the *shogun* and *daimyo,* who made up some 6–7 per cent of the population) and towards the emerging commercial sector. This shift was symbolized by the rise of the trading city of Osaka.

The pace of change in late Edo Japan produced numerous sources of social discontent. *Samurai* became jealous of the higher incomes and better lifestyles enjoyed by the more well-to-do merchant families, and status alone no longer determined wealth. Peasant protests over harsh taxes or local abuses were common, their violence often directed at oppressive village leaders rather than the *samurai* class (Sato, 1990: 59). Another source of dissatisfaction was that the Edo bureaucracy was not meritocratic, but reserved higher positions for the well-born, blocking career prospects for lower-ranking but more able young *samurai*. Tensions within the shogunate were well-established long before the challenge of the West hit home in 1853, characterized by acute internal political contestation. With the onset of international pressures, doubts about the effectiveness of *samurai* rule undermined the hierarchical ideology of Tokugawa Japan. Yet to see the Edo period as essentially 'feudal', static and backward would be much too simplistic: the tensions which emerged during these two-and-a-half centuries reflected vast social and economic changes, which had an enormous impact on early modern Japan.

## The Meiji period (1868–1912)

The economic and political crisis brought about by the arrival of the Americans precipitated the collapse of the *shogun* system. In finally agreeing to 'open up' Japan to foreign trade, the ruling elite saw this as a strategy to create a strong Japan, capable of mastering western science and technology, and thereby emulating western power. At the same time, the external challenge from foreign powers offered new solutions to the social problems that had afflicted late-Tokugawa Japan. In 1867, the Emperor Meiji was 'restored' to head a new government. This 'restoration' meant that after many centuries without any effective power, the Japanese Emperor regained a central political role. The significance of the restoration is contested: some historians see it simply as an elite manoeuvre on the part of a small group of ambitious *samurai,* whereas more recent scholarship has supported the view that it reflected a growing social movement for revolutionary change, which dated back to the eighteenth century. As Pyle explains: 'The role of the foreign crisis was to bring into sharp focus the impotence of the old system and to prompt revolutionary action to create a new order' (Pyle, 1996b: 74).

A period of rapid modernization followed, as Japan sought to 'catch up' with the West. Seeing the imperial powers as a serious threat, Japan sought to learn from western countries, partly in order to fend off the dangers of colonization. Missions were sent to study western states and societies (particularly those of Britain, France, Germany and the United States), and to identify models that Japan could adapt. During the early Meiji period, Japan established a wide range of new institutions, including a British-style navy and postal system, a French-style police and judicial system, American-style banking and primary school systems, and a German-style army (Pyle, 1996b: 79). More than 3,000 foreign advisers were employed in Japan during the Meiji period, many of them engineers and technologists: Japan did not become reliant on these expatriates, however, but sought to replace them with Japanese personnel as soon as these had been trained.

Over 11,000 Japanese people were sent to study abroad during the Meiji period, primarily to the USA and Germany. Japan benefited from a relatively young leadership, and, importantly, the ruling elite were urban-dwellers who derived their power from their formal positions, not from landed estates; this made them far more open to change, since they did not have to fear that they might lose property and wealth under new social arrangements (Pyle, 1996b: 79–80). Under these conditions, 'civilisation and enlightenment' took place during the Meiji period. Salient features of this enlightenment included a negative view of Japan's traditions, considerable optimism about the prospects for Japan to catch up with the West, a belief in the inexorability of progress by emulating western examples, and 'a wholehearted commitment to science, technology, and utilitarian knowledge' (Pyle, 1996b: 93).

During the Meiji period, Japan emerged as the first non-western industrial power. The government gradually developed a state-led industrial policy emphasizing the establishment of heavy industries such as mining, steel and railways; pursued a strategy of import substitution, coupled with the purchase of the best available western industrial technology; and established a dynamic export sector. Foreign debt was avoided wherever possible. By the end of the Meiji period, Japan was successfully competing with Britain as a leading exporter of textiles. At the same time, some scholars argue that the role of the state in fostering Japan's industrialization should not be overplayed: individual entrepreneurs were also central to this complex process, which government could facilitate but not imple-

### Box 2.1 Key dates in modern Japanese history

| | |
|---|---|
| 1603 | Tokugawa shogunate established |
| 1635–9 | Seclusion policy adopted |
| 1774 | Rise of so-called 'Dutch studies' |
| 1853 | Commodore Perry's 'black ships' arrive in Tokyo Bay |
| 1868 | Meiji Restoration (reversion to imperial rule) |
| 1889 | Meiji Constitution |
| 1890 | Imperial rescript on education, beginning of parliamentary government |
| 1894 | Sino-Japanese War |
| 1895 | Annexation of Taiwan |
| 1902 | Anglo-Japanese alliance |
| 1904 | Russo-Japanese War |
| 1910 | Annexation of Korea |
| 1918 | First party government formed; 'Taisho democracy' begins |
| 1923 | Tokyo earthquake |
| 1925 | Universal manhood suffrage |
| 1931 | Manchurian incident |
| 1932 | Puppet state of Manchukuo established in Manchuria; assassination of Prime Minister Inukai by rightist naval cadets |
| 1937 | Invasion of China begins |
| 1940 | Japan signs Tripartite Pact with Germany and Italy |
| 1941 | Attacks on Pearl Harbor and the Malay peninsula; United States enters the war |
| 1942 | Philippines taken; Allied victory at the Battle of Midway |
| 1944 | Allies recapture the Philippines |
| 1945 | Atomic bombing of Hiroshima and Nagasaki; surrender, beginning of Allied Occupation and reforms |
| 1946 | Political purges begin |
| 1946–8 | Tokyo war trials |
| 1947 | New Constitution and major political reforms; Socialist government takes office |
| 1948 | 'Reverse course' begins |
| 1949 | 'Dodge line' implemented |
| 1950 | Korean War breaks out |
| 1951 | San Francisco peace treaty; US-Japan security pact |
| 1952 | End of Occupation |
| 1954 | Self-Defence Forces established |
| 1955 | Liberal Democratic Party is formed and takes power; industrial production back to 1942 levels |
| 1956 | Diplomatic relations restored with Soviet Union; Japan admitted to the UN |
| 1959 | Minamata disease first confirmed |
| 1960 | Mass protests against renewal of US-Japan security treaty; income-doubling policy announced |
| 1964 | Tokyo Olympics held |

| | |
|---|---|
| 1967 | Incomes doubled after only seven years; first anti-pollution legislation passed |
| 1971 | Environment Agency established |
| 1972 | Okinawa reverts to Japanese administration; diplomatic relations restored with China |
| 1973–4 | First oil shock |
| 1976 | Ex-Prime Minister Tanaka arrested over Lockheed scandal; National Defence Programme Outline announced |
| 1977 | Fukuda doctrine announced |
| 1978 | Narita airport protesters destroy control tower; airport finally opens |
| 1979 | Second oil shock |
| 1983 | Prime Minister Nakasone takes office with a conservative agenda |
| 1987 | New union federation Rengo formed |
| 1988 | Record trade surplus with the USA: bilateral trade disputes peak |
| 1989 | Death of Emperor Hirohito; Showa period ends, and Heisei era begins. Many leading politicians involved in Recruit-Cosmos scandal |
| 1990 | End of 'bubble' economy based on land and stockmarket speculation |
| 1991 | Gulf War raises questions about Japan's defence policy |
| 1992 | Sagawa Kyubin scandal breaks |
| 1993 | LDP loses power in 1993 general elections, replaced by anti-LDP coalition |
| 1994 | Electoral reform legislation implemented. Anti-LDP coalition collapses, hybrid alliance based on the LDP and the Socialist Party takes over |
| 1995 | Kobe earthquake; sarin attack by Aum Shinrikyo cult in Tokyo |
| 1996 | LDP leader Hashimoto becomes prime minister. First general election under the new electoral system sees little substantive change |
| 1997 | Asian financial crisis has an adverse impact on Japan's economy |
| 1998 | 1 April – start of 'Big Bang' financial deregulation programme |
| 1999 | SDF members join UN PKO in East Timor |
| 2000 | Landmark negotiations with North Korea in Pyongyang |
| 2001 | Populist conservative Junichiro Koizumi becomes prime minister |
| 2002 | Japan co-hosts soccer World Cup with South Korea |
| 2004 | Small unit of SDF deployed to Iraq |
| 2005 | Koizumi steps down, ushering in a period of one-year PMs |
| 2006 | SDF withdrawn from Iraq; Defence Agency upgraded to Ministry. Deaths exceed births, start of negative population growth |
| 2009 | LDP loses power, DPJ form new coalition government |
| 2010 | China overtakes Japan as world's second largest economy |
| 2011 | Tsunami and earthquake hit Japan's Tohoku region, leading to Fukushima nuclear crisis |

ment without the active participation of the private sector (Pyle, 1996b: 108–12).

Various steps were taken during the Meiji period to forge a more powerful and effective state, and to establish a strong sense of national identity. Conscription was introduced in 1873 for all men over the age of 20, and the monarchy was used as an important symbol of the nation, not just to the outside world but also to the Japanese population at large (Waswo, 1996: 26–33). This was seen in new national holidays associated with imperial dates, the use of impressive imperial edicts and proclamations, and an emphasis on the idea of serving the Emperor. School textbooks were controlled – and later directly written – by the Ministry of Education, and came to emphasize 'moral' themes such as loyalty to the throne and filial piety. Another important step entailed incorporating traditional localities into a national administrative structure. At the same time, the bureaucracy was made somewhat more open and meritocratic. The precise role of the Meiji Emperor himself in all these developments is difficult to assess, since he left no diary and few letters. Much of the writing about him is mere hagiography; Keene argues that few biographers have succeeded in 'creating a believable portrait of the man whose reign of forty-five years was characterized by the greatest changes in Japanese history' (2002: xi).

The most significant political development of the Meiji period was the promulgation of the 1889 constitution, which symbolized the forging of the first modern nation-state in Asia (for the best discussion, see Gluck, 1985: 42–72). The document was heavily influenced by German political and legal ideas, and established a bicameral legislature resembling those of European countries. There was an unelected upper house dominated by the nobility, and an elected lower chamber – though suffrage was limited to around 1 per cent of the population. These representative institutions were seen as instruments of nation-building and unity, and as 'safety valves' for popular discontent, rather than as instruments for establishing or managing democracy (Gluck, 1985: 49–50). In theory the 1889 constitution enshrined certain civil liberties, though in practice these provisions made little impact. This was a constitution imposed from above, rather than one explicitly reflecting broader political demands. A central feature of the 1889 constitution was its definition of the Emperor as the sovereign source of supreme authority. In practice, however, real power belonged to a group of influential leaders. Ministers were appointed by the Emperor, and cabinets were accountable to him rather than to parliament. The elected assembly – which featured political parties – was intended to play a merely consultative role (for a discussion, see Gluck, 1985: 60–7). Despite all these limitations and shortcomings, the 1889 constitution was a great step forward for Japan, establishing the political foundations of a modern nation-state. Following the formal promulgation of the constitution, it took roughly a decade for the constitutional system to be thoroughly institutionalized and established as a working entity (Banno, 1992: 200).

## Taisho democracy

In practice, the political system inaugurated by the Meiji constitution was one of competing elites. As Stockwin puts it:

> Cabinets, political parties, senior government bureaucrats, the House of Peers, the Privy Council, the tenno's [Emperor's] personal advisers in the Imperial Household Ministry, the chiefs of staff of the armed forces and directors of certain big business combines were all jockeying for power in a situation where it was unclear where power really lay. (Stockwin, 2008: 20)

This sense of contending forces reached its peak during the period of 'Taisho democracy' (corresponding to the reign of the weak and mentally ill Emperor Taisho from 1912 to 1926), when political parties grew in importance and there was greater political freedom than previously. From 1918 to 1932, parties were especially poweful, and prime ministers were generally selected from among the party leaders. Nevertheless, the political parties that existed were elite organizations, rather than mass-based ones (see Pyle, 1996b: 159–71), and party politicians were obliged to work in close collaboration with the court, the bureaucracy, and the military. However, the political system did seem to be moving in a democratic direction, though substantive change was limited by the nature of the Meiji constitutional order. Outside the elite, popular political consciousness was growing rapidly: unions flourished (including militant unions of tenant farmers), students became politically active, and a wide range of liberal and even radical reform movements emerged. One important political change occurred in 1925, when universal male suffrage was introduced, increasing the size of the electorate four-fold to more than 12 million. This carrot was offset by the stick of a draconian new Public Security Act, which curtailed civil liberties.

## Imperialism, militarism and war

The Meiji leadership placed considerable emphasis on military strength, recognizing that only a well-armed Japan could deal with the West on an equal footing. The success of its policies was first seen in the Sino-Japanese War of 1894–5, in which Japan destroyed China's navy and overwhelmed her army. Japan was then able to dictate the terms of a highly favourable treaty: China ceded the Pescadores, Formosa (later Taiwan) and the Liaotung Peninsula to Japan. The reality of China's weakness was exposed, and the war precipitated a 'scramble for China' among the imperial powers. However, the western powers were unwilling to see Japan reap the full benefits of her aggressive action, and in April 1895, Germany, Russia and France forced Japan to renounce the Peninsula. Japan then concentrated on building up sufficient forces to take on Russia, and succeeded in defeating the Russian navy in the Russo-Japanese War of 1904–5.

The defeat of Russia was a major turning-point, greatly emboldening Japan's leadership for the pursuit of further imperialist adventures. At the same time, the victory over Russia had been hard-won, leaving Japan feeling vulnerable and insecure. This persistent sense of insecurity was one of a compound of forces, which drove Japanese foreign policy over the following decades. Japan annexed Korea in 1910, and took advantage of the global upheavals of the First World War to seize German territories in Asia and the Pacific, and to increase pressure on China. The rise of militarism in Japan during the 1930s empowered the armed forces at the expense of other political institutions, leaving the military in a strong position to help shape Japan's domestic and overseas agenda.

Japan acted as an imperialist aggressor during the fifteen years from the September 1931 Manchuria Incident (in which the Japanese Army used the pretext of a small explosion to invade the whole of Manchuria, subsequently establishing the puppet state of Manchukuo) to the August 1945 surrender. During this 'Fifteen-Year War', Japan terrorized the population of China, carried out a surprise attack against the US Navy at Pearl Harbor in December 1941, invaded and conquered most of Southeast Asia, and fought a brutal war against the Allies. Japanese aggression only ceased following the terrible use of the atom bomb on Hiroshima and Nagasaki. The Fifteen-Year War was one of the darkest episodes in Japanese history, and any discussion of that history readily invokes intense emotions. Many of the actions of the Japanese forces – rapes and massacres of Chinese civilians, the abuse of so-called 'comfort women', and dreadful treatment of prisoners of war, to cite but a few examples – are difficult to comprehend, let alone to explain. But Japan's decision to pursue the imperialist policies that culminated in war with the Allies can be understood by reference to considerations of domestic and international politics.

One leading Japanese historian describes Japan's actions during the Pacific War as an 'imperialist war after the age of imperialism' (Nakamura, 1998: 248). The Versailles and Washington treaties signed at the end of the First World War had been intended to put a stop to imperialist rivalry, but the order they sought to define was one that greatly favoured the victors in that war, principally the United States, Britain and France. The rise of fascism in Germany and Italy reflected the attempts of the defeated nations to turn the tables on their victors. In Japan, the situation was both similar and different. The similarity was that Japan also numbered among the have-nots in the Anglo-American dominated global order – despite the fact that Japan had fought alongside the United States and Britain, and so was notionally on the winning side in 1918. The difference was that, unlike some countries of western Europe, Japan had not had the opportunity to form a great overseas Empire, a ready source of natural resources and raw materials to fuel rapid industrialization. In some respects, Japan had achieved its Meiji goal of 'catching up' with the West, transforming itself into a modern industrial society, yet Japan had not gained the prestige and advantages of great power status. In the minds of Japan's pre-war leaders, as Nakamura argues:

> The Allies were the 'haves', trying to preserve the post-World War I, post-imperialist order, and the Axis countries were the 'have-nots', envious of the Allies' vast territories and overseas possessions and eager for a redistribution of global wealth and power. (Nakamura, 1998: 249)

Although Japanese apologists for the Pacific War have sought to represent it as a war of liberation, designed to free Asia from colonialism and establish a 'Greater East Asian Co-Prosperity Zone', the reality was that the Fifteen-Year War reflected attempts by Japan to emulate western patterns of imperial domination and exploitation. In doing so, Japan singularly failed to recognize that the tide was already turning against colonization. Nationalist movements were flourishing across Asia: in India, in the Dutch East Indies (later Indonesia), in Vietnam, and above all in China. Imperialism was already past its sell-by date, and Japan's claims that it wanted to nurture Asian independence movements were highly suspect.

Questions concerning how and why Japan decided to invade Manchuria and later China, to sign a military pact with the Axis, and to launch attacks on US forces and British colonies in 1941, require long and careful answers. Significantly, throughout the 1931–45 period, the military was largely beyond the reach of civilian control. China policy was not primarily determined by the cabinet, but by the military. Although in broad sympathy with much of the policy, the prime minister and foreign ministers of the day often found themselves reacting to situations over which they had little control or influence. In addition, the tenure of civilian leaders was usually short-lived: there were thirteen cabinets and eleven prime ministers between 1932 and 1945. When politicians sought to rein in or to dissent from military actions, they were literally taking their lives in their hands: prime minister Tsuyoshi Inukai (who advocated a peaceful solution to the Manchuria dispute) was shot dead by uniformed naval cadets in his official residence on 15 May 1932 (Ienaga, 1978: 42–3). Several other prominent civilian leaders were also killed in plots hatched by young military officers, including the highly influential Finance Minister Takahashi Korekiyo in 1936.

The military insisted on vetoing cabinet appointments, and often completely refused to account for their actions. In making the decision to embark on war with the United States, 'the opinion leaders were the officers of a few key departments in the army and navy' (Nakamura, 1998: 252), not the prime minister or other members of the cabinet. During the war, the cabinet was not always kept informed of developments at the front: when several Japanese warships were lost at the disastrous Battle of Midway, Hideki Tojo (who was then prime minister and army minister, as well as a serving general) was not told for a month (Ienaga, 1978: 39). At times, Japanese military strategy seemed utterly perverse; this was exemplified in the terribly futile battle for the remote island of Iwo Jima, where an estimated 22,000 Japanese soldiers died in February and March 1945 (see Kakehashi 2007, as well as the magnificent Clint Eastwood film of the same title). The use of kamikaze aircraft on suicide missions in the latter stages of the war illustrated the same heady blend of courage and desperation (see Photo 2.1). The role of Emperor Hirohito during the war remains a matter of intense debate (see Box 2.2).

An expansionist military abroad was backed by political repression at home; the notorious secret police monitored the civilian population closely for signs of dissident views or behaviour, and acted swiftly and effectively against offenders. However, the same Keynesian policies of state-supported economic stimulation which helped pull Japan out of recession did provide significant economic benefits to much of the population during the late 1930s. Allinson argues that a combination of economic recovery and 'a more bellicose' nationalism helped ensure that the Japanese people accepted the expansionism in China, and later the Pacific War itself (Allinson, 1997: 26). This economic recovery helped forge a strong industrial sector led by a small number of powerful conglomerates, and so paved the way for the reconstruction of Japanese economic power after the war. Dower calls the conflict 'the useful war', arguing that war put into place the basic infrastructure for Japan's post-war economic ascendancy, building a strong capitalist state brokered by conservative interests (Dower, 1992: 49–70).

**Illustration 2.1 Kamikaze plane on display at Yasukuni Shrine, Tokyo**

**Box 2.2 Hirohito (1901–89): the controversial Emperor**

The role of the Emperor in the war remains highly contested: some scholars see Hirohito as a rather peace-loving man, 'the unwilling symbol' of war (Large, 1992: 216) placed in an impossible position by his commanders. Revisionists, by contrast, have denounced him as a war criminal. This long-running controversy was inflamed by the publication of Herbert Bix's Pulitzer Prize-winning biography *Hirohito and the Making of Modern Japan* in 2000. Bix argues that the military never completely controlled the political process. He sees Hirohito as the wartime 'helmsman' (Bix, 2000: 486), closely engaged in shaping military strategy, and thus directly responsible for many serious errors of judgement. Bix also believes that Hirohito was personally to blame for not bringing the war to a speedier end, given that defeat was inevitable after the unconditional surrender of Germany early in May 1945 (Bix, 1995: 223; 2000: 519–30).

Much praised in the United States, Bix's biography generated mixed reactions in Japan. In a lengthy review article, two Japanese academics accused Bix of lacking primary sources for his core assertions, and over-relying on secondary studies by left-wing Japanese scholars. One declared 'It seems to me that Bix simply failed to understand the imperial institution as a Japanese cultural tradition' (Matsumoto and Shoji, 2002: 68). This controversy seems unlikely to die down.

The American decision to drop atomic bombs on the Japanese cities of Hiroshima and Nagasaki was one of the most controversial issues of the Second World War (for a discussion, see Bernstein, 1995: 227–73, and other articles in the Spring 1995 special issue of *Diplomatic History*). Officials in the Truman administration claimed that dropping the bombs had foreshortened the war, rendering an invasion unnecessary, and so saving up to half a million American lives. Revisionist historians have argued that Japan was already on the verge of surrender, and that the nuclear bombing served little military purpose: Truman's real aim was to demonstrate US superiority over the Soviet Union. The official projections of American fatalities for the planned invasion were 25,000 to 46,000 – not hundreds of thousands. The bombs themselves eventually killed as many as three hundred thousand people (see Dower, 1995: 282), the great majority civilians. There is plenty of middle ground between the official and the revisionist views: arguably, a Japanese surrender might have been achieved without either dropping the atom bombs, or a full-scale invasion. And while a case can be made that the Hiroshima bomb expedited the Japanese surrender, the dropping of a second bomb on Nagasaki has never been convincingly justified.

Japanese memories of the Pacific War – the conflict with the United States and the Allies – loom much larger than the darker attacks on Manchuria and China from 1931 onwards; yet Japan began the Pacific War precisely to consolidate and build upon those conquests. Despite the fact that the rest of the world has generally regarded Japan as an aggressive power during the 15-year period of 1931 to 1945, within Japan there has often been a dominant perception of Japan as a victim of war. Not only was Japan uniquely victimized as the target of two atomic bombs, but the Japanese people saw themselves as the victims of militarism. Blame was shifted away from the nation as a whole, and onto the military and their elite supporters, especially the 28 leaders tried at the Tokyo War Crimes Tribunal (see Totani 2009). Tanaka writes:

> popular thinking in Japan remains strongly linked to the feeling that responsibility for the war lies overwhelmingly in the hands of the war leaders who deceived a gullible populace and led citizens into a war no-one would want to see repeated. Consequently people at large were made to feel they were victims. (Tanaka, 1996: 214)

Tanaka believes that in actual fact 'citizens at large eventually supported the war and as such bear responsibility' (Tanaka, 1996: 215). Many of Japan's leaders in turn claimed to be victims: they were only acting on behalf of the Emperor, who was not put on trial. As Gluck puts it 'neither the people nor the Emperor were arraigned' (Gluck, 1992: 13). As a consequence, many ordinary Japanese people were able to feel, in retrospect, that the war had little to do with them, whereas actually the kind of 'total war' in which Japan engaged involved the active or passive complicity of virtually the entire population (see Young 1998: 7–8). Max Hastings argues that 'By choosing to participate in a total war, the nation exposed itself to total defeat' (Hastings 2007: 5). In effect, the Japanese chose to believe that the totality of their defeat exonerated them from the totality of the war that they had waged.

In post-war Germany, trials of former Nazis continued for decades, whereas the Tokyo trials ended in 1948. Far more than the Germans, the Japanese people have engaged in collective denial of their wartime responsibility and culpability. Japanese right-wingers have lionized the Indian Tokyo tribunal judge Radhabinod Pal for his dissenting judgement, which criticized the war-crimes trials as 'victor's justice'. A statue of Pal stands at the Yasukuni Shrine in Tokyo. Bix argues that Japan's post-war denial was bound up in the Occupation's treatment of Emperor Hirohito, since 'as long as [the Japanese] did not pursue his central role in the war, they did not have to question their own' (Bix, 2000: 17). Nevertheless, Carol Gluck believes that since Hirohito's death in 1989, public discussion of 'war responsibility' (*senso sekinin*) has become more mature and reflexive (Gluck 2009: 94–100).

## The American Occupation

Much of the difficulty involved in evaluating the present-day Japanese political system hinges on the fact that, outwardly, the system appears to be a western one, largely because the Japanese constitution was imposed upon the country during the 1945–52 American Occupation. An understanding of the conflicting views and interpretations of the American role in post-war Japan is central in obtaining a sense of subsequent Japanese politics.

At the end of the war, Japan was in a state of *kyodatsu* (demoralization, exhaustion and despair), and much of the initial energy and optimism for reconstruction came from outside (Dower, 1999: 89). Ordinary Japanese people were preoccupied in a simple struggle for survival; their 'bamboo-shoot' lifestyle often involved 'peeling off' and selling all but the barest necessities (1999: 95). Yet the Americans demanded that the Japanese shoulder many of the costs of the Occupation (1999: 115).

In Allied circles, there was considerable disagreement over how Japan should be treated. Whilst Australia, for example, advocated punitive treatment of the Japanese, including the abolition of the Emperor system, many in the United States (such as Secretary of War Stimson) favoured an extremely limited intervention in Japan's affairs, confined to a programme of demilitarization and the trial of war criminals. In the event, General Douglas MacArthur, the American who was assigned the task of implementing post-surrender arrangements, was given a more ambitious brief: to introduce a system of 'democratic self-government' in Japan (see Box 2.3). MacArthur was also instructed, however, not 'to impose upon Japan any form of government not supported by the freely expressed will of

**Box 2.3 General Douglas MacArthur (1880–1964)**

MacArthur was a career soldier who had risen to the rank of Army Chief of Staff under Roosevelt, before being assigned as military adviser to the Philippines. Despite his ignominious 1942 retreat from Corregidor to Australia in the face of the Japanese advance (notoriously vowing 'I will return'), MacArthur was lionized by the American public. For all President Truman's reservations, he was chosen to receive the Japanese surrender in 1945, and to head the Allied occupation forces (Schaller, 1989: 118–19). MacArthur's personal vision for Japan loomed extremely large; Dower argues that he 'reigned as a minor potentate in his Far Eastern domain' (1999: 79), possessing both executive and legislative powers. Yet, ironically, MacArthur had very little contact with those over whom he presided during his five years as Supreme Commander Allied Powers. Not only did he never see how ordinary people lived, but only 16 Japanese people actually spoke to him more than twice, and all of these were very senior figures (Dower, 1999: 204). MacArthur's own commitment to reforming Japan wavered, partly because of his growing preoccupation with his own political ambitions. Yet in spite of his enormous influence over Japan's political direction, MacArthur's bid for the American presidency came to nothing. He took command of UN forces during the early stages of the Korean War; but his career ended abruptly in 1951 when he was dismissed by Truman. Some writers see MacArthur as a towering colossus, others as an heroic failure (Schaller, 1989: 252–3).

the people'. In other words, Japan was to become a democracy whether it wanted to or not, so long as everyone agreed. The aims of the Occupation were neatly framed in a document known as the 'Initial post-surrender policy', which emphasized 'the freely expressed will of the people' as its guiding principle (Dower, 1999: 77).

The American-drafted 1947 constitution was a very different matter from the Meiji constitution. The Japanese government had prepared its own draft constitution, based on the Meiji constitution, which was summarily rejected by the Supreme Commander for the Allied Powers (SCAP). Instead, during the eight days between 4 and 12 February 1946, American officials wrote an entirely new document, which a shocked Japanese government was effectively compelled to accept (Matsui 2011: 13–16). There was an intense debate in Occupation circles concerning the future of the Emperor, a debate influenced strongly by culturalist views that Japanese psychology was very different from that of westerners. MacArthur quickly saw that the Emperor could become an invaluable instrument of the Occupation; as Dower puts it: 'The pressing, immediate task was to create the most usable Emperor possible' (Dower, 1999: 299). To this end, the Emperor was not put on trial, but retained, stripped of all formal powers and designated the 'symbol of state' rather than head of state (for the full text, see www.solon.org).

Sovereignty now rested with the Japanese people, who elected a parliament (known as the Diet) to which the cabinet was answerable. The authority of the legislature was greatly enhanced, and women's suffrage was introduced for the first time. 'Local autonomy' was adopted as a central principle for local and prefectural government; a range of human rights was to be protected; an independent judiciary was established; and, most controversially of all, Article 9 decreed that Japan had forever renounced the sovereign right to wage war. The durability of the constitution was evidenced by the fact that it has yet to be revised; serious proposals for constitutional revision did not emerge until the 1990s (Hook and McCormack 2001).

In addition to the constitution itself, the Occupation forces also implemented various secondary reforms aimed at broadening and democratizing participation in politics. One of the most important secondary reforms was the re-establishment of the right to form unions and other interest groups, including left-wing political parties (communists had been jailed since the 1920s). Another was an extensive programme of land reform; no individual was allowed to hold more than about 7.5 acres of land, which had the effect of bringing rural landlordism to an end. A further reform gave new powers to local government in place of the old centralized system. Education was also reformed: nationalist textbooks were rewritten, the education system was decentralized, and many new degree-granting institutions were created. Many scholars have regarded the great majority of these reforms as highly successful.

Another significant aspect of the Occupation was the 'purging' (meaning, for the most part, forced retirement) of individuals held to have been important supporters of the war, including members of the secret police, religious officials and members of militaristic organizations, as well as military officers, ex-bureaucrats, around 3,000 prominent members of the business community, and about 300 national-level politicians. Twenty-eight men were tried at the Tokyo war trials from 1946 to 1948: seven were executed (including two former prime ministers), and eighteen received long prison sentences (Allinson, 1997: 52–5).

Nevertheless, the American Occupation did not pursue the same goals throughout: while there was considerable zeal for 'New Deal'-style social and political reform during the period 1945–7, by 1948 the dawning realities of the Cold War led to a change in US policy towards Japan, popularly known as the 'reverse course'. Democratization was downgraded as a priority: instead, Occupation policies concentrated on forging an economically strong and self-sufficient nation, which would form a robust bulwark against communism in Asia. MacArthur's early enthusiasm for building up countervailing left-wing forces in Japan was now reversed. Many 'purged' bureaucrats were duly reinstated. The main emphasis during the latter part of the Occupation was on reviving the Japanese economy, a task overseen by the American banker Joseph Dodge. The Occupation of mainland Japan formally ended in April 1952 – though Okinawa remained under American military rule until 1972.

A number of analysts have emphasized the limited achievements of the American Occupation. In particular, they note the failure of MacArthur decisively to purge the Japanese bureaucracy of those who had held key positions before the war – only a few score were removed, and many of these later regained important posts (see Pempel, 1987: 157–87) – and his parallel failure to break the dominance of pre-war large companies in the business sector, despite token attempts to reform the *zaibatsu,* or great conglomerates (Allinson, 1997: 74–5). If the Occupation did not displace old concentrations of power, it is difficult to see post-war Japan as a dramatically more democratic and open society than pre-war Japan.

How could a country such as Japan embrace a constitution apparently so different from its previous political direction? An answer favoured by some scholars is that the 1889 constitution marked the beginnings of more widespread political participation in Japan; something not dissimilar to the 1947 constitution was already evolving. Reischauer claimed that:

> An aversion to dictatorial power, or even to charismatic leadership, and a strong tendency to group co-operation were pronounced features of Japan's political heritage, and in my view they still constitute great political assets for Japan today. (Reischauer, 1977: 240)

Reischauer also cites universal literacy and a strong entrepreneurial spirit as reasons for Japan's successful creation of a 'mass democracy'. He suggests a continuity between the 1889 and 1947 constitutions; by implication, the period of Japanese militarism during the 1930s, which culminated in the Pacific War, was an aberration from a gradual process of democratization. Support for this argument may be drawn from an analysis of the workings of the post-1889 political system. Although the Meiji constitution was doubtless intended to keep political participation under control, in practice MPs and political parties did not prove as docile and ineffectual as had been hoped. Although the Great Depression of 1929 saw the military return strongly to the political ascendant, scholars such as Reischauer have argued that, during the Taisho era, Japan was evolving into a modern democratic state: the American-imposed 1947 constitution simply expedited a process of evolution which was already under way. Reischauer's view is disputed by other scholars, who argue that the Japanese elite were forced to make the best of a post-war political settlement which was little to their liking.

Considerable debate centres around the importance of the Occupation and 1947 constitution. For many American scholars, who suffer from what might be termed a 'constitution complex' reflecting the US historical experience, the new Japanese constitution was of the utmost significance. However, the Occupation has received more mixed reviews from non-Americans. Van Wolferen has forcefully questioned the assumptions of many Japan specialists and has called the idea that Japan made a break with its political past after losing the Pacific War 'a major hindrance to an accurate assessment of the Japanese system' (van Wolferen, 1989: 347). Like Reischauer, van Wolferen sees a great deal of historical continuity in the Japanese political order. But whereas Reischauer sees that continuity in terms of democratic tendencies, van Wolferen describes a continuity of bureaucratic control, a persistent pattern of curtailing opposition. For van Wolferen, the militarism of the Pacific War seems a logical development from the repressive, centralized nature of the Japanese system. He supports his argument by looking back at the Meiji period, arguing that bureaucrats in late nineteenth-century Japan practised a system of 'thought guidance', trying to prevent the growth of the dissident social forces which had emerged in Europe. Both the highly efficient Meiji-era police force and the introduction of conscription were measures designed to enforce 'order': in other words, to prevent dissent.

Kawai argued that there were three main hypotheses about Japanese modernization – and, by analogy, Japanese political development (Kawai, 1960: 234–48). According to the 'conservative hypothesis', in order to modernize successfully, Japan needed to preserve its cultural traditions as much as possible. The 'liberal hypothesis' contended that Japan needed to introduce all the changes which western societies had experienced so as to achieve the same degree of modernization. A third approach was expressed in Kawai's 'pragmatic hypothesis' – Japan needed to use a mixture of traditional values and imported western ideas in achieving modernization and political development. Culturalist scholars have argued that Japan's successes since the Occupation represented substantial vindications of the conservative or the pragmatic hypotheses. Revisionist critics of Japan's political system, on the other hand, have continued to find Japan wanting, usually for failing to measure up to liberal democratic ideals. Mainstream scholars, by contrast (using the same 'liberal hypothesis' as their baseline), have tended to see Japan as 'converging' with western liberal democracy.

It can be difficult to establish exactly what was – and was not – the result of the Occupation: for example, was Japan's political stability in the post-Occupation years a result of the reforms introduced by the Americans, or the economic growth during this period? Much of the academic work written on the American Occupation suffers from bias; many accounts are attempts either to vindicate the Occupation, or to repudiate it. There is no doubt that the new constitution and the political order it brought about resonated widely with the Japanese people and achieved a broad measure of acceptance. Outwardly, Japan accepted the American liberal democratic values contained in the 1947 constitution, but the deeper realities were more complex.

# 3

# The Changing Political Economy

The phoenix-like emergence of Japan from the ashes and rubble of the 1945 defeat to become one of the world's most powerful industrial economies by the 1980s has often been casually characterized as a 'miracle'. Yet, as with other aspects of contemporary Japan, both the origins and the nature of that 'miracle' are highly contested. For some scholars, Japan's success represents the triumph of market forces: they see Japan as engaged in a process of convergence, becoming more and more like the West. Other interpretations stress the special circumstances of Japan's economic rise, notably the external agency of the United States – with its technical assistance and know-how – and the fortuitous outbreak of the Cold War (and especially the Korean conflict) which provided the Americans with a compelling rationale to bolster the Japanese economy. Revisionists, led by Chalmers Johnson, emphasize the degree to which Japan's accelerated post-war industrialization was a state-led process, coordinated by key agencies such as the Ministry for International Trade and Industry. Johnson describes Japan as a 'developmental state' a view opposed by mainstream American scholars, who are generally uncomfortable with statist explanations for ideological reasons. Other explanations centre upon the quality of the Japanese workforce, based on high levels of education and training; culturalists take this view a stage further, arguing that Japanese cultural norms of diligence, teamwork and deferred gratification were the root cause of the country's economic transformation. Old debates about the sources of Japan's economic success have recently mutated into new controversies about the economic woes that have befallen Japan since the early 1990s: why did the winning formula begin to fail?

## The Occupation and after

> As American warships enter Tokyo Bay, Japan faces an economic, political and social crisis. The old political order is about to be dismantled, and replaced with an imported imitation of western models. In order to compete with the West, Japan needs to overhaul its economy, and engage in a rapid process of industrialization. Yet within a few decades, Japan will pose a vigorous challenge to the hegemony of the West.

The four sentences above are deliberately ambiguous: they could refer either to the Japan of 1853, or to the Japan of 1945. In many respects, the challenges faced by Japan after the end of the Pacific War replicated the challenges previously faced in the Meiji period. In both cases the ruling order was largely bankrupt, and had capitulated in the face of overwhelming foreign pressure. Yet in both cases, far-reaching socioeconomic changes that had taken place during previous decades laid the basis for Japan to tackle the challenges ahead. Despite the staggering destruction of Japan's cities and industrial capacity by American bombing, the task of reconstruction began almost immediately: once again, the imperative was to 'catch up' with the West. While much of the physical infrastructure of Japan's industrial economy had been destroyed (and some plant was confiscated as war reparations), the technical expertise to operate heavy industries such as steel and shipbuilding still existed.

The Occupation administration set out to 'democratize' the Japanese economy by promoting unionization, breaking up the big *zaibatsu* (or conglomerates) – 10 holding companies, 26 industrial companies and two trading companies were dissolved – selling shares to the public, and instituting a land-reform programme. Only the last of these reforms was substantially successful: in practice, the big companies which had formed the industrial core of Japan's war machine largely succeeded in recreating and reinventing themselves in the post-war era. This was especially true of the banks, which were barely touched by the dissolution programme: four of the biggest banks in the post-war period – Mitsui, Mitsubishi, Sumitomo and Fuji – had their origins in pre-war banks. *Zaibatsu* reform was criticized as a policy with no clear beneficiaries, and was controversial even within SCAP (Supreme Commander for the Allied Powers, a common abbreviation for the Occupation administration) (Allinson, 1997: 74–5).

Dower has argued that the Fifteen-Year War was a 'useful war', since 'modern Japanese capitalism was created in the crucible of conflict' (Dower, 1992: 49). During the war, Japanese industry underwent enormous expansion, and Japan was one of the world's fastest growing economies by the time of Pearl Harbor. Japan was already capable of building its own plants and producing many of its own chemical products: it was the world's fourth largest exporter. The period from 1937 to 1941 had seen colossal increases in production, including a 252 per cent increase in machinery production and, by 1942, 68 per cent of the industrial workforce was employed in heavy industry. In other words, Japan's economic recovery during the late 1940s and early 1950s began literally as a reconstruction, a programme to bring Japan back to the levels of industrial output which had been attained prior to 1942. Viewed in this light, what took place in the immediate pos-war period was no 'miracle', simply the continuation of a longstanding process which had been interrupted by the wartime defeat.

Dower argues that industrial technologies developed primarily for military purposes – ranging from automotive engineering and shipbuilding to optical equipment – formed the basis of many of Japan's most successful post-war businesses (Dower, 1992: 54–6). The industrial revival of the post-war period also capitalized on changes in the labour market during the war years, including a great increase in technical-school graduates. Another important factor was the existence of a strong core banking structure based on a relatively small number of sizeable banks. At the same time, not all businesses were large. Japan had a two-tier economic structure, in which large companies farmed out parts of their activities to subsidiary companies and subcontractors, giving rise to vast numbers of small and medium-sized enterprises. This dualism gave added flexibility to the economy, enabling the conglomerates to control costs, and inevitably weakening the bargaining position of workers.

During the early period of SCAP, the emphasis was on 'reform, revenge, and reparations' (Allinson, 1997: 76), an approach which did not bode well for Japan's economic recovery. During the later years of the Occupation, however, the USA became increasingly interested in building up a strong capitalist democracy in Japan, especially in the light of the rise of communism in China. Joseph Dodge, a Detroit banker, was sent to Japan in 1948 to devise a programme of measures aimed at securing financial stability. His nine-point 'Dodge Line' package of 1949 imposed an austere fiscal regime, involving cuts in spending and job losses, but thereby controlling credit and inflation.

The outbreak of the Korean War in 1950 provided a much-needed boost to Japan's economy, producing huge orders for uniforms and equipment which Japanese concerns were eager to fulfil. Japan was able to establish itself as the Asian powerhouse of the Cold War, and Japanese economic recovery was seen as an important element in US strategy to create bulwarks against communism in Asia. This role later continued during the Vietnam conflict: whilst the 'peace constitution' imposed by the Occupation rendered Japan conveniently *hors de combat,* Japan was able to reap considerable economic benefits from these surrogate 'hot wars' prosecuted in Asia by the superpowers and their local allies. The Korean War orders helped kickstart the Japanese economy at a crucial moment, boosting employment levels and wages, and helping to generate domestic consumer demand. Well-known companies such as Nissan, Toyota, Toshiba and Hitachi were among the leading beneficiaries, and by 1955 Japan's industrial output was back to pre-war levels (Allinson, 1997: 78–9).

The same was true of agricultural output; during the 1950s, government subsidies for infrastructure and irrigation helped farmers, who also began diversifying from rice growing into other areas such as fruit and vegetable production. In terms of contribution to gross domestic product, however, primary industries (mainly agriculture, forestry and fisheries) were in long-term decline relative to the manufacturing sector. Primary industries accounted for 26 per cent of GDP in 1950, only 12.9 per cent by 1960, and 6 per cent by 1970 (Lincoln, 1988: 85). Thereafter the decline of the primary sector slowed somewhat, but new growth was mainly in the tertiary sector at the expense of heavy manufacturing. By 1990, 2.9 per cent of the workforce was employed in agriculture, while agriculture accounted for only 6 per cent of GDP (Argy and Stein, 1997: 257).

Despite their limited contribution to the economy, farmers remained politically quite important: they were the recipients of sizeable government subsidies, administered through an arcane 'food control system' which supported large numbers of small-scale – often part-time - farmers (Yayama, 1998: 102–4) and limited imports. Rice production accounted for 40 per cent of Japan's agricultural land by 1990, but it was estimated in the late 1980s that over half of Japanese rice farmers' income derived from actual or *de facto* subsidies by the taxpayer and consumer (Argy and Stein, 1997: 268). Despite the generous rates of subsidy provided to Japanese farmers, and an increase in aggregate agricultural production of 43 per cent from 1960 to 1985, Japan's food self-sufficiency rate fell from 90 per cent in 1960, to 67 per cent in 1990 (Argy and Stein, 1997: 269–70). Faced with considerable foreign pressure, especially from the United States, Japan has been gradually liberalizing the import of agricultural products.

## Consolidating growth

The year 1955 can be considered something of a turning point for Japan: ten years after the momentous wartime defeat, the economy was back to 1942 levels of production. The merger of two conservative parties to create the Liberal Democratic Party (LDP) in 1955 marked the beginning of a period of one-party dominance (popularly known as the 1955 system) which lasted almost four decades. The emphasis was now on a remarkable degree of economic growth, which brought vastly increased living standards and elevated Japan to economic superpower status. Indeed, some analysts have argued that Japan was driven by 'economism', a quasi-ideological preoccupation with economic success. McCormack describes the post-war Japanese state as 'a kind of joint venture by General MacArthur and Yoshida Shigeru' (Box 3.1), characterized by an economist orientation and a weak, subordinated nationalism (McCormack, 1986a: 39–40). Critics described the Japanese as 'economic animals' who had abandoned their culture, their principles, and (implicitly) even their humanity in the pursuit of material gains. French President de Gaulle famously remarked after the visit of a Japanese prime minister in 1963 'Who was that transistor salesman?' (Horsley and Buckley, 1990: 64).

In reality, the late 1950s and much of the 1960s were characterized by intense ideological conflict in Japan. During the 1950s, there was a wave of crippling strikes organized by militant unions, and 1960 saw huge demonstrations against the renewal of the Security Treaty with the USA. Rapid economic growth offered a means of buying-off dissent, an implicit bargain offered to the populace by the Japanese state. Never was this more apparent than when Prime Minister Hayato Ikeda announced his 'income-doubling plan'. Unveiled shortly after the Security Treaty demonstrations, the plan (politically inspired, and based on dubious statistics) called for Japan's GNP and the personal incomes of the Japanese to be doubled in the next 10 years (Masumi, 1995: 67). In other words, people should keep their

**Box 3.1 Shigeru Yoshida (1878–1967)**

Yoshida was a former diplomat from a prominent political family. He played a crucial role in shaping the direction of Japan during the early post-war period, when he served as prime minister for a total of seven years (1946–7, and 1948–54). Yoshida excelled at dealing with MacArthur and the American occupiers, satisfying their demands whilst securing favourable terms for his country. The 'Yoshida doctrine' formed the basis of Japanese foreign policy: Japan relied on the United States to provide for its national security needs, concentrating instead on economic growth and national reconstruction. In other words, Japan integrated itself into the economic and political international order created by the USA.

heads down, work hard, and watch their salaries grow, rather than engaging in political protest or industrial disputes: it was 'a social contract on a grand scale' (Horsley and Buckley, 1990: 62). Contrary to many predictions, the plan proved a great success, and average incomes actually doubled within seven years rather than ten.

In the years that followed, consumer demand increased considerably as most families sought to equip themselves with the 'three sacred treasures' (television, fridge and washing machine): by 1964, 90 per cent of households possessed all three items (Horsley and Buckley, 1990: 76), and many new blocks of flats were constructed to accommodate workers in rapidly expanding urban areas. Not all the extra income generated by rapid growth was spent on consumer goods or housing, however: small savers were a crucial source of the funds lent by Japan's banks and financial institutions. An average Japanese family was saving 25 per cent of its disposable income by 1974, which represented a 'savings-doubling' since 1955 (Allinson, 1997: 101). Japan's new post-war affluence was aptly symbolized by the 1964 Tokyo Olympics, the first Olympic Games to be held in Asia (Photo 3.1). The Games were accompanied by showcase infrastructure and technological projects, notably the inauguration of the first high-speed 'bullet train' (*shinkansen*) route, from Tokyo to Osaka.

Several factors drove Japan's high-speed growth during this period. One was the high rate of investment: the contributions of small savers were matched by those of industry itself, which reinvested a large proportion of gross national product in productive capacity, especially capital goods industries (Pyle, 1996b: 245). Another factor was a well-educated labour force, boosted during the

**Illustration 3.1 The Olympic logo from a bridge built in 1964**

1960s by post-war baby-boomers. The population rose from around 72 million in 1945 to 93.4 million in 1960, 103.7 million in 1970, and 117 million in 1980; thereafter, population growth began to level off (*Japan Almanac*, 1999: 286–7). There was a large shift of labour away from agriculture and into manufacturing, accompanied by sizeable migration into urban areas, especially the Kanto (Tokyo–Yokohama–Kawasaki), Chubu (Nagoya) and Kansai (Osaka–Kyoto–Kobe) regions on the Pacific coast of Honshu. Japan's workforce was widely seen as highly motivated, preoccupied by the imperatives of economic recovery and growth.

A further factor driving increased productivity was widespread technological innovation, as a large contingent of engineers and specialists sought to regain the competitive edge that Japan had lost because of the war. A great deal of foreign technology was bought in by Japanese concerns (often at bargain prices, from western companies that saw no competitive threat from Japan), though some foreign products were simply copied (Pyle, 1996b: 245; Horsley and Buckley, 1990: 63). Japan gradually moved away from labour-intensive textile production, and into heavy industries. Japanese electronics companies began by quietly vacuuming up global markets for consumer electronics such as televisions, radios and hi-fis, while their American counterparts were concentrating on pioneering large-scale capital goods for the high-prestige space programme and the military-industrial complex (Horsley and Buckley, 1990: 144–50).

During the 1970s, companies such as NEC and Fujitsu concentrated on acquiring and developing cutting-edge integrated-circuit technology and semiconductors, spearheaded by a MITI (Ministry of International Trade and Industry) 'national plan' for the semiconductor industry from 1972, later organizing a consortium of five leading Japanese computer firms, which succeeded in developing their own 64k-RAM superchips by 1979. In 1971, MITI had published a report setting out a new technological agenda for Japan, based on a shift to 'knowledge-intensive' industries, a 'vision' which formed the basis of Japan's industrial strategy in the decades that followed. Japan's commercial banks underwrote the necessary investment with low-interest long-term credit.

Aside from domestic factors such as these, broader international conditions played a part in Japan's remarkable economic rise. After the war, trade restrictions were reduced, world markets were opened, and international trade entered a highly expansionist period – so providing a favourable climate for Japanese exports. Japan joined the newly established GATT (General Agreement on Tariffs and Trade) in 1955, and membership helped Japan gain access to export markets. The establishment of the International Monetary Fund (IMF) in 1945 helped create a stable international currency regime, and Japan was able to obtain secure supplies of raw materials for its industrial output (Allinson, 1997: 98–9). Given the limited domestic sources of raw materials, Japan was exceptionally dependent upon such supplies, and highly vulnerable to external pressures in consequence. Japan's exports increased by about 17 per cent per annum from 1953 to 1965 (Pyle, 1996b: 246), reflecting a growing world demand for manufactured goods. The total global volume of manufacturing exports increased sixfold from 1953 to 1973, while the dollar value of Japanese exports increased by 25 times from 1955 to 1974 (Allinson, 1997: 99). Japan became a leading supplier of goods ranging from steel and ships, to cars, and audio and video equipment. At the same time, 90 per cent of what Japan produced from 1955 to 1974 was for the domestic market (Allinson 1997: 100): huge consumer demand at home was the primary engine behind the growth of Japan's industrial capacity.

## Savings

Like the importance of domestic consumer demand, the importance of savings in the Japanese economy can hardly be understated (see Table 3.1). Savings rates are very high, and rose steadily during the 1960s to peak in the 1970s (for a technical discussion, see Ito, 1992; 259–77). Levels of savings are consistently high across different parts of the country, and among the various age groups. Explanations offered for these high savings rates include culturalist interpretations ('Confucian' thriftiness), deficiencies in the social security system, the bonus system (whereby employees receive a sizeable proportion of their annual pay in the form of half-yearly bonuses), tax incentives, the need to save for the high costs of purchasing a home, and the desire to pass on inheritances to relatives. Garon argues that high levels of savings reflect systematic government promotional efforts led by the Central Council for Savings Promotion, which used radio, television and poster campaigns in a sophisticated programme of moral suasion (Garon, 1997: 153–7).

In the recent period, another factor supporting high levels of savings has been popular concern about the ageing society and falling birthrates: with fewer children to take care of the elderly, many Japanese people want to be assured of financial security in their old age. One very important form of savings is the postal savings system,

*Table* 3.1 Net household saving as a percentage of disposable household income

| | *1960* | *1975* | *1985* | *1990* | *1997* | *2000* | *2005* | *2007* |
|---|---|---|---|---|---|---|---|---|
| United States | 7.2 | 8.9 | 6.6 | 4.9 | 4.7 | 3.0 | 1.5 | 1.7 |
| Japan | 14.5 | 22.8 | 15.6 | 14.1 | 11.0 | 3.9 | 3.8 | 3.8 |
| United Kingdom | 4.5 | 11.4 | 5.4 | 4.4 | 5.9 | 0.1 | -1.3 | 4.3 |
| Germany | 8.6 | 15.4 | 11.4 | 13.9 | 10.1 | 9.2 | 10.5 | 11.2 |
| Italy | 16.5 | 26.9 | 17.8 | 15.6 | 15.1 | 8.4 | 9.9 | 8.2 |
| Canada | 3.8 | 12.7 | 15.6 | 10.5 | 4.9 | 4.8 | 2.2 | 2.6 |

*Note*: From 1997–2007, I reflected the OECD data (above resource).

*Sources*: OECD, *Economic Outlooks 2002*; OECD (1989) *Historical Economic Statistics 1960–1990*; *Bank of Japan* (1997), *Comparative Economic and Financial Statistics*; OECD, *Statistics, Main Economic Indicators (2002)*, http://www.oecd.org/EN/statistics/ OECD (2010) 'HOUSEHOLD SAVINGS', Available: http://www.oecd-ilibrary.org/docserver/download/fulltext/3010061ec014.pdf?expires=1286112911&id=0000&accname=freeContent&checksum=C59333CFE453DDAE999DC14C0636E651.

which offers tax-free savings accounts: by 1980 this system held deposits four times larger than the Bank of America, then the world's biggest commercial bank (Johnson, 1982: 210). High levels of savings provided a ready source of capital for industrial development, yet the very low interest rates prevailing by the late 1990s undermined incentives to save, weakening a longstanding strong point of Japan's economy.

## The developmental state?

Just as scholars of Japanese politics have often debated whether politicians or bureaucrats have the upper hand in governing the country, so scholars of the Japanese economy often disagree profoundly about the relative degrees of state and market influence in shaping the country's economic and industrial policies. Many mainstream American scholars display a touching faith in the primacy of democracy, the constitution and the free market: they typically seek to portray the politics and the economy of Japan as resembling those of the United States. Such views were robustly challenged in one of the most important and controversial books ever published about Japan: Chalmers Johnson's (1982) *MITI and the Japanese Miracle: The Growth of Industrial Policy, 1925–1975*. Johnson identified four core elements in his model of Japan's 'developmental state':

1 A small, inexpensive, but elite bureaucracy staffed by the best managerial talent available in the system.
2 A political system in which the bureaucracy is given sufficient scope to take initiative and operate effectively.
3 The perfection of market-conforming methods of state intervention in the economy.
4 A pilot organization like MITI. (Johnson, 1982: 315–19)

He argues that the powerful bureaucracy in Japan served as an 'economic general staff', planning and directing Japan's industrial policy through direct and indirect forms of administrative guidance. Japan's shift from labour-intensive declining industries such as textiles, to new high-growth areas such as shipbuilding, machinery, and later electronics, was superintended by MITI, while the restructuring of companies and industries was carried out by MITI and the Ministry of Finance. These same ministries also established the Japan

Development Bank in 1951, a bank with access to the resources of the country's postal savings system (Johnson, 1982: 210) and which offered inexpensive capital to selected industries, thereby bankrolling long-term growth. The Japanese government practised 'preferential credit allocation', turned a blind eye to monopolistic practices, coordinated investment strategy, and created a variety of non-tariff barriers (Pyle, 1996b: 248). Gibney argues that economic growth replaced war as Japan's national preoccupation:

> Practically speaking, the economic ministries – principally the Finance Ministry and MITI – were to serve as Japan's Pentagon; and bureaucrats, rather than politicians, were to be its generals. (Gibney, 1998: 70)

Johnson (1987) has extended his arguments about Japan to account for the rapid industrialization of other economies in the region, including Singapore, South Korea and Taiwan, views which have been elaborated by other authors. These economies are held to have pursued similar policies of 'developmentalism', characterized by features such as strong government, a close public/private-sector relationship, foreign direct investment, 'deferred gratification', and the US security umbrella (see McCargo, 1998: 130–7). These ideas reflected an important 'developmentalist' school of thought concerning the rise of East Asian economies.

Since Johnson's arguments directly contradict analyses that stress the pre-eminence of the market, they have met with considerable criticism. The 'market school' stresses different factors to account for Japan's industrial success, arguing that private enterprise in Japan was able to take advantage of:

> the rates of savings, investment, and taxation; the high level of skills and education in Japan; the huge stock of advanced western technology; the unparalleled export opportunities created by the expansion of world trade, and the availability of capital. (Pyle, 1996b: 248)

Johnson himself counter-argues that:

> American economic theory and Cold War strategy interacted to produce an environment of condescension toward and self-delusion about the Japanese economy. (Johnson, 1995: 56)

Much recent debate has been less concerned with the rights and wrongs of Johnson's original argument (which covers the period to 1975), and more concerned with the degree to which the 'developmental-state' model holds true for the last quarter of the twentieth century. During the 1980s and 1990s, the Japanese economy underwent a rapid transition away from traditional heavy manufacturing ('smokestack industries') and towards cleaner, high-technology industries such as information technology and electronics. At the same time, there was a parallel shift away from manufacturing and into the service sector. With the decline of those industries traditionally shepherded by MITI, the developmental-state model became gradually less appropriate. Writers such as Okimoto (1989) and Callon (1995) argue that MITI has gradually declined in influence, as have private-sector bodies such as the employers' organization *Keidanren*.

The result has been a more flexible and complex set of relationships between the public and private sectors, rather than the relatively fixed pattern described by Johnson. A common view is that Johnson may have been broadly correct about the 1950s and 1960s, but his ideas are not as helpful in explaining the 1980s and 1990s. Calder, taking the developmental-state model as a starting-point, argues that Japan has evolved a hybrid public–private system of 'corporate-led strategic capitalism', especially after the 1973–4 oil shock (Calder, 1993: 268). This system is characterized by higher levels of clientelism than the purely technocratic developmental-state model acknowledges, and partly arises from the hollowing out of state capacity resulting from 'the globalization of industry and finance, combined with escalating research costs, risk factors, and market-scale economies' (Calder, 1993: 268–9). The result is a continuing tendency for 'systematic partnerships' between Japanese enterprises, which may involve some secondary collaboration with government agencies. Calder emphasizes the importance of *keiretsu*, industrial and business networks which generate 'private-sector-dominated strategic capitalism'. He stresses that the Japanese state is rather risk-averse; the shortcomings of statism are offset by 'a creative, organized private sector, with a powerful sense of long-term objectives' (Calder, 1993: 277). Johnson himself later described Japan's 'Asian capitalism' as a combination of 'a strong state, industrial policy, producer economics, and managerial autonomy' (Johnson, 1995: 68), a description which offers some concessions to his critics.

## The structure of Japanese business

The most popular international images of Japanese business centre on major industrial giants such as Toyota or Sony. Japan is often portrayed as an economy dominated by large trading companies with huge workforces and complex structures, which are engaged in a diverse range of activities. Although big companies are very important players in the Japanese economy, most Japanese companies are small or medium-sized, and many have very limited operations. Small family concerns, ranging from mum-and-dad shops to tiny factories, abound in Japan. There are elaborate networks of relationships between larger companies and the sub-contractors which supply them.

Much of the academic research on Japanese business has focused on big firms, which make use of interlocking alliances known as *keiretsu,* of which there are two main forms – horizontal *keiretsu* (alliances across different industries), and vertical *keiretsu* (alliances between specific industrial concerns, their suppliers and their distributors) (Argy and Stein, 1997: 107). Horizontal *keiretsu* have been defined as:

> associations of large corporations which are clustered around a group city bank, a trust bank, a real-estate agency, a life and casualty insurance firm and one or more trading companies. (Argy and Stein, 1997: 107)

The best-known examples are the 'big six' horizontal *keiretsu*: Mitsui, Mitsubishi, Sumitomo, Daiichi Kangyo, Sanwa and Fuji. Such groupings have often subscribed to a 'full-set' mentality, seeking a wide range of holdings in areas ranging from shipbuilding to chemicals. They have typically placed less emphasis on profitability, and more on the 'safety and security' associated with their size and privileged positions (Katz, 1998: 157–8). These groupings have a loose structure, and are not subject to central control. Nevertheless, members promote each others' business interests, both directly and indirectly: for example, by ordering products and services from one another. They hold shares in each other's companies, and consult regularly on strategy and collaborative endeavours. Cross shareholding is an important feature of the Japanese economy, creating an 'institutional complementarity' that provides the foundations of the *keiretsu* system, the relationships between business firms and their bankers, and the relationships between employers and employees (Okabe, 2001: 82). While *keiretsu* may appear to be vast and monolithic, in practice they do most of their business with non-member companies, and the amount of business done within *keiretsu* has been in decline since the early 1980s (Argy and Stein, 1997: 112). Nevertheless, the six big *keiretsu* remain very influential in certain sectors, with more than 80 per cent of market share in chemicals, construction, drugs, electrical machinery, petroleum, rubber and shipbuilding. This sectoral dominance reflects the central role of MITI in protecting major players, by creating barriers to entry which have prevented both domestic and foreign competitors from entering key markets (Katz, 1998: 89).

Newer 'vertical' *keiretsu,* such as Honda, Sanyo and Canon, have had more impact in high-technology businesses, such as electronics. Vertical *keiretsu* are defined as 'a collection of input manufacturers and or distributors (mainly small firms) attached to a large corporation' (Argy and Stein, 1997: 108). Each large concern has a group of core sub-contractors, which in turn have their own relationships with secondary and tertiary suppliers. Japanese companies produce fewer of their components in-house than their western competitors.

### *Features of large business organizations*

Banks are a key element in *keiretsu*; indeed, all Japanese companies seek to establish special relations with a 'main bank', which may even hold shares in the company. This bank plays a leading role in raising loan capital for the company as required, based on its detailed knowledge of the company's finances. During the 'catch-up' period, most of the investment for industrial expansion was funded by around 15 major banks, which in turn were dependent upon loan funds channelled through the powerful Bank of Japan (Katz, 1998: 86). There was little scope to raise private finance through the stockmarket, so maintaining good relationships with bureaucrats and politicians who could influence the approval of expansion plans and loans was essential for large companies. Hoshi and Kashyap suggest that the costs of this financing system rose and benefits declined, until 'the regime became unsustainable and was overhauled' through a process of deregulation from the 1970s onwards (2001: 210, 259–63). Many larger firms, especially those engaged in manufacturing, began rapidly to replace bank finance with bond financing, often linked to equities (2001: 248).

Whereas many western companies recruit most of their directors from outside, internal appointees constitute the majority on the boards of all Japanese companies. Japanese companies are headed by a president, who appoints the board of directors: directors often have direct experience of production and technology, in contrast to the accountant-dominated boards of many Anglo-American concerns. Much has been written about the practices of collective decision making said to be followed by Japanese companies. These include the system of '*ringi-sei*', or circulating consultative memos designed to achieve consensus, and suggestion systems where workers are encouraged to propose improvements, ideas which are supposedly taken on board by higher management. However, most Japanese organizations are firmly based on a top-down hierarchy, and many large companies are controlled or dominated by a single key individual (Argy and Stein, 1997: 119). Small shareholding is less common in Japan than in the West, and the majority of shares are held by institutions. Many companies purchase shares in partner firms such as customers or suppliers, not so much to obtain good share returns as to cement business relationships and procure favours. As a result, the managers of Japanese companies are less directly accountable to their shareholders than, say, American managers.

Whereas many western companies are preoccupied with the (often short-term) goal of profit maximization, partly as a result of pressures from shareholders, Japanese companies have tended to be more concerned with the (usually long-term) goal of increasing their market share. The standing and reputation of Japanese firms is based largely on market share, rather than profitability, which may lead to highly aggressive marketing and sales policies. Distribution agents for the three main daily newspaper groups (Asahi, Mainichi and Yomiuri), for example, are notorious for their high-pressure sales tactics, which 'often makes it less trouble for consumers to subscribe to a daily newspaper than to continue to fend off salesmen' (Westney, 1996: 54). In many sectors, this kind of competition has resulted in cut-throat pricing, relying on economies of scale which drove out all but the largest players. Some analysts describe this as 'excess competition', a trend which was fuelled by high-growth rates in the immediate post-war period, and by a desire on the part of companies to lower average labour costs by expanding their operations, and bringing in cheaper, younger workers.

Traditionally, Japanese companies have concentrated on core businesses, and have been reluctant to diversify. However, there has been a growing trend towards diversification since the 1980s; companies have increasingly shifted their core production to overseas locations with lower labour costs, and have diversified their activities at home. Mergers and acquisitions have been much less common than in the West. However, creating subsidiaries (initially owned entirely by the parent company) is common practice; as core companies become too large to manage their activities efficiently, secondary aspects of the business are typically farmed out to subsidiaries. Subsidiaries, which may be located in cheaper regions of Japan, or even overseas, usually have lower labour costs than core companies. Senior staff who are underperforming are quite often 'kicked upstairs' to nominally higher posts in subsidiaries, transfers which may encourage them to retire early.

The rise of *keiretsu* in certain key industries was associated with growing inter-*keiretsu* collusion and the emergence of cartels that limited competition and restricted the penetration of imports (Katz, 1998: 160). At the same time, Okabe argues that since the late 1980s cross shareholding has been declining quite rapidly in Japan, and he anticipates an 'accelerated and drastic change' in this pattern of shareholding and the cosy corporate relationships it earlier spawned (Okabe, 2001: 83). The days of the classic Japanese *keiretsu* may soon be numbered.

### *Features of small companies*

The sub-contracting of production is highly institutionalized in Japan. As Francks notes, this practice may be regarded:

> either as embodying all that is exploitative in the 'dual structure' of Japanese industry or alternatively as an expression of the hierarchical but personalised long-term relationships of trust and patronage that make Japanese business culturally unique and impenetrable to foreigners (Francks, 1999: 252).

Sub-contracting became very widespread during the inter-war period, allowing large firms to hive off much of their production to smaller firms that used 'cheaper and more dispensable labour'. By the early 1980s, 82 per cent of companies with over 300 employees used sub-contractors (Francks, 1999: 252). Francks compares what is often referred to as Japan's 'small and medium enterprise sector', with what development economists call the 'urban informal sector'

(Francks, 1999: 183). While the existence of family-owned factories and garage-sized sweatshops producing goods for a single larger customer tends to be treated as a 'third world' phenomenon, businesses of this kind remain widespread in Japan. In the 1990s, almost 90 per cent of private-sector Japanese workers were employed in organizations with fewer than 300 employees (Sugimoto, 1997: 79–80), 60 per cent of the Japanese labour force worked in companies employing fewer than 100, and only 13 per cent in companies employing more than 1,000. In 1993, over 70 per cent of factory workers were employed in concerns with fewer than 300 workers (Whittaker, 1997: 3). In 1986, the same applied to 96 per cent of construction workers, 76 per cent of miners, and 88 per cent of transport workers (Argy and Stein, 1997: 126). Twenty-nine per cent of all workers in the early 1980s were employed in family-only or one-person concerns, compared with 9 per cent in the USA and 8 per cent for the UK (Argy and Stein, 1997: 125).

Classifying businesses is a contentious affair. Kiyonari suggests that there are four main business types in Japan: enterprise-type businesses, enterprise-type family businesses, livelihood family businesses (where profits and wages are not accounted separately), and side businesses or house-based working (cited in Whittaker, 1997: 5). There is some evidence that the first two types constituted a growing proportion of businesses as a whole, given the high rate of enterprise-type start-ups during the 1970s and 1980s. At the same time, some small family-oriented businesses were able successfully to upgrade themselves into fully fledged enterprises. Whittaker argues that despite popular images of the Japanese as preferring to work for large companies, a significant proportion were 'motivated by the desire to be their own boss' (Whittaker, 1997: 6).

The pressure gauges for certain machinery used in Toyota factories, for example, might all be manufactured by a single supplier (with fewer than a dozen employees) in an eastern suburb of Nagoya: if the orders from Toyota ever ceased, the enterprise would be instantly wiped out. Everything rests on a wholly unequal business relationship between the two enterprises, one of total dependency on the giant manufacturer by the small business. While many small businesses in Japan are too preoccupied with sub-contracting to develop more entrepreneurial activities, over 40 per cent of manufacturing small and medium-sized enterprises (SMEs) do no sub-contracting at all (Whittaker, 1997: 1). Some small enterprises, however, have grown into much larger ones: Honda and Sony are among the best-known examples. Revisionists have criticized Japan's economy for having a 'dual structure': the large 'modern' manufacturing sector is said to exploit the 'traditional' small sector. This view is rejected by some analysts, who see more integration (and greater reciprocal benefits) among the two sectors than this dualistic model implies (Francks, 1999: 254, 271). Katz notes that business cartels are not confined to *keiretsu,* but operate widely among small enterprises in Japan; over decades of LDP rule, many regulations were created that helped small businesses to maintain high prices and excess employment. At the same time, the authorities turned a blind eye to endemic tax evasion by small businesses. This was a 'conservative socialist' mechanism by which the LDP rewarded its urban support base, so ensuring that 'the fruits of Japan's high economic growth were spread among all of society's members' (Katz, 1998: 105). While deregulation and other changes in the Japanese economy post-bubble created some new opportunities for SMEs, by the late 1990s there were fewer SME start-ups than closures in many sectors of the economy. As proprietors of small family businesses approached retirement, many lacked successors. Hopes of a 'paradigm shift' towards a new Japanese economy in which small business served as a major engine of regeneration have failed to bear much fruit. As Whittaker puts it, 'Japan has lost its small firm "problem" – too many, too small – only to be confronted by another, namely how to nurture dynamic, new small firms' (1997: 206–7). Ironically, the entrepreneurial culture that produced so many earlier SMEs now seems on the wane in Japan, despite some notable counter-examples.

### *Employment and labour*

The best-known aspect of Japanese employment, internationally, is the idea of lifetime employment. According to this model, an employee is provided with job security until around the age of 55. Pay is determined largely by seniority within the organization (in other words, the longer you stay and the older you get, the more you are paid), rather than by job performance. In fact, there are often two parallel modes of promotion in Japanese organizations: promotion to more senior and responsible positions, and promotion based on rather loosely defined 'skill qualifications'. People who never attain senior management roles nevertheless see their pay gradually increase in line with their accumulated experience (Sako, 1997: 6–7). Associated with lifetime employment and payment by seniority is the idea of paternalistic management: the company assumes a very direct responsibility for the welfare of its employees. The opposite side of this coin is an expectation that employees will demonstrate reciprocal 'loyalty', and dedicate themselves to the higher needs of the company. This loyalty may include doing unpaid overtime, passively accepting disagreeable temporary transfers to far-flung branches, not normally moving to work for rival companies and not using holiday entitlements. These three elements of the Japanese employment system were first discussed by James Abegglen (1958) in his classic book *The Japanese Factory,* and have often been emphasized by culturalist scholars who see Japan's industrial relations as culturally distinctive. For culturalists, Japan's economic success has been largely predicated on this special pact between employers and employees, a pact based on Japanese notions of deference and paternalism. Even scholars who reject such explanations may be prepared to see Japanese firms as 'communities' bound together by a sense of shared interests (Sako, 1997: 5).

Broadly speaking, most categories of workers and age groups in Japan have more limited job mobility than in other countries, though there are exceptions. In larger concerns, long-term employees are typically taken on straight from school, college or university. Many new employees are hired on the basis of general educational level; often the most important factor in hiring decisions is which school, college or university applicants attended. Vocational training is largely the responsibility of employers, who generally emphasize job-specific skills within a company-specific context, rather than transferable skills. It is still quite unusual for executives to change company in mid-career, and a major mid-life career change (for example, switching from working in a company laboratory to teaching science in a secondary school at the age of 44) is quite rare. Disillusioned executives typically see starting a small business – such as a coffee shop – as the only alternative to remaining with their company. This pattern is changing amongst younger executives in fields such as financial services, however, especially in sectors where foreign companies have gained an important foothold. Yet most Japanese organizations still prefer new recruits to those with previous work experience, since they like to socialize their staff into the prevailing organizational culture. Rather than specializing in particular fields, the majority of junior executives are regularly rotated to different jobs in various sections of the organization, learning about the way the company works, instead of gaining an in-depth knowledge of any one area of work.

Abegglen saw 'lifetime employment' and limited job mobility as a reflection of Japanese culture, a view that has been challenged in some of the subsequent literature (Francks, 1999: 218). To begin with, the 'lifetime-employment' model is far from universal in Japan. It applies most completely to male white-collar employees in large companies: relatively few women benefit from lifetime employment, many manual workers are employed on a 'temporary' basis even by large companies (and so do not receive the same pay and conditions as their permanent counterparts), and most smaller enterprises do not offer the same long-term job security and benefits as major concerns. Blue-collar workers often change jobs in pursuit of higher wages or better conditions. In other words, the benefits package generally understood by the term 'lifetime employment' probably never applied in full to even a quarter of Japan's workforce.

Japanese employees typically receive up to 30 per cent of their annual salaries in the form of twice-yearly bonuses, a system that helps promote high levels of savings. 'Lifetime' employees may receive subsidized company housing, an extremely valuable benefit given the high rent levels and exorbitant property prices in urban Japan. At the same time, company life has drawbacks: many executives put in very long hours (see Figure 3.1), and there have been some well-publicized cases of *karoshi,* death from overwork (Sugimoto, 1997: 94). Male executives often spend many of their evenings in work-related drinking and social activities, and while most Japanese men enjoy these activities, opting out is usually impossible. Exhausted salarymen often find solace in *pachinko* parlours, where they unwind by spending many hours gambling on a kind of upright pinball machine (see Photo 3.2).

The rotation system has serious personal drawbacks for career-track employees, who are often expected to relocate to regional offices or even overseas at short notice, generally without their families. On balance, however, there is little evidence to suggest that the Japanese work harder than, say, Americans: western Europe, with its high levels of unionization, short working hours and month-long summer vacations, is far more 'culturally distinctive' globally in its working practices than is Japan.

In the Japanese context, 'working' and 'being at work' are two different matters. Many Japanese organizations are overstaffed by international standards: secondary-school teachers often give only 16 lessons a week, department stores are full of supernumerary sales assistants, and every roadside construction site has a flag-waving

**Illustration 3.2 Playing *pachinko* – leisure activity for office workers**

safety marshal standing on the pavement, as shown in Photo 3.3. Senior bureaucrats at government ministries in Tokyo may spend part of the morning reading the newspapers, so that they will have some work left to do during their compulsory overtime in the evenings: they are obliged to be available every evening when the Diet is in session, on the off-chance that a parliamentary question might be asked about the work of their department, and an instant response has to be drafted. Most Japanese firms and organizations have long-winded consultation and decision-making processes. The Japanese 'work ethic' is not always an ethic of intensive and efficient work (though such work certainly often takes place), but an ethic which entails spending long hours in the workplace or with work colleagues, engaging in work, quasi-work or work-related socializing. The art of looking busy is an important one in every Japanese organization. As Masao Miyamoto, an outspoken psychiatrist and senior bureaucrat who was eventually fired from the Japanese Health Ministry, put it:

> 'Don't be late' . . . means you must be at work – that is, at your desk, before anyone else; you don't actually have to be working. You could be reading the paper, or looking at a comic book, or

**Illustration 3.3 A safety crossing marshal**

> having a cup of coffee. The important thing is to let people around you know that you arrived before starting time. (Miyamoto, 1994: 157)

To regard lifetime employment as a product of Japanese culture is rather problematic. The practice is of recent origin and was clearly shaped by the industrialization process, rather than itself facilitating rapid industrialization. Similarly, it is highly doubtful whether the Japanese are possessed of a special, culturally distinctive work ethic. Like other people, the Japanese can and do work hard when circumstances require, but they are by no means a nation of out-and-out workaholics, with an exclusive dedication to the interests of their company or organization. Indeed, surveys of Japanese employees reveal high levels of dissatisfaction. The stereotyped Japanese 'corporate soldiers' who receive a disproportionate amount of attention in much of the literature on Japan actually constitute a small minority of the workforce; many Japanese workers are sceptical about the paternalistic rhetoric of their companies, or else are excluded from the benefits of 'corporationism' on account of their inferior conditions of employment (Sugimoto, 1997: 121–3). For

*Figure* 3.1 Average annual hours actually worked per worker (2010)

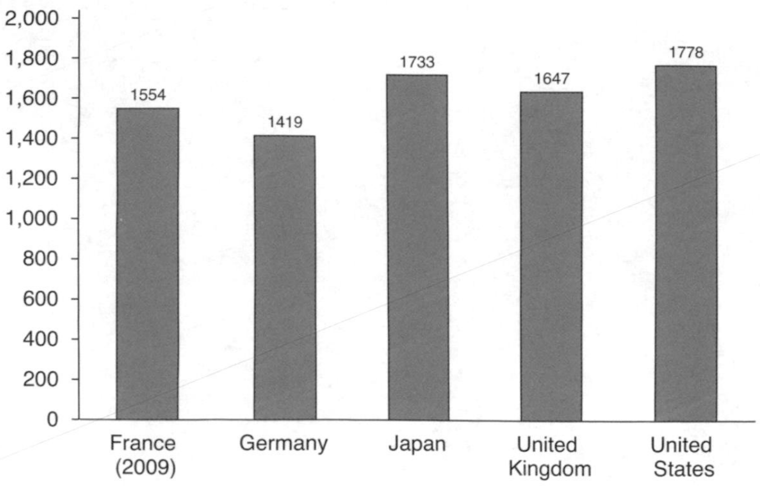


*Source*: OECD, *Labour Force Statistics*, http://stats.oecd.org/Index.aspx?DataSetCode=ANHRS (accessed 26 March 2012).

many of the footsoldiers of Japan's post-war industrialization, the corporation was less a benevolent and holistic patron than an oppressive hierarchy demanding absolute obedience and submission (on the life of ordinary car factory workers, see Kamata, 1982). Sako argues that although earlier culturalist views of Japanese industrial relations now seem outmoded, Japan has not simply converged with western models. Understanding Japanese patterns of employment requires nuanced interpretations that acknowledge underlying social and cultural differences, by examining a range of 'interlocking and mutually reinforcing' elements (1997: 2).

## *Unionization*

Trade unions existed in early twentieth-century Japan, but independent trade unionism was suppressed in the late 1930s and early 1940s. In the immediate post-war period, Japanese unions were seen by the US Occupation forces as an important counterbalance to militarism, and were actively supported. During the late 1940s and the 1950s, unions staged numerous major strikes, pursuing a highly adversarial strategy in a quest for improved pay, benefits and working conditions for their members. Notable strikes included Yomiuri Newspapers (1946), Nissan Motors (1953), and the Mitsui coal mine strike (1960).

The Nissan strike was an important turning point: to undermine the industry-wide National Car Workers' Union, Nissan established a company-specific union and thereafter never experienced a single day of lost production due to industrial action (Argy and Stein, 1997: 148). Company unions (also known as enterprise unions) became the dominant form of unionization in the private sector; these unions largely eschew confrontation, holding ritualized 'spring offensives' in which demands for higher pay are backed by such innocuous actions as strikes held during the lunch hour. Union officials recruited from the shopfloor are given privileged treatment by management, and some even become directors of the company. Despite a significant number of industrial disputes in Japan, very few days are lost through strike action. Some analysts argue that enterprise unions are quite assertive and effective in representing employee interests (Argy and Stein, 1997: 149), but revisionists believe that the enterprise-union model reflects a strategy for co-opting and manipulating workers by company managements. One writer calls these unions 'an "auxiliary instrument" of personnel administration' (Kawanishi, 1986: 151).

Enterprise unions have certainly done little to support temporary workers in their companies, emphasizing building relations of trust between management and long-term employees. This has led to criticism of enterprise unions as overly deferential towards the agendas of management. Sako argues that the major challenges for these unions involve adapting from a homogeneous to a heterogeneous workforce, and 'how to redefine their role in the workplace in such a way which is transparent to the members' (Sako, 1997: 17). Much of the international literature on enterprise unions questions the extent to which they can be considered unions at all. From a Japanese perspective, however, they play an important role in monitoring the activities of company managers. Shareholders typically receive much lower rates of return in Japan than in Britain or the USA, a trend that reflects the greater relative importance of rewarding 'loyal' employees for contributing to the firm's community (Sako, 1997: 8). Nationally, labour unions have not proved particularly effective in recent decades, as a result of declining memberships and inter-union conflicts. Rengo, the main union federation, was backed by only 62 per cent of Japan's unions in 1993. Yet Kume argues that despite these shortcomings, Japanese labour unions have been much more successful than is generally recognized. He argues that unions form part of 'flexible networks' which workers helped create, and which bring them considerable benefits (1998: 227).

## Busts and booms

The oil crisis of the 1970s was the first serious setback to Japan's post-war high-growth policies, and Japan's reliance upon imported supplies of raw materials – especially oil from the Middle East – was abundantly illustrated. The first abrupt rise in oil prices in 1974 led to 24.5 per cent rises in consumer prices and, in consequence, Japan was plunged into recession. When a second hike occurred in 1979, Japan was much better able to withstand the impact. Nevertheless, the mid-1970s marked a turning point for the Japanese economy – as for most industrialized economies – when high-speed growth began to decline (Ito, 1992: 69–72). Four years of double-digit GDP growth from 1967 to 1970 were followed by much lower GDP growth rates (typically from 3 to 5 per cent) during the 1970s and 1980s.

However, despite the fact that Japan was far from the world's top-performing economy during the late 1980s and the beginning of the 1990s, land and share prices rose at exponential levels during this so-called 'bubble' period. Asset values rose five times over from 1981 to 1989 (Argy and Stein, 1997: 46). Much of Japan's new super-wealth, symbolized internationally by the Japanese purchase of the Rockefeller Center in Manhattan, and of a Van Gogh painting for a record-breaking $83.9 million, was based on excessive speculation. Part of this 'paper' Japanese wealth derived simply from the exceptionally high value of the yen, in contrast to the weakness of other major currencies, especially the US dollar. The turning point came in 'black August' of 1990 (Ito, 1992: 433–4), when the value of the Japanese stockmarket fell by over 16 per cent in a single month – a development precipitated by the Iraqi invasion of Kuwait. From then on, the bubble began to burst, share and asset prices tumbled, and many newly acquired overseas companies and assets were sold off by their Japanese owners (see also Figure 3.2). The overly rapid pseudo-expansion of the economy during the bubble period produced significant pockets of bad debt, and within a few years the unthinkable began to happen, as big-name Japanese companies and financial institutions went belly-up. Downsizing and retrenchment involved the 'unravelling' of the lifetime-employment system, as the first white-collar redundancies were announced (Yamamoto, 1993: 381). A 1993

*Figure* 3.2 Japan's real economic growth rate (1983–2009)

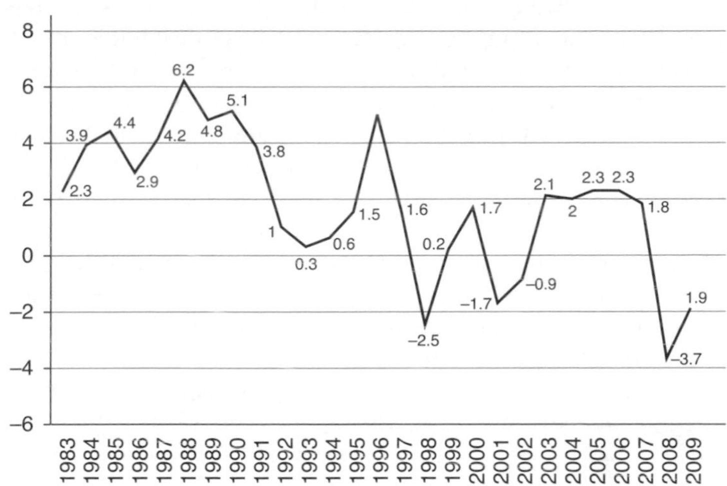


*Source*: The Cabinet Office, Japan; http://www.esri.cao.go.jp/jp/sna/toukei.html#qe.

survey showed that 15 per cent of Japan's top 400 companies had already shifted from seniority-based pay to individual, performance-related salaries. Higuchi argued that without a wholesale shift to merit-based pay, Japan would be unable to achieve the flexible and effective workforce required in the ageing society of the early twenty-first century (1997: 50). Whittaker and Kurosawa, however, note that various Japanese and foreign commentators have been predicting the demise of lifetime employment and 'managerial familialism' since the early 1960s (1998: 767).

One structural problem in the Japanese economy by the beginning of the 1990s concerned the high rate of personal savings and consequently lower levels of consumer demand. By the late 1970s, 'excess' savings meant that lack of domestic consumption proved an obstacle to continuing economic growth. However, during the early 1980s, this problem was solved by a shift towards exports, which in turn generated large trade surpluses – incidentally leading to growing international trade friction. But the high value of the yen soon meant that Japan's exports were overpriced, and industrial production actually began to fall (Katz, 1998: 213). Faced with strong competition from other economies in the region, exports collapsed. Yet calls for fundamental changes in the economy to counter the problem of excess savings were rejected as politically unacceptable. Japan responded by reinvesting considerable amounts of capital in the form of direct foreign investment, as well as in portfolio investments in other financial assets, such as US government debt (Francks, 1999: 9). This overseas investment brought some short-term advantages, but the Japanese preference for savings over spending sapped the core strength of the domestic economy: capital was not being invested in productive new businesses. At the same time, interest rates were cut, producing a temporary surge in investment and fuelling a short-lived 'bubble' from 1985–91. However, much of this investment was in overpriced real-estate projects that brought in few returns. As Katz puts it: 'Some of the "bubble buildings" are the loveliest in all of Tokyo. Yet, in far too many cases, they were the economic equivalent of digging ditches and filling them up again' (Katz, 1998: 216). Borrowers had no way of repaying the banks and bondholders who had underwritten their spending. Asset prices plummetted, and financial institutions were left with vast portfolios of non-performing loans. Faced with the resulting recession of the early 1990s, the government could not make the classic response of cutting taxes in order to stimulate demand: Japanese people already had enough money to spend, but were choosing instead to save it. The bubble period left Japan with a serious banking crisis. Katz argues that Japan's financial sector reflected a 'pre-capitalist' order in which capital was never allocated to the most efficient uses for investment purposes (Katz, 1998: 218–19). While 'patient', 'dedicated' use of capital to foster long-term growth could be highly positive, Japan had seen this kind of lending assume troubling characteristics. Despite the downturn of the post-bubble era, the Japanese economy continued to perform quite impressively on a comparative study of GDP per capita (see Figure 3.3).

As problems began to emerge, serious questions were raised about the competence (or lack thereof) with which the Finance Ministry and Bank of Japan had regulated the financial sector. A series of scandals and investigations revealed well-established practices of collusion between bank officials and the bureaucrats who were supposed to supervise them. Major companies were found to have paid large sums of money to racketeers. The Finance Ministry has never been headed by an economist, and is run largely by a self-reinforcing elite of Tokyo University law graduates who are suspicious of economics specialists. Two of Japan's leading economists have

*Figure* 3.3 GDP per capita (based on purchasing power parities, 2009 estimate)

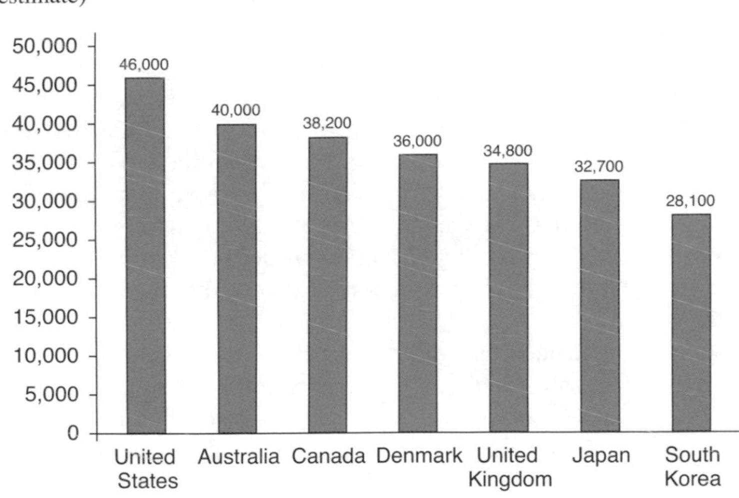


*Source*: CIA, *CIA World Factbook 2009*, https://www.cia.gov/library/publications/the-world-factbook/rankorder/2004rank.html.

argued that the Japanese government does not employ even a single professional economist (Hartcher, 1997: 9). While a reliance on well-rounded generalists may have served Japan well during the period of post-war reconstruction and high growth, it created serious difficulties as financial markets became more complex and more globalized. The Ministry retained high levels of regulation that stifled the successful development of financial services in Japan, yet these regulations did not serve the purpose of properly safeguarding the integrity of the banking system. Very few Japanese bankers were even forced to resign over their mistakes and misdemeanours, let alone faced criminal charges. However, Wright's meticulously-researched study of the Ministry of Finance did not hold bureaucrats primarily responsible for Japan's fiscal crisis: he rather stressed the 'inherent constitutional and practical limitations' on the Ministry's controls, and the politicization of the policy process by the LDP (Wright, 2002: 5).

While Japan's vast and inadequately supervised banking and financial sector was left in appalling shape following the end of the bubble era, the industrial sector was also suffering. The high costs of pay and production in Japan had led to large-scale shifts of production to low-wage foreign markets, such as Southeast Asia and the United Kingdom. The result was a 'hollowing out' of the Japanese economy. The corporate shells – head offices, senior management, bank accounts, deposits and debts – remained in Japan, but many core employment and revenue-generating activities had been shifted out of Japan. Nissan Motors was now selling British-made Nissans (bearing Union Jack stickers) in Kobe: Japan was importing Japanese cars. One analyst suggested that 15 per cent of Japanese manufacturing would be carried out overseas by the year 2000; certainly, very few Japanese companies were increasing domestic production (Hartcher, 1997: 169). These shifts in production weakened the domestic manufacturing base.

Meanwhile, the declining value of the Japanese yen during the late 1990s, coupled with problems in the economy, meant that, for the first time, Japanese companies began selling-up to foreign concerns. The economic nationalism upon which Japan's post-war industrialization had been predicated was now under threat. Ironically, the financial sector was also hollowing out: international companies were shifting their trading out of Tokyo by the early 1990s (Hartcher, 1997: 180–1), while Japanese companies were establishing trading operations in Hong Kong and elsewhere. When the Thai government effectively devalued the baht on 2 July 1997, a crisis in confidence was precipitated, which led to dramatic economic crashes in Thailand, South Korea and Indonesia, with knock-on effects across the region and the globe. Much of the public and private debt owed by the affected Asian countries was to Japanese banks, by far the largest lenders in the region. This wider financial meltdown put the Japanese economy under severe strain, leading to a decline in the value of the yen, company closures, and layoffs.

Despite a series of bank insolvencies and failures, these issues were dealt with on a case-by-case basis, typically using 'convoy operations' rather than any decisive comprehensive package of measures (Hoshi and Kashyap, 2001: 267–77). In 1996, Hanwa Bank became the first Japanese bank in the post-war period to be dissolved by the Ministry of Finance; shortly afterwards, four Kansai banks were wound down. Meanwhile the process of financial deregulation continued apace, culminating in the 'Big Bang' of the late 1990s. The Japanese 'Big Bang' was less of a 'bang' than its 1986 London predecessor, in that changes were phased in more gradually; nevertheless, it was 'bigger', in the sense that the package of reforms was more extensive and far-reaching. The overall effect was to transform 'a heavily regulated bank centred system to a liberalized market-based system' (Hoshi and Kashyap, 2001: 290). The main provisions involved expanding investor choice, increasing corporate fundraising options, allowing financial institutions to offer a wider range of services, creating a fair and efficient market, and improving the stability of the financial system (2001: 290–3). The Big Bang led to a wave of mergers among major Japanese city banks, resulting in only four major financial groups by 2001: Mizuho, Mitsubishi Tokyo, Sumitomo Mitsui, and United Financial. These bank mergers were accompanied by a similar round of insurance group mergers, and a series of agreements between major international financial services providers and Japanese counterparts. A novel feature of the bank mergers was that many cut across traditional *keiretsu* lines. Some of these mergers were primarily 'defensive', based on the belief that larger financial institutions would be less likely to fail, or to fall victim to hostile takeovers by foreign competitors. Adopting a mainstream stance, Hoshi and Kashyap argue that the twenty-first century will increasingly see Japan's financial system converging with Anglo-American models, as banks decline in both size and significance, and securities markets gain in importance accordingly (2001: 324–7).

Another problem for many Japanese manufacturers was the extent to which their profits during the bubble period had derived from financial speculation and other 'non-operating revenues'. Such sources accounted for 40 per cent of Toyota's profits in 1987, 65 per cent of Nissan's profits, and 63 per cent of Sony's profits (Katz, 1998: 221). For some of these large concerns, traditional 'core businesses' had become secondary activities in terms of their profit base, distorting their priorities, and making them extremely vulnerable to short-term financial pressures.

## Accounting for the end of the 'miracle'

Why did Japan's economy start to falter with the bursting of the bubble in the early 1990s? The answer to this question clearly hinges on your preferred explanation for Japan's post-war economic successes. Gao offers a useful summary of core explanations from the English-language literature, adding his own for good measure (Gao 2001: 2–19). Most scholars emphasize specific causal explanations, with major reference to either domestic or international factors;

others, such as Brenner, Katz, Pempel and Gao himself, favour more elaborate structural interpretations:

1 *Specific international factors*. These include 'Reaganomics, the liberalization of finance, the coordination of multinational foreign policy, and rules promulgated by the Bank of International Settlements' (Gao, 2001: 20). Leading scholars in this camp include Chalmers Johnson (1998) and Paul Krugman (1999). Arguments here focus on 'international political economy' readings; Japan's economic rise was facilitated by certain international conditions, and once these no longer obtained, decline set in.
2 *Specific domestic factors*. These include failures of particular institutions (notably regulatory failures by the Bank of Japan or the Ministry of Finance), or shortcomings in specific areas such as corporate governance, 'window guidance' or fiscal policy. Writers in this group include David Asher (1996), Aikyoshi Horiuchi (2000), R. Taggart Murphy (1996) and Adam Posen (1998).
3 *Crisis of capitalism*. Robert Brenner (2002) sees Japan's economic woes as simply a function of giant contradictions in the global capitalist system, which entered a 'long decline' during the second half of the twentieth century.
4 *Logic of 'development stages'*. Richard Katz (1998) sees Japan's state-mandated economic growth as an appropriate strategy during the 'catch-up' period, but one that became 'cartelized', inefficient, and stifled further growth.
5 *Regime shift*. T.J. Pempel (1998) argues that Japan's post-war economic growth both legitimated and was fostered by conservative LDP rule. From the 1970s, however, electoral politics became more fragmented, economic policy making was politicized, and Japanese corporations began to act as 'international investors'. Japan lost its way and stumbled economically.
6 *Institutional failure of corporate governance in a changing global context*. Gao (2001) argues that the changing global economy produced a contradiction between growing domestic calls for protectionism, and international pressures for deregulation and liberalization. Japan was torn between strong coordination and weak monitoring and control; this led to excessive competition, the bubble, and its subsequent burst.

These suggested explanations are only examples, and the extensive literature on the subject covers many others. At the core of each explanation lie certain key questions:

(a) How far did Japan's economic decline reflect long-term structural failings of institutions and regimes, rather than misplaced policies or strategies?
(b) How far was Japan's economic decline the result of a failure to converge with Anglo-American modes of business?
(c) How far was Japan's economic decline an essentially domestic affair, and how far was it shaped by international dimensions beyond Japan's control?

In analysing the causes of Japanese decline and suggesting prognoses for the future, simple distinctions between mainstream, revisionist and culturalist perspectives become extremely blurred. Insofar as 'revisionism' was based upon a sense that Japan's rise threatened to undermine the pre-eminence of the United States, the end of the bubble left revisionists deflated. Japan no longer constituted a substantial economic threat to American or western interests. However, revisionists' criticisms of Japanese shortcomings in areas such as corporate governance were vindicated by the country's mounting economic problems. Mainstream scholars could argue that Japan's economic troubles showed how Japan needed vigorously to pursue liberalization and deregulation. Mainstream analysis of the origins of the 'miracle' might have been faulty, but these analysts had always been right to assume that Japan did not pose a long-term threat, and would ultimately need to seek convergence with western models and practices. The result was that the revisionist–mainstream divide, while still salient, became extremely indistinct. Chalmers Johnson, famous for emphasizing the central role of the Japanese state in promoting industrial development, suggested Japan's crisis stemmed from American reluctance to let the Cold War end. In a 1998 article, he complained that he and other revisionists stood accused of having failed to highlight the dark side of East Asian capitalism (Johnson is singled out for severe criticism by Asher – see 1996: 232–3). He responded that 'It was the so-called revisionist writers who first outlined the differences between East Asian and American capitalism' (1998: 655). But Johnson acknowledged that revisionists had failed to appreciate just how far the end of the Cold War would affect the Japanese economy.

Meanwhile, Richard Katz, who had criticized the antagonism towards Japan expressed by many revisionists, produced a classic characterization of the sclerotic Japanese 'system' that had strong overtones of Karel van Wolferen. Though uncomfortable with revisionist perspectives, Katz recognized that revisionists were 'in certain ways descriptively correct' (www.japanreview.com). Both mainstream and revisionist perspectives were somewhat vindicated by economic developments in the 1990s, but culturalist views were greatly weakened: if culture largely determines economic performance, and culture is largely unchanging, how could such a dramatic downturn in Japan's economy be explained?

The general expectations of good and secure employment which framed Japan's post-war politics were already beginning to unravel well before the new millennium, and now belong to a previous era. Although fully fledged unemployment remains relatively low by international standards, under-employment and incomplete employment are huge problems. Many Japanese people in their twenties and thirties have never held a long-term job. Instead, they have followed alternative employment paths as casual hourly paid workers, temps and seasonal contract-holders, living with their parents, or in very modest apartments on wages that barely maintain them at a subsistence level. Others work online from home, or run tiny businesses. For such people, conventional goals such as marriage, starting a family or home ownership seem permanently out of reach. They are often known as 'freeters', which may be a play on 'freelance' or 'freeloader', or as NEETs ('Not in Employment, Education or Training', a term first used in Britain). Greatest attention has been paid to those *freeters* who have deliberately opted out of pursuing conventional goals, though most became *freeters* for lack of any good alternatives: the number of secure longer-term jobs has greatly declined. David Slater, who sees *freeters* as the new face of the working class, argues that the term is misleading:

> For many, freeter is a label that has built into it a narrative of agency, choice, freedom, and individuality. In some more romantic renderings in the popular and academic press, a freeter can even be a rebel making a political statement. (Slater 2010)

In other words, the idea of *freeters* is a middle-class construct; for many lower-class Japanese people, casual employment has long been a way of life, previously. Moral panic about the casualization of labour in Japan was only aroused when the middle classes were more visibly affected in the late 1990s. To some extent, the work now done by so-called *freeters* was previously the less visible domain of older women, who had sought casual employment after raising families and returning to the workplace. While *freeters* are very hard to quantify, Kosugi suggests that there were between three and four million in 2002 (Kosugi, 2006), while some estimates suggest that they may number ten million by 2014. The rise of *freeters* among well-educated social classes that previously enjoyed much greater economic opportunities has had a dampening effect on the domestic consumer demand which drove the Japanese economy during its heyday.

### *New kinds of Japanese company*

Despite the ossification of many traditional big Japanese conglomerates, some entrepreneurs have been able to create extremely successful and fast-growing start-ups that seem to owe more to Silicon Valley than to Nagoya or Osaka. Financial analyst Jesper Koll points to dynamic Japanese entrepreneurs such as Tadashi Yani of Fast Retailing (best known for its Uniqlo clothing stores), Yoshikazu Tanaka of the GREE social networking site, and those behind such technology start-ups as Mixi, DeNA and Rakuten (Koll, 2011: 115). Other examples include SoftBank, Nitori and Nihon Densan. Typically, these companies were led by high-profile mavericks who set out to break the mould in their fields, were much more cosmopolitan and culturally adept than their precursors, and were able to write their own rules in new areas of emerging business. Nevertheless, many such entrepreneurs have not had it easy, facing constant sniping from the staid and mainstream Japanese media. One of Japan's most famous start-ups, internet provider Livedoor, suffered a spectacular collapse and subsequent takeover in 2006, when its founder Takafumi Horie was arrested for trading law violations. Horie has protested his innocence; whatever the rights and wrongs of the legal case, his punishment was widely seen as the revenge of the Japanese establishment on an uppity interloper (Son 2011: 58). The challenge for Japan is to create the space and conditions to grow a new generation of creative business leaders who will shake up the existing order across a range of fields. So far, such space remains tightly curtailed.

### *Post-tsunami challenges*

The terrible tsunami, earthquake and nuclear crisis that began in northern Japan on 11 March 2011, eventually claiming almost 20,000 lives, created a set of complex interlocking challenges (see

*Earthquake Report*, 2011). The greatest of these were the economic and human costs of rescue, clean-up and reconstruction; and the disastrous impact on Japan's nuclear power industry. Over 900,000 buildings were damaged or destroyed. Estimating costs on this scale, including the losses due to permanent or temporary closure of thousands of businesses, is extremely difficult. One authoritative source suggests that direct losses will total around $280 billion, with between $110 and $220 billion in additional indirect losses (*Earthquake Report*, 2011). The Japanese government has embarked on a huge reconstruction programme, one that will further increase the country's high levels of public debt. Nevertheless, funds for this task can be raised largely from within Japan and do not expose the country to substantial external risks. In some respects the reconstruction programme will serve as a much-needed stimulus to some sectors of the economy, though again pandering to the special interests of Japan's over-indulged construction industry. Hopes expressed by commentators such as Bill Emmott that the disaster might shake Japan's economy out of stagnation soon seemed over-optimistic (Emmott, 2011).

The position of Japan's nuclear power programme is much more troubling. The botched handling of the meltdown at the Fukushima nuclear power plant revealed a disturbing level of collusion between TEPCO, the utility which owns the plant, and the bureaucrats who were supposed to regulate the nuclear industry. Safety procedures had been extensively violated, and there was a dark history of accident cover-ups by TEPCO. As Paul Scalise put it 'TEPCO painfully transformed from the "secretly sick man of Japan" to the walking undead in a matter of months' (Scalise, 2011: 210). The company's lies and deceits had destroyed its public credibility, yet the nuclear power industry which TEPCO controlled provided around 30 per cent of Japan's electricity needs. A country so lacking in natural resources in Japan could ill-afford to ween itself away from nuclear power; yet Japan's acute seismic vulnerability made ensuring nuclear safety exceptionally difficult. All 54 of Japan's nuclear reactors are located on coastlines, in locations that could easily be struck by future tsunamis (Scalise, 2011: 214). On one level, the Fukushima crisis vindicated many revisionist critiques of the Japanese system, with its lack of accountability and privileging of elite interests over the public good. With many nuclear plants shut down and plans to build more on hold, Japan now faces the prospect of a looming energy crisis.

## Conclusion

In the post-bubble era, it is no longer possible (if it ever was) to see Japan simply as a land of economic miracles. The rapid reconstruction and economic growth that post-war Japan experienced was based on a particular set of historical circumstances. Some analysts argue that Japan's industrial rise was primarily governed by state intervention; others see it more as a triumph of market forces. Still others emphasize the cultural aspects of Japanese business, with its distinctive patterns of industrial relations, as a central explanatory variable in accounting for the country's economic rise. However, the decline of Japanese economic strength since the end of the bubble calls all of these explanations into question. The very same structural or cultural assets which helped Japan to gain such immense economic power by the end of the Cold War seem also to have contained within them deep-rooted shortcomings. While Japan's bureaucrats and *keiretsu* bosses thrived during the hothouse conditions of high growth, they struggled to adapt to the changing international economic environment of the post-Cold War period. Katz makes this argument very clearly in a useful appendix, claiming that Japanese industrial policy only worked in the 'catch-up' period, but became a burden once Japan had achieved full industrialization, and the economies of scale involved diminished (Katz, 1998: 349–57). So long as Japan could use exports to sustain production, the problems of the economy were not insuperable. But as export markets flagged in the 1990s, those problems became acute and eventually amounted to a crisis.

The rapid shift from a world economy dominated by conventional manufacturing and trade to a 'global information society', which required the ruthlessly effective management of cutting-edge financial services, appears to have caught Japan off-guard. Some Japanese companies seem to have lacked the flexibility and independence required to compete successfully with western rivals in changing market conditions, and accordingly lost comparative advantage. Like Katz, Iwao argues that Japan's economic rise was based on a 'catch-up' approach that is only suitable for developing countries (Iwao, 1998: 37–9). Japanese companies placed 'excessive' emphasis on building group-learning capacity, to the detriment of fostering individual talent. Yet the current global enterprise culture requires allowing scope for individual creativity. Only by abandoning their trademark hierarchical organization can major Japanese companies perform effectively as innovative organizations. Iwao concludes: 'The Japanese economy of the 1990s is missing the massive "third industrial revolution" (or the information revolution) being led by the United States' (Iwao, 1998: 39). Iwao's analysis, however, fails to explain continuing areas of technical innovation by many Japanese companies, or the runaway global success of highly creative new products such as computer games and animated films.

Some time back, the independent economist Tadashi Nakamae suggested three possible future scenarios for Japan: a 'long hollowing' (structural problems are not addressed and Japan gradually declines economically); 'crash and rebirth' (under which the economy virtually collapses, producing an inexorable demand for structural changes, and leading ultimately to regeneration); and 'Hercules departs', under which the US withdraws its military support, leaving Japan increasingly challenged as an Asian economic power by a resurgent China (*The Economist*, 21 March 1998; http://www.nier.co.jp). Despite tensions between the post-2009 DPJ government and the United States, Hercules has singularly failed to depart. 'Crash and rebirth' remains the most optimistic of Nakamae's scenarios: given Japan's successful track record in transforming calamities (such as the arrival of the 'black ships', and the 1945 defeat) into opportunities, a combination of domestic crisis and global 'foreign pressure' could offer the ideal catalyst for transformation. It was briefly hoped that the 2011 tsunami and associated disasters might provide just such a catalyst, but weak political leadership has meant that Japan still seems intent on continuing to with what Gao calls 'muddle-through' (2001: 274); some change, but too little reform, enacted too slowly, resulting in continuing stagnation. Japan did enjoy an extended post-bubble phase of financial recovery from around 2002 to 2008, characterized by higher levels of productivity (Posen, 2011: 104), but failed to seize this opportunity to push through more serious structural changes.

By the second decade of the new millennium, Japan has settled into a 'long hollowing', a kind of collective resignation to the country's gradual eclipse by China, and an extended *sayonara* to earlier aspirations of beating the United States at many – if not all – of its own games. Neither the long-ruling LDP nor the supposedly reformist DPJ that came to power in 2009 had a realistic plan to overcome Japan's long-term economic challenges. The greatest of these is Japan's alarming level of public debt, by far the highest of any advanced economy (Schwab, 2011: 121). The combination of an ageing population, low birthrate, higher life expectancy, low immigration and limited female participation in the workforce remains extremely troubling; while both immigration and female employment policies could readily be changed, this would require a bold and imaginative political leadership.

To be sure, there are more optimistic views. Koll argues that if the state deregulated other areas of the economy such as telecommunications and healthcare, opening them up to more foreign competition, Japan could see the same kinds of successes that have already emerged in the retail and digital media sectors (Koll, 2011: 115–17). He suggests that the long-postponed and highly contentious increase in consumption tax from a mere 5 per cent should be pushed through, with the specific aim of boosting pension and health benefits and so firm-up consumer confidence. The Noda government did try to grasp this nettle when it drafted new measures to increase Japan's consumption tax rate in early 2012. Posen argues that while Japan will never return to the glories of the bubble years, its economy is 'becoming British', characterized by a strong financial system, good flows of foreign direct investment, some high value manufacturing onshore, and a key role for cultural industries and tourism (2011: 107) – all in all, a respectable, if not stunning economic future.

# 4

# Social Structure and Social Policy

How far does Japan's social structure differ from those of other societies? Mainstream scholars identify numerous points of similarity, arguing that Japan has been engaged in a process of modernization and convergence with western models. Revisionists tend to emphasize the shortcomings and the dysfunctional aspects of Japanese society, challenging the dominant view of Japan as overly rose-tinted. For culturalist analysts, Japanese social structure can only be understood through the study of distinctive patterns of order and behaviour that reflect longstanding cultural norms and mores. One view that borrows from all three perspectives is the metaphor of Japanese society as an onion, where the bulk of the population can be viewed in terms of different concentric rings. At the core of the onion are the most privileged members of Japanese society: male, permanent employees of large companies. In the outer ring are disadvantaged groups such as migrant labourers and minorities. The middle rings contain blue-collar males, women, the elderly, people hired on short-term contracts, the self-employed, and employees of small enterprises. Generalizing about the Japanese is difficult, since those at the core of society are vastly more privileged and comfortable than those on the margins.

## Cultural characteristics

Discussions of Japan's cultural characteristics can be highly contentious. 'Culturalist' approaches to understanding Japan typically emphasize certain core values and beliefs which are held to underpin society. These include: collectivism (an emphasis on the interests of the family, village, company or nation rather than those of the individual); consensus (a preference for harmony and agreement over open dissent and disputation); and hierarchy (accepting the importance of seniority and status). Much of the debate about Japanese culture centres around the question of where culture originates. If culture is seen as an inherent and largely immutable set of values passed on from one generation to the next, culture offers an explanation for the nature of society. However, if culture is seen as a construct, an artefact created by the state (especially through the education system), then culture is less an explanation for society than a manifestation of it.

Status is a core concept in Japan, where even university students have a strong sense of their position on the social ladder; second-year students refer to third-year students as their *sempai* (seniors), and to first-year students as their *kohai* (juniors). In Japan, everyone knows the age of everyone else, and many organizations produce seniority lists for internal distribution. Vertical ranking, based mainly on age, pervades virtually all Japanese institutions, determining everything from the location of each individual's desk to the order in which cups of tea are distributed (Japan National Tourist Organization, 1986). These rankings are reinforced by all kinds of linguistic constraints, since the Japanese language designates different ways of addressing one's social superiors and inferiors. In a system such as this, it is difficult for outstanding individuals to be accorded recognition, since this would upset the apple cart of hierarchy. It also makes open debate and disputation difficult; inferiors cannot easily challenge the opinions of their superiors, but often feel obliged to defer to their supposed higher wisdom.

The scholar who has done most to popularize the idea of group-based explanations of Japanese society is Chie Nakane. She argues that:

> At a group meeting a member should put forward an opinion in terms that are safe and advantageous to himself, rather than state a judgement in objective terms appropriate to the point at issue ... Freedom to speak out in a group is determined by, as it were, the processes of human relations within the group; in other words, it goes according to status in the group organization. (Nakane, 1970: 35)

Nakane's arguments, though extremely influential, have been widely criticized as misleading and dated. As well as vertical relations of seniority, horizontal relations of group solidarity are profoundly important in Japanese society. Traditionally, the Japanese place great emphasis on the importance of *wa,* or group harmony. Activities in Japanese schools, notably within particular 'homerooms' or sports clubs, are organized around teaching students to work together collectively, to subsume their own interests to those of the group. Later, these principles are applied to the workplace, where the group might be defined by a specific department of a company.

In general, positions of power in Japan are held by men in their fifties, sixties, and seventies, even where it might be widely recognized that a particular individual in his thirties or forties has greater talents than his bosses. Relatively few women have achieved senior positions in politics, the bureaucracy, or business. The ambitious younger person must be extremely patient, since openly to challenge a superior would cause the superior to lose face. The difference between appearance and reality is a key element in Japanese society. Whatever people's true feelings (*honne*) about a given situation, the facade of appearances (*tatemae*) must be kept up. To western observers critical of Japan, the idea of *honne* and *tatemae* often looks like a form of dishonesty or hypocrisy. To the Japanese, however, operating on two levels of 'reality' may seem entirely normal. Some scholars see Japanese cultural characteristics as 'natural' phenomena that have arisen over a long historical period.

Revisionist scholars prefer to see Japanese culture as an 'artificial' construct, created and perpetuated by the state, by ruling elites, and by the needs of the capitalist order. Marxists see an emphasis on culture as a crude attempt to obscure the class relations that they believe underpin all societies. Mainstream scholars tend to emphasize convergence, arguing that Japanese culture is becoming less important in the face of modernization and social change. Some writers have even argued that certain features of Japanese culture (such as managerial methods or working practices) might profitably be exported to the West and to the developing world.

## Family structure

Traditionally, Japan had an extended family structure, and it used to be common for three generations to live together in the same household. The *ie,* or traditional Japanese household, operated according to strict social norms, which clearly defined the roles of each member. However, rapid urbanization in the post-war period, combined with high land prices and poor standards of housing, mean that most Japanese people now live in much more cramped conditions than their counterparts in Europe and North America. The nuclear family, packed into a 'rabbit hutch' of an apartment or house, has become commonplace, though there are also numerous 'new extended families' comprising a nuclear family, plus one or more parents-in-law. Many single people, young and old, live alone in tiny flats. The average ages of first marriage for Japanese people have risen steadily from 26.6 for men and 23.8 for women in 1955, to 28.8 for men and 27.0 for women in 2000, to 30.4 for men and 28.6 for women in 2009 (Ministry of Health, Labour and Welfare). The old Japanese adage that an unmarried woman of twenty-six is like 'Christmas cake' (a play on the idea of 26 December, suggesting an item past its prime) no longer applies.

There has been a steady decrease in the number of marriages since 1972 (see Table 4.1, p. 83). While this can be linked to the rise of individualism and more freedom of choice, Masahiro Yamada also notes that 'it is not about an increase in the number of people who want to stay single, but an increase in those who want to get married but can't, mainly due to 'social obstacles to marriage' such as 'decreases in men's salaries, more women who desire to be a housewife only, and the rise of "parasite singles"' (cited in Ito, 2009). There are two common patterns of marriage for women: one is to marry early, soon after finishing high school or a two-year college; another is to marry later, often after working for several years on a short-term contract as an 'office lady', or temporary employee. Kelly (2002) argues that Japan is characterized by a phenomenon of 'female marriage resistance': Japanese women find that employment opportunities are increasing, but men are largely unwilling to share domestic chores and often expect their wives to care for elderly parents. The solution for many women is to marry later, if at all.

Many private Japanese high schools are single-sex institutions, and even at mixed high schools there is considerable segregation and self-segregation of boys and girls. Similarly, in the workplace men and women typically socialize in single-sex groups, resulting in a 'quasi-homosexual' society (Miyamoto, 1994: 48, 61). Only for a relatively brief period (roughly from the ages of 18 to 25) do men and women mix together socially and some Tokyo commuter trains have special 'women-only' carriages to reduce sexual harassment (see Illustration 4.1). It is relatively rare for husbands and wives to entertain other couples at home, or to meet them for evenings out: often men and women have separate social lives and groups of friends. There is a common Japanese saying that 'a good husband is healthy but absent'; marriage is looked upon as an economic arrangement that lends form and respectability to adult existence, but not as the central institution around which a person's inner life revolves. While 'love matches' are now the norm, some marriages are still arranged through formal or informal introductions by go-betweens. Social, economic and educational status are still important criteria for decisions concerning marriage. Many companies in Japan assign male employees to branches and offices away from their home for months or years at a time. Partly because Japan has a very limited housing market – it is too expensive and impractical to buy and sell a home each time a new transfer comes – these men typically leave their wives and children behind in their home city, returning only at weekends (Jolivet, 1997: 70–2). Traditional gender roles within marriage are rather persistent; for example, a nationwide survey conducted by NHK in 2005 showed

**Illustration 4.1 Sign for a women-only carriage on the Tokyo underground**

that 'women spend considerably more time (daily average of 4.26 hours) in doing housework compared to men (1.38 hours) in 2005', and similarly in respect of childcare, 'on average, Japanese mothers spend approximately 46 minutes whereas fathers spend only 13 minutes per day in taking a physical care of their children' (Ishii-Kuntz, 2008: 3).

Despite the numerous shortcomings of marriage, the divorce rate in Japan remains negligible by international standards (2.3 divorces per thousand in 2002, falling to 2.01 divorces per thousand in 2009), reflecting a high degree of outward social conformity. Nevertheless, an April 2007 change in the pension laws enabled 'divorced women to access up to half of their ex-husbands' future pension payments, making divorce more financially feasible for women who have not held full-time jobs... This legal change coincides with the oldest baby-boomers turning sixty and is generally predicted to create a boom in "later-life divorce" (*jukunen rikon*)' (Alexy, 2007: 169). Although the overall divorce rate has dropped, the number of divorces among couples married for more than 35 years reached 5,507 in 2007 (the largest number in Japanese history), a 16.0 per cent increase over 2006 (*Asahi Shimbun*, 6 June 2008). According to a private detective agency, the top three reasons for divorce in 2001 were: personality conflict (46 per cent), violence (30.8 per cent), and adultery (27.5 per cent) for women; and personality conflict (63.2 per cent); adultery (19.3 per cent); and bad relationships with families and relatives (17.6 per cent) for men.

Nevertheless, low divorce figures disguise the fact that some Japanese marriages are little more than conveniences, maintained for pragmatic reasons by couples who would separate or divorce in other societies. Sugimoto notes that the Japanese system of 'family registration' (*koseki*) makes divorce difficult (Sugimoto, 2010: 160). Under this system, the husband is usually designated head of the household, children born out of wedlock are effectively 'second-class' citizens, children of divorced people may be stigmatized, all members of a family are expected to assume the same surname, and the ashes of women are usually placed in the family cremation tomb of their husband. Family registration documents are publicly available, and it is common for the families of couples who are becoming engaged to inspect these documents for evidence of irregularities. Any 'stain' on the family register can make it difficult for people to find respectable marriage partners. All in all, maintaining facade marriages is often the path of least resistance.

## Dating and relationships

Traditionally, eligible young people were typically introduced by friends of the family or professional intermediaries through a formal *o-miyae* (matchmaking) process. 'According to the National Institute of Population and Social Security Research, about 70 per cent of all marriages before the war were arranged. Sixty years later, the percentage had plunged to 6.4 per cent' (Ito, 2009). Due to long working hours and little opportunities to meet marriage partners, there has been a growth in the matchmaking and dating industry; 'The Ministry of Economy, Trade and Industry estimated in 2006 that the sector saw sales of between ¥50 billion to ¥60 billion'(Ito, 2009). Another phenomenon is the huge increase in international marriages: 44,701 out of 730,971 marriages in 2007 were between Japanese and foreign spouses compared to 27,727 out of 791,888 in 1996 (Ministry of Health, Labour and Welfare). Table 4.1 shows two major trends in international marriage: the tendency for growing numbers of Japanese men to 'import' brides – often from China or Southeast Asia – and the increased tendency for Japanese women to 'export' themselves, in order to marry foreign husbands (often westerners) and then live abroad.

Increasingly, young people are tempted to delay marriage – sometimes indefinitely – in order to enjoy the greater freedoms and higher disposable income associated with extended singlehood. This has led to some criticism of so-called 'parasite singles', 20- and 30-somethings dedicated mainly to their own consumerist pleasures, whose parents often continue to accommodate them and so subsidize their comfortable lifestyles. In 2009, 2.8 million older single people, aged between 35 and 44, were still living with their parents (*Yomiuri Shimbun*, 24 September 2010). Masahiro Yamada, the sociologist who coined the term 'parasite single', refers to them as 'pension (*nenkin*) parasites' – middle-aged singles who depend on their ageing parents' pensions.

Pre-marital sexual activity is common, and as in western countries, many Japanese men and women seek extra-marital liaisons or relationships. Numerous 'telephone clubs' exist, providing a means for men to contact available women, who may include high-school students or housewives: free tissue packets advertising these clubs are handed out to commuters at busy stations. A 1994 survey suggested that one in three teenage girls had contacted such clubs (McGregor, 1996: 241).

*Table* 4.1 Marriages of Japanese citizens, inside and outside Japan, 2009

| | *The number of marriages within Japan (ratio)* | *The number of marriages outside of Japan (ratio)* | *The total number of marriages (ratio)* |
|---|---|---|---|
| Japanese husbands and Japanese wives | 689,137 (about 95%) | 2,215 (about 18%) | 691,352 (about 93.5%) |
| Japanese husbands and non-Japanese wives | 28,720 (about 4%) | 1,635 (about 13%) | 30,355 (about 4%) |
| Non-Japanese husbands and Japanese wives | 8,249 (about 1%) | 8,686 (about 69%) | 16,935 (about 2.5%) |
| Total | 726,106 | 12,536 | 738,642 |

*Sources*: Ministry of Health, Labour and Welfare (2009) 'Summary of Japanese demographic-transition in 2009'; Nikkei Business (in Japanese) [online] available: http://business.nikkeibp.co.jp/article/topics/20101105/216965/?P=2.

'Compensated dating', where a man provides money or gifts to a woman in exchange for dates or sexual favours, is quite widespread (see Liddy, 2002). So-called 'love hotels', garish buildings renting rooms by the hour, are widespread throughout Japan, providing facilities for clandestine encounters. This kind of behaviour exists just below the surface of Japanese society, widely known and understood, but rarely discussed in public. Some studies suggest that as much as half of all sex in Japan takes place in the country's 30,000 love hotels – where many Japanese people were conceived (Chaplin, 2007: 2).

The term *soushoku-kei danshi* (herbivorous/grass-eating boys), coined by popular columnist Maki Fukasawa in 2006, defies ready definition. But it is generally used to describe young men who 'earn little and spend little, and take a keen interest in fashion and personal appearance' (Neill, 2009). In some recent surveys, half of Japanese men in their twenties and early thirties identified themselves as herbivorous: many were close to their mothers, uninterested in women (especially in bed), lacked self-confidence, were often alone, and were not good at communicating face-to-face. These lifestyle choices reflect a rejection of their fathers' values as sexually competitive 'economic animals', who were typically salarymen in the business sector. While some herbivore men are gay or metrosexual, most simply lack any libido. Many also lack conventional career ambitions. Quite similar to herbivores are so-called *otomen*, or girly guys.

Half of all unmarried Japanese men between 18 and 34 have no close friendship – let along sexual relationship – with a woman. The same applies to 40 per cent of women in the same age category. According to a 2010 survey, 84 per cent of 20-year-old Japanese men said they were not dating anyone and 49 per cent had never had a girlfriend. Another survey found that 36 per cent of Japanese males between 16 and 19 had no interest at all in sex (Osaki, 2011). While many Japanese men with *otaku* (computer geek) tendencies have relatively limited social lives and spend a lot of time alone, an extreme form of this behaviour is known as *hikikomori*, or reclusiveness. *Hikikomori* have become so absorbed in their private worlds that they stop going to work or school, developing a form of agrophobia (see Zielenziger, 2006: 15–92). Some estimates suggest that there may be a million *hikikomori* in Japan, though others argue that the real figure is in the thousands. As a large-scale social phenomenon, their emergence has worrying implications.

Some women seem to be excited by fantasies about these new-style men: there is a new genre of 'boys love' comic books, magazines and computer games about close relationships between men, which are consumed largely by women. But in general, women and girls are becoming more *nikshoku-kei joshi* (carnivorous girls), with completely opposite traits to *soushoku-kei* guys. Young Japanese women are much more confident than their mothers' generations, and are often well-travelled, romantically adventurous, and deeply underwhelmed by their emasculated herbivorous counterparts, whom they sometimes describe using the derogatory term *ojou-man* – 'overly refined' men. Some carnivorous women take a special interest in pursuing grass-eating guys, but the popularity of sexual vegetarianism among young Japanese men does not bode well for most women, nor for Japan's declining birthrate. A popular form of dating in Japan is the *gokon*, or group blind date, mostly commonly at a restaurant but also sometimes for a ski-trip or for golf (*golfkon*). Some young working people prefer alternative forms of socializing, such as visiting 'cat clubs' (see Illustration 4.2) to unwind after hours by petting an assemblage of cute feline creatures.

While social norms make it difficult to live an openly gay lifestyle, homosexuality is not uncommon – although many gays are nominally

**Illustration 4.2 Relaxing at a Tokyo 'cat club'**

in heterosexual marriages, as a result of family and social pressures (Harada, 2002). McLelland found that most Japanese gay men were very reluctant to 'come out' to their families, friends and colleagues about their sexual preferences, even when their real orientation must have been obvious. Typically, the issue simply remained unmentioned for years. For most such men, cohabiting was out of the question (McLelland, 2000: 218–21). Much the same applies to lesbians. Same-sex marriage remains prohibited, but Japan is a rather liberal society in that homosexual acts have always been legal.

At the same time, homosexuality is both satirized and celebrated in Japanese popular culture. *Okama* is a derogatory term used to describe homosexuals, transgender, transvestite and transsexuals in Japan. They are also referred to as the 'new half'. McClelland (2000), for instance, notes 'what is called a "gay boom"', with 'homosexual-themed movies, television programs, novels, and academic discourse' during the late 1980s and early 1990s' (cited in Furnham and Saito, 2009: 302). This boom has continued through the popularity of transgender/transsexual TV personalities, models and singers such as Ikko, Ayana Tsubaki, and Ai Haruna.

In the past, living together before marriage was very rare: in the 1987 Japanese National Fertility Surveys, only 3 per cent of unmarried respondents reported that they had lived in a cohabiting union, (Raymo *et al.*, 2009: 787). However, there has been a rapid increase in cohabitation in recent years; about 25 per cent of 25- to 34-year-old female respondents (both married and unmarried) in the first rounds of the Japanese Generations and Gender Survey and the National Survey on Population, Family, and Generations reported that they had lived in a cohabitating union (Isawa, cited in Raymo, 2005; Tsuya, 2006 cited in Raymo *et al.*, 2009: 787). Despite the considerable growth in cohabitation, many couples cohabit discreetly and informally, and few chose long-term cohabitation. Heuveline and Timberlake (2004) suggest that 'cohabitation was a marginal experience for earlier cohorts of Japanese women but can be described as a prelude to marriage for women born after 1965' (cited in Raymo *et al.*, 2009: 793). 'Cohabiting unions in Japan may be best viewed as a prelude to marriage rather than as an alternative to marriage or singlehood' (Raymo *et al.*, 2009: 800).

Childbearing outside wedlock is still very rare in Japan and it remains only 2.5 per cent compared to 45 per cent in the United Kingdom and 65 per cent in Iceland in 2007 (OECD, 2010). There are a number of reasons for the strong emphasis on legitimacy. 'The legal rights of legitimate children generally take precedence over the rights of illegitimate children in Japan' (Hertog, 2009: 81); for instance, according to a controversial provision of Japanese civil law (article 900), illegitimate children are entitled to only half of what legitimate children inherit. In addition, the 'family register – the main legal document used for personal identification in Japan –makes unwed mothers and their children easily identifiable', by 'making unwed mothers and illegitimate children identifiable, the family registry opens the possibility to treating them differently and thus may discourage women from opting for unwed motherhood' (Hertog, 2009: 77–8). At the same time, Japanese single mothers lack state support and face considerable structural economic difficulties (Hertog, 2009: 5). Hertog also found considerable evidence that many biological fathers responsible for illegitimate pregnancies pressured their girlfriends to have an abortion (2009: 37).

## The urban–rural divide

Patrick Smith argues that the divide between urban and rural Japan is central to understanding the country and its politics (Smith, 1997:

164–86). Japan's main cities – such as Tokyo, Yokohama, Nagoya, Kyoto, Osaka and Kobe – are largely concentrated in *omote nihon* (the front of Japan) on the Pacific coast, in the central part of the main island of Honshu. Nearly half of Japan's population lives in three areas: Kanto (around Tokyo), Kansai (around Osaka) and Tokai (around Nagoya). Whereas in the pre-war period, Osaka was a merchant city that rivalled Tokyo, in the post-war period many Osaka-based companies moved their head offices to the capital, and Yokohama became the second largest city in Japan. The urban–rural divide is in some respects an outdated concept because most Japanese live in areas that are by any definition urban, but there are differences between semi-urban areas which retain older social practices, and urban or suburban areas which are more atomistic. Some social facts about Japan are summarized in Box 4.1.

Clammer notes that cities such as Tokyo and Osaka might be considered 'world cities' in terms of their populations and their

**Box 4.1 Key social facts about Japan**

| | | |
|---|---|---|
| Religion | Shintoism 83.9%, Buddhism 71.4%, Christianity 2%, other 7.8%<br>*Note*: total adherents exceeds 100% because many people belong to both Shintoism and Buddhism (2005) | |
| Life expectancy at birth | Average<br>male:<br>female: | 82.12 years<br>78.8 years<br>85.62 years (2010 est.) |
| Infant mortality rate | 2.79 deaths/1,000 live births (2002 est.) | |
| Literacy | 99% ( 2002) | |
| Doctors per 1,000 of population | 2.02 (2000) | |
| Beds per 1,000 of population | 14.69 (2002) | |
| Education continuance rates | Upper Secondary School<br>University | 98% (2010)<br>54.3% (2010) |

*Sources*: CIA (2010), *The World Factbook 2010*; Statistics Bureau, Ministry of Public Management, Home Affairs, Posts and Telecommunications, Japan, *Japan Statistical Yearbook 2010*; Ministry of Education, Culture, Sports, Science and Technology (2010), *School Education Report*, http://www.mext.go.jp/b_menu/toukei/chousa01/kihon/kekka/k_detail/__icsFiles/afieldfile/2010/08/05/1296403_2.pdf.

economic and cultural power. He also identifies several other categories of Japanese city (Clammer, 1997: 28–30): the 'old capitals' of Kyoto, Nara and Kamakura, with mixed economies based partly on tourism; 'traditionalized' old towns with a high-class character, such as Kurashiki and Kanazawa; modern industrial cities such as Toyota City (home to the car manufacturers), Kawasaki and Kitakyushu; provincial cities that combine various administrative and commercial functions, and which are also educational and cultural centres, such as, Sapporo, Sendai and Kagoshima; and science cities, such as Tsukuba (outside Tokyo). Clammer is sceptical about the efforts of some urban anthropologists to emphasize the political and cultural vitality of traditional urban neighbourhoods and administrative units, arguing that this vitality is being displaced by new forms of network-based consumerism (Clammer, 1997: 30–1). He argues that although neighbourhoods do still exist in urban Japan, 'except in pockets still dominated by members of the old middle class, they do not mean the kind of things that many anthropologists of Japan ascribe to them' (Clammer, 1997: 33). He prefers to see many areas as 'epitome districts', a mish-mash of residential accommodation, restaurants, cafes, entertainment outlets, convenience stores and other shops, with considerable life, but limited sociological coherence.

The Japan Sea coast, along with the other islands of Japan, is far less developed and urbanized: this is *ura nihon,* a politically incorrect term meaning the back of Japan, or hidden Japan. Hidden Japan is an example of – but is not synonymous with – *inaka,* the countryside, regarded by urban dwellers as the sticks, the boondocks, the back of beyond. Whereas wealthy Europeans or North Americans frequently aspire to live in the countryside, for urban Japanese people (as for many other Asians) the countryside often represents an uncivilized place, sentimentalized but largely avoided. During the Meiji period, Tokyo exploited the countryside, turning rural people into impoverished tenant farmers lorded over by wealthy landowners. The Occupation land reforms gave rural people their own fields to till, and during the post-war period successive governments provided a range of benefits to the countryside:

> Tokyo made rural life manageable, even comfortable, with price supports, import protection against foreign farm products, subsidies, and vast public-works budgets. This was a great reversal. In effect, the countryside began to live off the capital after centuries during which it was the other way around. (Smith, 1997: 169)

Rural communities were romanticized as *furusato,* 'old home towns', the source of traditional Japanese culture and wisdom. Yet Smith sees this reversal as a hollow one: the Japanese countryside became dependent upon state beneficence, the province of pork-barrel politics and electoral gerrymandering. The 'back of Japan' missed out on the economic transformation which was taking place on the Pacific coast, becoming instead an 'internal periphery' (Smith, 1997: 171). Massive government-funded projects to 'develop' the countryside form the core of what McCormack calls 'the construction state', a political system based on large-scale structural corruption, in which major construction companies enjoy enormous power (McCormack, 1996: 25–77). By the early 1990s, over 6 million people were employed in the Japanese construction industry (more than in the entire manufacturing sector), while Japan's public-works budget continued to exceed the US defence budget at the height of the Cold War (McCormack, 1996: 32–3). Smith describes Kakeya, home town of former Prime Minister Noboru Takeshita (which received at least ¥200 million a year from the Construction Ministry and other government agencies, amounting to nearly half the town's annual budget) as 'a well-dressed welfare case' (Smith, 1997: 170), with problems typical of many towns in rural prefectures. Rural depopulation has been a serious problem: although Japan's population has increased by almost three-quarters since the war, some prefectures actually have a lower population today than in 1949. Rural areas of Japan are often in direct competition with low-wage Southeast Asian economies to become the location of factory investments, competitions they frequently lose.

At the political level, Japan's over-centralization means very little autonomy for prefectural governments: as former Prime Minister Hosokawa famously complained, a prefectural governor needs permission from Tokyo even to move a bus stop. Localities have been engaged in a movement towards rural revitalization, involving developing and marketing distinctive local agricultural products, stimulating rural industries and promoting tourism (Knight, 1994: 634–46). Although there are some claims of a 'U-turn' trend of urban dwellers moving back to the countryside to enjoy a higher quality of life, these revitalization efforts have met with limited success. Knight found that many of the prime-movers in village revitalization campaigns were 'return migrants' from urban areas, supported by local authorities: for all the rhetoric of self-reliance, the movement was largely reliant on external agency (Knight, 1994: 645–6). There have been numerous demands for wholesale decentralization, such as former Prime Minister Hosokawa's proposal for a 'United States of Japan' (Smith, 1997: 185–6), calls echoed by globalization guru Kenichi Ohmae during his unsuccessful 1995 campaign for the Tokyo governorship (McCormack, 1996: 19–20).

Sugimoto notes that the urban–rural divide is reinforced by what he calls 'ideological centralization': because the mass media and book-publishing industries in Japan are dominated by a small number of Tokyo-based companies, it is difficult for non-Tokyo voices to be heard:

> Thus the Japanese public is constantly fed views of the world and the nation that are constructed, interpreted and edited in Tokyo. Outside the capital, local situations draw attention only as sensational news stories, or as provincial items exciting the 'exotic curiosity' of the Tokyo media establishment. (Sugimoto, 2010: 72)

While this situation is certainly not unique to Japan, the degree of capital-city centralization in Japan is unusual, especially in a nation that boasts such important competing secondary cities as Osaka and Nagoya.

## Women

Despite Japan's remarkable economic growth during the post-war period, very few Japanese women have obtained positions of power and authority within the country's political, bureaucratic or economic structures. Women do perform some quite heavy manual jobs, working on building sites and driving trucks, for example, but although the labour of women workers has long been immensely important to Japan (40.6 per cent of the paid workforce were women in 1999), that labour is deeply subordinated to male power. Discrimination against female employees is thoroughly institutionalized in Japan; many women are technically part-time workers, and so are not entitled to the same benefits as male colleagues. Often women are obliged to take care of elderly relatives, especially in-laws, and have difficulty in balancing these demands with those of the workplace. For these women, unskilled part-time work is a common alternative; another is running a small business. Sugimoto argues that most women who work part-time are not frustrated would-be career women, but women who are not sufficiently well-off to become full-time housewives: their ideal is to become women of leisure. Affluent middle-class women in Japan can achieve comfortable lives, balancing family demands with hobbies and friendships: for the majority of women, however, this ideal is impossible to attain. Another alternative for women is to concentrate on voluntary work in community-based organizations, working on environmental or other issues.

Contraceptive practice in Japan lags behind both western countries and most developing countries: condoms are the most common form of birth control, and abortion is both legal and widespread. Numbers of abortions remain high but are falling fast: there were officially 341,164 abortions in 2000 and 221,980 in 2009, but in both years this represented just over 22 per cent of pregnancies. Nevertheless, real numbers of abortions may be much higher. The contraceptive pill long remained effectively banned, its distribution blocked by the interests of doctors who benefited from the abortion trade: liberalization finally took place in 1999. According to one survey, 72.9 per cent of women between 40 and 49 admitted to having had an abortion (Jolivet, 1997: 127).

Studies suggest that Japanese women hope to have well-behaved and docile children, whereas similar studies of American women suggested a desire for independent children. This preference for docility partly reflects lack of childcare support from fathers: in 2005, the Japanese fathers spent on average only 13 minutes per day (91 minutes per week) 'taking physical care of their children' (Ishii-Kuntz, 2008: 3). While Jolivet claims that 'The majority of Japanese men have the extraordinary ability of living as though no one else was there' (Jolivet, 1997: 62), many Japanese men – especially younger ones – are very family-oriented. However, the assumption that a man should be at work may make it difficult for men to fit into family life; a retired man with no job may be seen by his family as a 'wet dead leaf, difficult to peel off the ground' (Jolivet, 1997: 68).

For many women, the pressure of living with in-laws is considerable and, in particular, women are often reluctant to live with their husbands' mothers. While mother-in-law tensions are universal, the importance of seniority in Japan means that mothers-in-law have traditionally played a powerful role in the household hierarchy, a problem compounded by the prevalence of 'mother complexes' in Japanese men. Jolivet quotes one source as saying 'most of the country women who come to see me want to divorce their in-laws rather than their husbands' (Jolivet, 1997: 160). Smith argues that the position of women has improved dramatically during the post-war period, stressing that survey evidence supports the view that more than two-thirds of Japanese women are satisfied with their lot (Smith, 1987: 25). The figures for 2010 from the Cabinet Office suggested that Japanese women were generally happier than men, and 59 per cent rated their happiness higher than seven out of 10 (Cabinet Office, 2010) However, Lock (whose survey data Smith used) demonstrates that some of the women who claimed to be satisfied actually led dreadful lives, exploited and oppressed by husbands and in-laws: 'The kind of misery that these women have endured is simply filtered out in both survey research and ideological constructions about the homebody' (Lock, 1996: 93).

Nancy Rosenberger used an anthropological approach to explore the roles of women in both Tokyo and northeast Japan during the 1970s, 1980s and 1990s. Drawing sharp contrasts between the three decades, Rosenberger charts the flow of what she calls women's '*ki* energy', arguing that:

> Amidst great variation, new hybridities of self and personhood emerge as Japanese women negotiate the story lines of personal, local, national and global plays. Women use their culturally learned abilities to develop inner strength of character, to adjust their *ki* energy, and to stretch the stages of their societal theatre in all directions. (Rosenberger, 2001: 239)

This study demonstrates the ways in which cultural approaches to understanding Japan can be given a new lease of life, endowed with a greater degree of flexibility than older interpretations such as the group model. What Rosenberger emphasizes is the sheer difficulty of generalizing convincingly about such a large and diverse group as Japanese women.

## Minorities

Japan is often described as a uniquely homogeneous society, as though its relative lack of ethnic diversity was one of its social and economic strengths. Nevertheless, this image of Japan as homogeneous and undifferentiated has been criticized by revisionists and others as a misrepresentation (see Weiner, 1997: xii–iv). Sugimoto (2010a: 15) argues that Japan is actually a multicultural society. There are several significant minority groups in Japan, including: *burakumin* (who are physically indistinguishable from other Japanese), Japanese-born Koreans, Ainu, and foreign residents, especially migrant workers.

The phenomenon of *burakumin* is peculiar to Japan, though there are parallels with 'untouchables' in the Hindu caste system. *Burakumin* (of whom there are roughly three million, or about 1 in 40 Japanese) are descended from those 'specialists in impurity' who traditionally performed low-class occupations such as butchery, working in slaughterhouses and tanneries, grave-digging and rubbish collection. In Tokugawa Japan, *burakumin* (who had their origins in earlier medieval times) became an outcast class. They were physically segregated from the mainstream community, lived in designated areas, and were unable to inter-marry with other people (see Pharr, 1990: 76–80). It was widely believed that they were ethnically different from other Japanese. There are still estimated to be up to 6,000 *burakumin* neighbourhoods in Japan, and it is quite common for the parents of prospective marriage partners to investigate their respective family backgrounds, in order to uncover any *burakumin* ancestry (see Smith, 1997: 277–83). Many companies use similar practices to screen new employees. In the post-war period, the Buraku Liberation League has campaigned against social and economic oppression and demanded special measures to improve the social status of *burakumin*. Other *buraku* organizations have different orientations and objectives (Neary, 1997; Takagi, 1991). In response to political pressures, national and local governments have provided sizeable grants and subsidies to improve *burakumin* areas, and in addition far more *burakumin* now inter-marry with *non-burakumin*. Nevertheless, the government has failed to pass legislation outlawing *burakumin* discrimination. Smith argues that the continuing existence of the minority serves the purposes of the Japanese state: 'the illusion of homogeneity is reinforced when there are islands of difference in the sea of sameness' (Smith, 1997: 283).

Japan's Korean minority numbers around 565,000; like the *burakumin,* Koreans are heavily concentrated in Honshu, especially the Kansai district. The Korean population of Japan dates from Japan's colonization of Korea in 1910, after which many Koreans were brought to Japan to provide low-cost labour (Sugimoto, 2010: 202). Most Koreans are second, third or fourth-generation residents for whom Japanese is their first language. While another nearly 300,000 have so far become Japanese nationals, the remainder still retain the status of foreigners, with no voting rights and limited access to employment, promotion and pensions except in a few municipalities; they cannot become civil servants or local government employees and so are largely barred from many jobs, including permanent teaching posts in many prefectures. Until 1993, all Koreans were obliged to undergo regular fingerprinting as part of official 'alien registration' procedures, and previously Koreans were forced to take Japanese names. The political situation of a Korean peninsula divided into a communist North and capitalist South has resulted in a split in the Japanese Korean community: about two-thirds carry South Korean passports, whilst the remaining third are loyal to the Pyongyang regime (on North Koreans, see Ryang, 1997). Mass organizations mobilize the two Korean communities along national lines, and Korean businesses in Japan, such as Nagoya pachinko parlours, have provided substantial revenue for the North Korean economy. However, while some Koreans remain strongly attached to their Korean identity, more than 80 per cent of Koreans now marry Japanese partners, and the majority of young Koreans are integrated into wider Japanese society despite the persistence of prejudice and discrimination. Hester argues that many Koreans living in Japan are becoming less attached to their distinctive status and beginning to adopt a new 'Korean-Japanese' identity, while inter-marriage means that the total number of Koreans in Japan has been declining since reaching just under 700,000 in 1991 (Hester 2008: 139–50).

Other minority groups in Japan include the Ainu, and Okinawans. Around 25,000 people in Hokkaido are officially designated as Ainu, but this figure does not include Ainu who have moved to other parts of Japan, or people who are reluctant to identify themselves as Ainu. The Ainu are an indigenous people, often compared with Native Americans and Australian aborigines: they are ethnically and culturally distinct from other Japanese. They have also faced discrimination and loss of lands at the hands of the state (see Siddle, 1996). Okinawa, an island prefecture where the majority of American military bases on Japanese soil are located, possesses a distinct culture and language; there is some dispute as to whether Okinawans are descended from 'mainland' Japanese. The residents of Okinawa have borne the brunt of the negative aspects of the US–Japan security relationship, and some scholars view this as a form of systematic discrimination against a peripheral area and its people (see Taira, 1997). Tensions between Tokyo and Okinawa came to a head following the gang-rape of a Japanese schoolgirl by American soldiers in 1995, an incident which triggered strong calls for a reduction of the US military presence in Okinawa. They re-emerged in a controversy over the location of the Futenma airbase in 2009–10.

## Immigration

Labour shortages in Japan during the bubble period of the 1980s led to a rise in the use of immigrant labour from overseas. Nearly 800,000 foreign workers are employed in Japan; more than two-thirds are employed legally, but around 250,000 are illegal immigrants. The majority perform dirty, difficult and dangerous jobs, which the Japanese are reluctant to do, such as working on construction sites, in factories, and in restaurants and bars (including the 'hostess' industry). After Koreans, the second largest group of foreign nationals in Japan is the Chinese, who numbered over 381,000 in 2001. Chinese immigration has a long history in Japan, and Japanese cities such as Kobe and Yokohama have 'Chinatown' areas dating back to the Meiji period. However, most of the Chinese residents of Japan are recent arrivals. Many are legitimately studying in Japan, though some Chinese arrive in Japan ostensibly to enrol in language schools, but then overstay their visas and become illegal workers. There are also well-established smuggling routes for illegal Chinese immigrants to enter Japan (Oka, 1994: 17–22).

Well-known Japanese automotive companies such as Toyota have hired large numbers of Japanese Brazilians to work in their plants: there were over 267,000 Brazilians in Japan in 2009. Other sizeable companies bring in workers from Southeast Asian subsidiaries for periods of 'training'. But the great majority of foreign workers are hired by small and medium-sized enterprises. There are significant numbers of illegal immigrants from several Asian countries, including Thailand, China, South Korea, Malaysia, the Philippines, Bangladesh, Iran and Pakistan. Foreign residents may become popularly associated with criminal activities; for example, during the mid-1990s, many Iranian nationals were arrested around Yoyogi Park in Tokyo for selling narcotic drugs and illegally produced, cut-price telephone cards. However, the telephone cards themselves were manufactured by Japanese *yakuza* gangs, who used the Iranians as a front for distribution. This trend reflects the way in which Japanese organized crime has been modifying its tactics and operations following the passage of anti-gang legislation in 1992. Illegal foreign workers who have lost their jobs as a result of the economic recession may have many incentives to turn to crime; nevertheless, there is evidence that figures for foreign criminal activity in Japan are inflated, reflecting government attempts to blame crime on outsiders (Sugimoto 2010: 214f; Friman, 1996: 970–1). Deportations of foreigners (mainly for overstaying) reached a peak in 1993, and have since declined to 32,661 in 2009. Japan is a major destination for human trafficking, especially of women from developing countries for prostitution, and the Japanese government has been criticized for its persistent failure to address the issue seriously. Most human trafficking in Japan is controlled by elements of the *yakuza*.

In recent years Japanese companies have tried to reduce their reliance on imported labour. In 2009, the number of foreign immigrants actually dropped for the first time since 1961; some companies began laying off Brazilian workers, who were offered Japanese government assistance to return home (Messmer, 2010). Brody argues that, to date, Brazilians of Japanese descent have not been successfully integrated into Japanese society; many are confined to ethnic enclaves, and effectively inhabit a 'Brazilian' world within Japan (Brody, 2002: 104–13). Brody advocates the creation of a clear 'social contract' according to which the Japanese state would make a number of policy changes (such as promoting bilingual schools and outlawing housing discrimination), while immigrant communities would adopt a greater willingness to learn the Japanese language. Yet any such contract would require a widespread recognition that Japan is a multicultural society, something many Japanese people have not yet accepted. As Japan's population ages, however, one category of foreign workers is in growing demand: care workers and nurses. In 2008, the Japanese government set up special schemes to bring in more nurses and care-givers from Indonesia and the Philippines, but those coming to work in Japan via this route are obliged to leave after three or four years if they cannot pass fiendishly difficult national examinations (Noguchi and Takahashi, 2010).

## Religions

Unusually, Japan has two main religions: Shinto and Buddhism. These religions exist literally side by side, and most Japanese nominally subscribe to both of them (see Hendry, 1995: 115–32). However, these notional syncretist affiliations are not typically matched by any clearly definable religious beliefs, or by any personal commitment to reli-

**Illustration 4.3 The controversial Yasukuni Shrine**

gious practice. While religiosity is widespread in Japan, religion in a deeper sense is much more rare: only about a tenth of Japanese people are 'actively' religious. However, token participation in some religious rituals is increasing in Japan; for example, a growing number of Japanese people pay festive visits to temples and shrines at New Year. Although this could be seen as evidence of religious revival, some scholars argue that Japanese religion is turning into a set of social customs, or simply a leisure activity, while others regard it as part of a quest for identity in an increasingly complex world (see *Religion in Japan Today,* 1992: 15). By contrast, some more inconvenient and less enjoyable religious rituals (such as the practice of visiting ancestors' graves during the August O-bon period) are declining.

Shintoism is based on the worship of *mana,* which Sugimoto describes as 'the supernatural or mystical power that resides not only in human beings, but also in animals, plants, rivers, and other natural things' (1997: 231). Shintoism, therefore, includes some animistic elements. An indigenous religion that teaches myths about the special origins and destiny of the Japanese people, Shinto was previously associated with the cult of the Emperor and with militarism (Davis, 1991: 793). One of the best-known (and most controversial) shrines in Japan is the Yasukuni shrine in Tokyo, where many of Japan's war dead are buried (see Illustration 4.3). Shinto shrines, with their distinctive *torii* (gateways, often red), are a common sight all over Japan; as with many Buddhist temples, the smaller shrines are often family concerns, passed down from father to son.

Japanese Buddhist temples are cultural centres, some of which house important images, manuscripts and art objects. Most Japanese people visit temples mainly for tourism or for funerals, and many Japanese priests earn most of their living from the funeral business. Despite the worldwide fame of Zen, as seen in Illustration 4.4. showing the Ryoan-ji Zen garden in Kyoto, the majority of Japanese Buddhist priests do not engage in meditation, though the practice of '*nembutsu*' (chanting) and reading Buddhist texts has always been more common in Japan among the most popular sects. Unlike their more ascetic, celibate Theravada counterparts in Southeast Asia, Japanese Mahayana priests are free to marry, and most now lead consumerist lives which are barely distinguishable from those of secular Japanese people.

During the post-war period, many 'new religions' have sprung up in Japan, most of which are new Buddhist sects rather than entirely new religions. The most important include Rishho Kosei-kai, and Soka Gakkai, a mass organization linked to the Komeito (Clean Government) Party. Soka Gakkai claims a worldwide membership of 12 million, though this may be an overestimate by about three or four million. The movement has a primary appeal to those socially marginalized and economically disadvantaged during Japan's rapid post-war urbanization and growth. Davis describes Soka Gakkai as 'perhaps opportunistic rather than fundamentalistic' (Davis, 1991: 804). Nevertheless, the power and influence of some new religions made the Japanese authorities reluctant to interfere with questionable practices by religious sects.

This became a major issue with the rise of the apocalyptic terrorist group Aum Shinrikyo, which exploited its religious status for the purpose of protection, whilst building up a large arsenal of chemical and other weaponry (Kaplan and Marshall, 1996). Despite substantial evidence linking the cult to the deaths of seven people in a gas attack in Matsumoto in June 1994, it was not until the group released deadly sarin nerve gas into the Tokyo subway system in March 1995 – killing another twelve people – that police finally took action against the movement. The preoccupation of the group with illegal activities has led some commentators to describe Aum as a 'criminal religion', rather than a new religion as such (Metraux, 1995). However, leading Japanese novelist Haruki Murakami has produced a classic account of

**Illustration 4.4 A Zen garden in Kyoto**

the sarin attacks, organized around interviews with both survivors and cult members. He is critical of arguments emphasizing the evil nature of the movement, and concludes that most Aum members were not abnormal, disadvantaged or eccentric, but ordinary Japanese people living average lives (Murakami, 2000: 364). According to Murakami: 'We will get nowhere as long as the Japanese continue to disown the Aum "phenomenon" as something completely other, an alien presence viewed through binoculars on the far shore' (2000: 227). He compares the rise of Aum with the active complicity of many well-educated Japanese people in the pre-war Manchurian puppet administration. The clear implication is that the emergence of such a movement has wider lessons for a critical understanding of Japanese society. However, nothing comparable with Aum has yet to appear.

## Health and demography

Japanese people enjoy exceptional longevity. In 2009, estimated life expectancy was nearly 86.4 years for women and 79.5 for men, the highest in the world (McCurry, 2010) partly because of their excellent low-fat diet. Japan has a good healthcare system, supported by a national health insurance scheme that allows low-cost access to medical services. Despite the excellent life expectancy currently enjoyed by Japanese people, future trends are more difficult to predict: changes in the Japanese diet (which have produced substantial increases in the average height of young people in recent decades) may lead to much higher rates of cardiovascular disease. Similarly, the increases in cigarette smoking by young women since the 1990s will undoubtedly take a heavy toll on female health in the twenty-first century. Overall, smoking rates are now falling slightly, though nearly 37 per cent of men still smoke (Hondro, 2010).

If Japanese life expectancy and the current low birthrate continue at their present levels, Japan may end the twenty-first century with only around half of its present population. Since 2006, there have been more deaths than births in Japan, making Japan the only non-European in the world with negative population growth. Raising and educating children is an expensive and stressful business in Japan; as women marry later and have more scope to pursue work and other interests, enthusiasm for child-rearing has declined (Suzuki, 1995). Official injunctions to Japanese women urging them to produce more children have fallen on deaf ears. A falling number of active working people is now faced with supporting an ever-growing elderly population: Japan is an 'ageing society' (see Table 4.2). This demographic time-bomb looks set to undermine Japan's long-term economic and political standing. One result of this trend will be to make Japan ever more reliant on female labour, and on that of immigrant workers (legal or illegal) from abroad. Nevertheless, there are not quite as many old people in Japan as statistics suggest – a

*Table* 4.2 Share of people aged 65 and over in total population (per cent)

| | *1950* | *1960* | *1970* | *1980* | *1990* | *2000* | *2010* | *2020* |
|---|---|---|---|---|---|---|---|---|
| Japan | 4.9 | 5.7 | 7.0 | 9.1 | 12.0 | 17.2 | 22.6 | 28.5 |
| United States | 8.3 | 9.2 | 9.8 | 11.2 | 12.3 | 12.4 | 13.0 | 16.1 |
| Germany | 9.7 | 11.5 | 13.7 | 15.6 | 15.0 | 16.4 | 20.5 | 23.0 |
| France | 11.4 | 11.7 | 12.9 | 14.0 | 14.2 | 16.1 | 17.0 | 20.9 |

*Source*: Population Division, Department of Economic and Social Affairs, United Nations: *World Population Prospects*, available: http://esa.un.org/unpp/index.asp?panel=2.

number of recent cases have revealed that families had failed to report the deaths of elderly relatives in order to continue to claiming their pensions. Hundreds of centenarians had gone missing (McCurry, 2010).

## Welfare

Volunteer welfare officers play an important role in identifying welfare needs; these volunteers comprise the main form of direct social welfare provision for marginalized groups such as the destitute, the disabled and single mothers. There are around 190,000 such volunteers – mainly retired people with an average age of 60 – each of whom makes around 120 household visits per year (see Goodman, 1998: 139–58). This volunteer system is clearly extremely cost-effective, but Goodman argues that these untrained, paternalistic volunteers sometimes play an intrusive, moralistic role, and have helped ensure that take-up rates of welfare benefits remain extremely low.

Unemployment benefits in Japan are limited, and depend upon age and period of employment; they are markedly less generous than in most European countries. Unemployment rates in Japan long remained low compared with some other industrialized nations, rose sharply during the 1900s, reached 5.1 per cent in 2010, but fell to 4.3 per cent by August 2011 (see Table 4.3). Pension benefits vary widely, based on length of pensionable service and type of employment. A basic universal pension is provided by the National Pension System, while supplementary pensions are provided through various employee schemes, the largest of which is the Employee Pension Scheme (which includes all company pensions). Changes made to the pension system in 2007 made it easier for divorced women to lay claim to part of their ex-husbands' pensions, so fuelling the divorce rate (Alexy, 2007: 169). Pensioners solely reliant on the National Pension System are not well-provided for, though those in receipt of supplementary pensions could receive in the region of 50 per cent of their pre-retirement income. However, the rapidly ageing population, combined with the recent economic downturn, means that the major pension schemes may soon be unable to meet their current obligations. Whereas in 1990 the ratio of working people to retirees was 6:1, by 2025 it will be almost 2:1 (BBC News, 2007). Many young people in Japan now have little expectation of receiving good pension provision when they retire.

*Table* 4.3 Standardized unemployment rates (per cent)

| *Time* | *2001* | *2002* | *2003* | *2004* | *2005* | *2006* | *2007* | *2008* | *2009* | *2010* | *2011* |
|---|---|---|---|---|---|---|---|---|---|---|---|
| *Country* | | | | | | | | | | | |
| Japan | 5.0 | 5.4 | 5.3 | 4.7 | 4.4 | 4.1 | 3.9 | 4.0 | 5.1 | 5.1 | 4.6 |
| United States | 4.7 | 5.8 | 6.0 | 5.5 | 5.1 | 4.6 | 4.6 | 5.8 | 9.3 | 9.6 | 9.0 |
| France | .. | .. | 8.5 | 8.9 | 8.9 | 8.8 | 8.0 | 7.4 | 9.1 | 9.4 | .. |
| United Kingdom | 5.1 | 5.2 | 5.0 | 4.8 | 4.9 | 5.4 | 5.3 | 5.7 | 7.6 | 7.9 | 8.1 |
| Germany | 7.8 | 8.7 | 9.6 | 9.8 | 11.2 | 10.3 | 8.7 | 7.5 | 7.8 | 7.1 | .. |
| Denmark | 4.6 | 4.6 | 5.4 | 5.5 | 4.8 | 3.9 | 3.8 | 3.4 | 6.0 | 7.5 | 7.6 |

*Source*: OECD (2011), *Labour Force Statistics*, http://stats.oecd.org/Index.aspx?DataSetCode=MEILABOUR (accessed 26 March 2012).

Health insurance in Japan is provided by several officially recognized non-profit funds, one of which all citizens are obliged to join. Most of these cover 70 or 80 per cent of healthcare costs (which are based on a standardized scale of charges); the patient pays the remaining 20 or 30 per cent up to a maximum ceiling (Argy and Stein, 1997: 299–301). In April 2000, a new Long-Term Care Insurance Plan was launched to fund supplementary nursing care for the elderly, evidence of a growing recognition that families could not bear sole responsibility for such a large-scale need. Given the decline of traditional expectations of job security, there were also calls for a stronger, less paternalistic social security system.

## Class and inequality

Social class is a contested issue in Japan. Kelly argues that the myth of a new middle class formed part of a 'mainstream consciousness' propagated by post-war state and society in Japan, and was an ideological construct rather than an empirical depiction (Kelly, 2002). Sugimoto suggests that Japan is becoming increasingly class divided or *kakusa shakai*, 'disparity society' (Sugimoto, 2010b). It has become much harder to ignore the underclass of homeless, unemployed and casual labourers, who have been the greatest losers during the economic stagnation that set in since around 1990. The decline of the old myth of middle-class equality has contributed to the weakening of the LDP's electoral base.

## Conclusion

Mainstream scholars emphasize what they see as the positive features of Japanese society: relatively low divorce rates, exceptional longevity, cost-effective healthcare and welfare systems, a high degree of popular satisfaction, widespread self-identification as middle class, an increasing recognition of women's roles in the workforce, considerable social homogeneity, improving conditions for minority groups, growing internationalization and evidence of religious revivalism and rural revitalization. Culturalist scholars see many of these achievements as reflections of a highly distinctive culture and history, especially core Japanese values such as harmony, consensus and hierarchy. Revisionists stress the oppressive nature of many Japanese families, the dysfunctional character of male–female relationships, the ageing society and falling birthrate, the persistence of discrimination against women, minorities and foreigners, the questionable nature of some new religions, the imbalance between urban and rural areas, and limited scope for social mobility.

Clammer argues that Japanese society is actually something new, that 'traditional' ways of understanding Japanese society need to be revised in the light of rampant consumerism, and that products are being consumed primarily for their symbolic value. He poses the rhetorical question: 'What kind of social organization exists here: does the consumer society in Japan constitute a definable social structure, or do we need to reconceptualize it in fresh terms?' (Clammer, 1997: 47). In a similarly provocative fashion, Sugimoto argues that Japan is a different kind of society. He makes the case for a new understanding of Japan as a 'multicultural' society characterized by widespread internal variations which are obscured or concealed by dominant patterns of 'friendly authoritarianism' (2010a: 290). Another alternative analysis is to view the Japanese social order as an 'onion', centred on a Tokyo-based elite of white-collar males, but made up of numerous different concentric layers. These multiple layers give Japan far more richness and diversity than conventional explanations, stressing the relative homogeneity of the society, would suggest.

# 5

# Governing Structures

Under the 1947 Constitution, sovereignty rests with the people rather than with the Emperor. The Emperor serves as the 'symbol of state': technically speaking, Japan has no 'head of state', a legacy of post-war attempts to strip the throne of all power. The Diet contains two houses: the Upper House (House of Councillors), and Lower House (House of Representatives), both housed in the Diet Building (see Illustration 5.1). However, the lower house is much the more important of the two. Both houses are filled by elected members. In many respects, the formal structures of the Japanese parliamentary system reflect the British model, with executive power concentrated in the hands of the cabinet and the prime minister. At least 50 per cent of ministers must be members of the Diet. There is an independent judiciary, and local governments at the prefectural and municipal level enjoy autonomy. Civil and social rights, including freedom of speech and assembly, are incorporated into the constitution. Citizens are equal before the law; public officials are accountable to the people, who have the right to choose and dismiss them. Despite some criticism of the 1947 Constitution as a 'foreign' import imposed on Japan by the Occupation forces, no formal motion to amend it has yet been put before the Diet.

## Electoral system

Prior to the reforms of 1994, the House of Representatives had 511 members, chosen from 129 electoral districts for four-year terms (the number of seats and constituencies was revised five times in the post-war period). Electoral districts were therefore multi-member

**Illustration 5.1 The Diet (parliament) building, Tokyo**

constituencies, with between two and six Diet members representing each district. Voters had a single non-transferable vote; in other words, despite the fact that constituencies elected more than one Diet member, individual voters had only one vote. In practice, governments usually called elections before their four-year terms were up, taking advantage of favourable political conditions.

The 242 members of the House of Councillors are elected for six-year terms by two different methods; 146 are elected by districts corresponding to the 47 prefectures of Japan (each prefecture electing from two to eight members, based on size), while another 96 members are chosen in a national constitueuncy – a form of proportional representation. Upper-house elections take place on fixed dates, and half of the membership of the chamber is replaced every three years. Theoretically, members of the upper house represent broader constituencies than those of the lower house, and they are therefore somewhat 'above the fray' of day-to-day politicking. In practice, however, the composition of the upper house closely reflects that of the lower house (Bingham, 1989: 5). The Diet is in session for much of the year and, as in Britain, makes use of full parliamentary debates; as in the USA, an important role is given to a set of standing committees.

The multi-member district system of the lower house was often criticized for promoting factionalism, since often much of the electoral contestation would take place between rival LDP candidates rather than rival parties. In 1991, attempts to reform the electoral system were scuppered by opposition from within the LDP but, following the collapse of LDP rule in 1993, the pressure to reform the system became irresistible. In 1994, the short-lived Hosokawa government was able to push through an electoral reform package very similar to the 1991 proposals (Foreign Press Centre, 1995, 1997). Under the original reformed system (which did not affect the upper house), the lower house had 500 seats, 300 of them assigned to single-member constituencies, and 200 (divided into 11 blocs) allocated by proportional representation. In 2000, the number of proportional representation seats was reduced to 180, and the total number of lower house seats thereby reduced to 480. This was a deliberate ploy by the governing LDP to reduce the strength of small parties, which had been major beneficiaries of the reformed system.

Voters cast two ballots in the election. Constituency seats may be contested by independents, but only candidates backed by a party may compete for the proportional representation seats. Dual candidacies are also allowed: parties may include candidates for single-seat constituencies on their lists of candidates for election by proportional representation. For candidates from large parties this can easily serve as a fall-back plan: unsuccessful candidates from the constituency elections may stand a good chance of entering the lower house via the proportional representation route. In the 1996 lower-house elections (the first held under the new rules), 84 of those elected under the proportional representation system were defeated candidates from the constituencies, an outcome which many voters found very unsatisfactory. Initially, the new system produced very similar results to the old one, and was widely criticized. However, over time, the full effects of the reforms have been felt, leading to a concentration of lower-house seats in the hands of two major parties, the LDP and the DPJ. Rosenbluth and Thies argue that these 1994 reforms were the development that led Japanese politics to adopt a new *modus operandi* in the twenty-first century (2010: 101).

Malapportionment – in the form of unfair weighting of rural constituencies at the expense of urban ones – continued to be a significant issue even after the lower house reforms of 1994. In 2007, some minor changes were made to ease the much greater levels of malapportionment in the upper house, but this remained a very serious problem (Stockwin, 2008: 178). Electoral campaigning in Japan operates under various restrictions: in particular, door-to-door canvassing is banned, since in the past candidates used to offer 'gifts' or payments to voters during canvassing. Under the 1994 reforms, requirements for the financial disclosure of campaign contributions have been tightened up, and public funds to the tune of around ¥30 billion per election were allocated to underwrite the cost of party campaigns (Stockwin, 2008: 176–7).

## The prime minister

In theory, Japanese prime ministers (Box 5.1) are very powerful individuals: with a tiny number of short-lived exceptions, since 1955 they have been the leaders of the LDP, as well as being designated by the Diet and holding a range of executive powers. Yet in practice most Japanese premiers have found themselves heavily dominated and influenced by the political, business and bureaucratic interests which provide their support. Factors producing weak prime ministerial leadership include suspicion of 'aggressive' leadership styles, a tradition of 'consensus articulation' by prime ministers, the relative strength of the bureaucracy *vis-à-vis* the executive, and the importance of inter-factional negotiating skills (rather than clear policy stances) as a qualification in obtaining the post (Angel, 1989: 583). However, notable exceptions to the usual style of premiership include consummate machine politician Kakuei Tanaka, and the high-profile conservative ideologue Yasuhiro Nakasone. Nakasone succeeded in reorganizing the Cabinet Secretariat and Security Council in 1986,

**Box 5.1 Japanese prime ministers in the post-war period**

| | *From* | *Party* |
|---|---|---|
| Prince Higashikuni | August 1945 | None |
| Kijuro Shidehara | October 1945 | PP |
| Shigeru Yoshida | May 1946 | JLP |
| Tetsu Katayama | May 1947 | JSP |
| Hitoshi Ashida | March 1948 | DP |
| Shigeru Yoshida | October 1948 | DLP/LP |
| Ichiro Hatoyama | December 1954 | JDP/LDP |
| Taman Ishibashi | December 1956 | LDP |
| Nobusuke Kishi | February 1957 | LDP |
| Hayato Ikeda | July 1960 | LDP |
| Eisaku Sato | November 1964 | LDP |
| Kakuei Tanaka | July 1972 | LDP |
| Takeo Miki | December 1974 | LDP |
| Takeo Fukuda | December 1976 | LDP |
| Masayoshi Ohira | December 1978 | LDP |
| Zenko Suzuki | July 1980 | LDP |
| Yasuhiro Nakasone | November 1982 | LDP |
| Noboru Takeshita | November 1987 | LDP |
| Sosuke Uno | June 1989 | LDP |
| Toshiki Kaifu | August 1989 | LDP |
| Kiichi Miyazawa | November 1991 | LDP |
| Morihiro Hosokawa | August 1993 | JNP |
| Tsutomu Hata | April 1994 | JRP |
| Tomiichi Murayama | June 1994 | SDPJ |
| Ryutaro Hashimoto | January 1996 | LDP |
| Keizo Obuchi | July 1998 | LDP |
| Yoshiro Mori | April 2000 | LDP |
| Junichiro Koizumi | April 2001 | LDP |
| Shinzo Abe | September 2006 | LDP |
| Yasuo Fukuda | September 2007 | LDP |
| Taro Aso | September 2008 | LDP |
| Yukio Hatoyama | September 2009 | DPJ |
| Naoto Kan | June 2010 | DPJ |
| Yoshihiko Noda | September 2011 | DPJ |

*Parties*: DLP, Democratic Liberal Party; DP, Democratic Party; DPJ, Democratic Party of Japan; JDP, Japan Democratic Party; JLP, Japan Liberal Party; JNP, Japan New Party; JRP, Japan Renewal Party; JSP, Japan Socialist Party; LDP, Liberal Democratic Party; LP, Liberal Party; PP, Progressive Party; SDPJ, Social Democratic Party of Japan.

thereby greatly enhancing the potential for executive control, especially in crisis situations (Angel, 1989: 601). Nevertheless, with the exception of Junichiro Koizumi, subsequent prime ministers have generally been much more in the traditional, low-profile mode than Nakasone.

Since 2001, many of the central government agencies that formerly reported directly to the prime minister's office have been combined with relevant ministries; the whole system has now been streamlined, and the Cabinet Office given more authority. Nakasone and Koizumi both argued that Japan should hold direct prime ministerial elections to strengthen the hand of the country's chief executive officer, but it seems unlikely that this radical proposal would gain support from the LDP or DPJ grandees, whose power would be greatly undermined by such a change. The 2001 administrative reforms did enhance the powers of the prime minister, but much also depended on the personality and power base of individual incumbents. The reforms certainly did not stabilize prime ministerial turnover, which grew more rapid after 2006 than at any time since the 1940s.

## The Cabinet and the ministries

One important function of the Diet is to designate the prime minister (who then appoints the cabinet); the cabinet is held to be accountable to the Diet. Although the Diet is usually dissolved by the prime minister, the government can also be brought down in a no-confidence vote, which then precipitates a general election. Since reforms implemented in 2001, the cabinet has contained no more than 17 ministers of state, plus the prime minister. In principle, there are supposed to be only 14 ministers of state, but the number may be increased to 17 if a special need arises – which seems often to be the case. The average cabinet lasts only around nine months, as frequent reshuffles are common. However, in many cases the reshuffle will be only a partial one: this does not mean that all individual ministers are moved on average every nine months. While there has recently been a trend towards longer spells in office, during the 1980s, 57 per cent of ministers lasted less than a year, and 77 per cent less than two years (Bingham, 1989: 18). However, it is not necessary to hold a cabinet position to exert enormous influence in Japan, since parties such as the LDP are dominated by faction bosses and power-brokers. Ministerial posts are generally rotated among these power-brokers and their protégés. Cabinet meetings in Japan are notoriously short, sometimes no longer than 15 minutes.

After years of debate, the Japanese bureaucracy was restructured in January 2001, reducing the number of central government agencies from 23 to 13; agencies with overlapping or closely related responsibilities were merged (see Figure 5.1). This was accompanied by a reduction in the number of cabinet ministers. A typical cabinet of 17 includes 10 heads of ministries (Environment; Land, Infrastructure and Transport; Economy, Trade and Industry; Agriculture, Forestry and Fisheries; Health, Labour and Social Welfare; Education, Culture, Sports, Science and Technology; Finance; Foreign Affairs; Justice; and Public Management, Home Affairs and Telecommunications), along with the Chief Secretary of the Cabinet, the heads of the Defence Agency and the National Public Safety Commission, plus three additional ministers as appointed by the prime minister. In 2007, the Defence Agency was upgraded to be the Ministry of Defence.

While these reforms were supposed to generate efficiencies, they involved the creation of large super-ministries which produced new administrative challenges. In addition, effective political oversight of these vast organizations could prove difficult. To support the work of cabinet ministers, 48 new posts of junior ministers were created. The creation of junior ministers was supposed to help make ministries more accountable to the legislature – previously, top bureaucrats (so-called administrative vice-ministers, the civil servants heading ministries) often accounted directly to parliament for the work of ministries. Bureaucrats are now no longer permitted to take part in Diet Committee debates on behalf of their ministries, and this role has been assumed by junior ministers (Takenaka, 2002: 929). In an associated reform, a National Basic Policy Committee was introduced in the Diet, modelled on the British Prime Minister's Question Time. These weekly Wednesday afternoon meetings, lasting 40 minutes offer a forum in which the prime minister can be grilled by the leaders of opposition parties. These changes reflected attempts to strengthen the quality of parliamentary scrutiny of the executive branch, and of the policy process. The changes were driven by demands from non-LDP parties for reforms which would enhance their relative power *vis-à-vis* the LDP (Takenaka, 2002: 939), but the effectiveness of the reforms will take more time to evaluate. Creating a large number of junior ministers offered more scope for prime ministers to employ patronage powers to satisfy the demands of coalition partners. Neary

*Figure* 5.1 Japanese government organization*

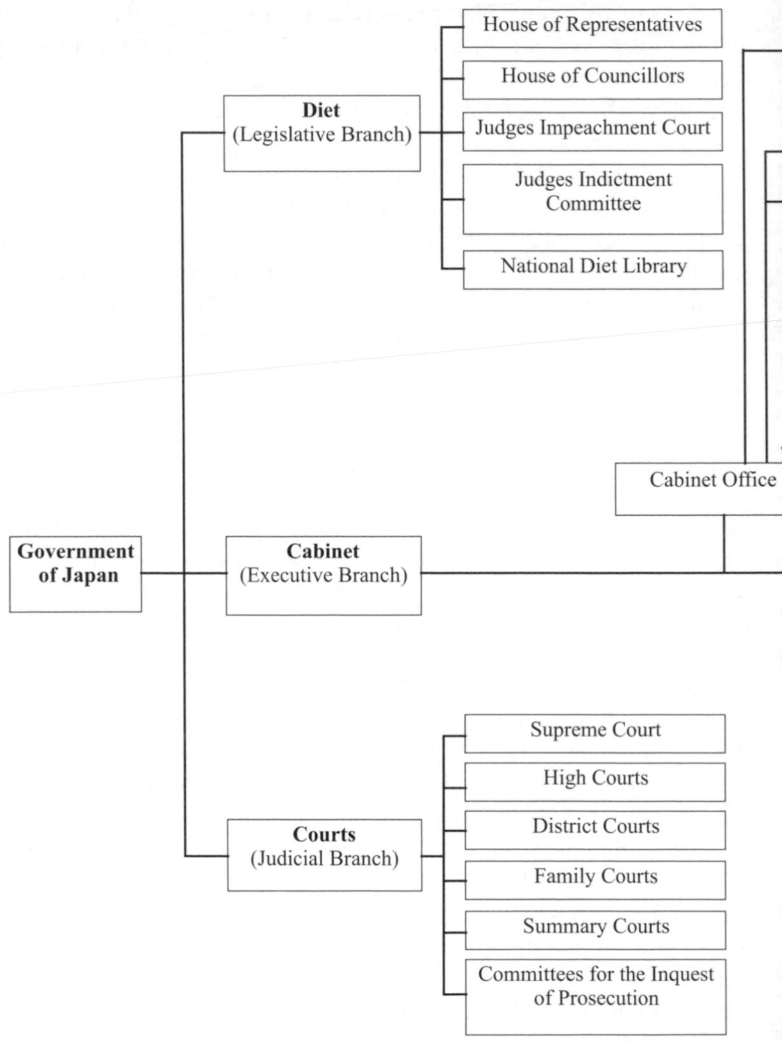


* Adapted by the author from *Japan Echo* (8, 1, February 2001: 58) and the website of Prime Minister of Japan and His Cabinet (http://www.kantei.go.jp).

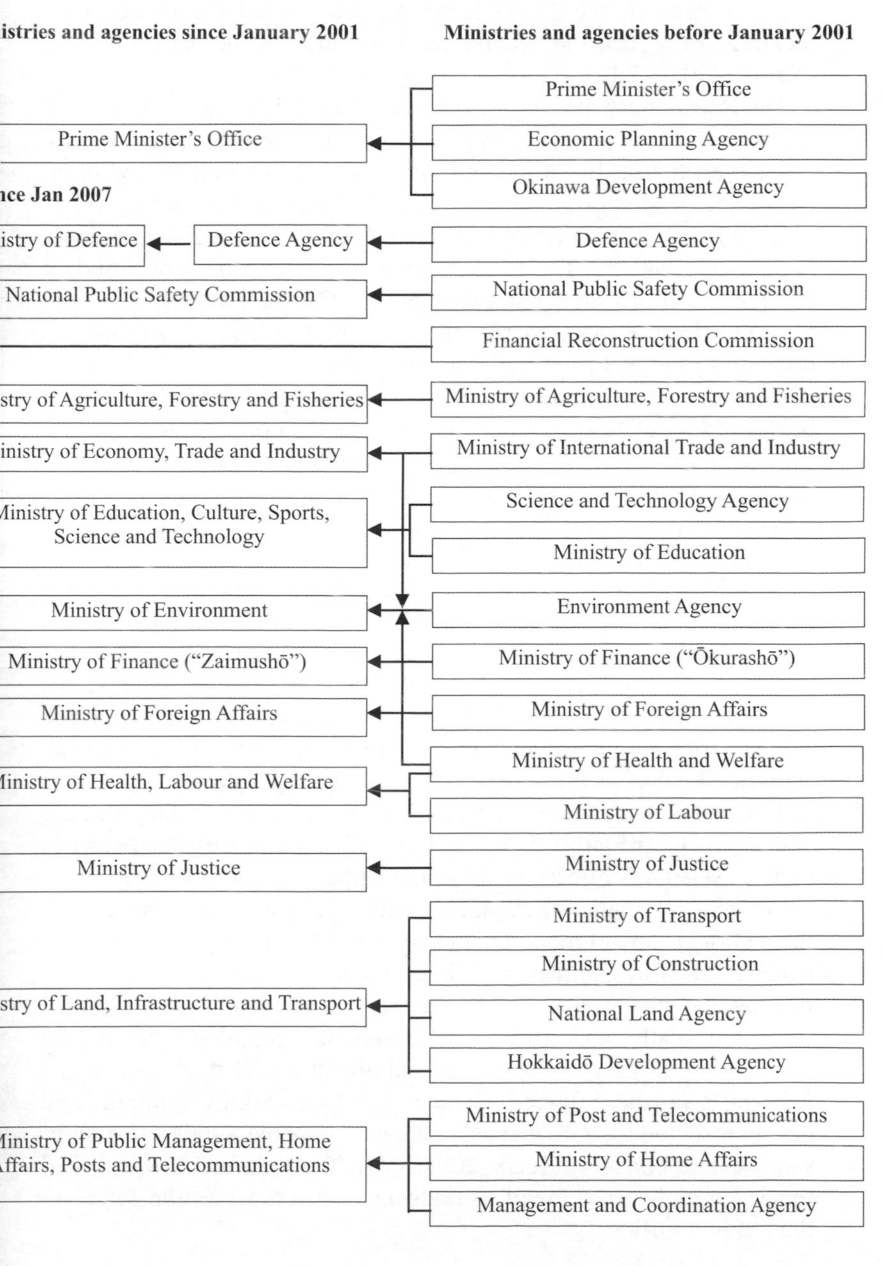
istries and agencies since January 2001
Ministries and agencies before January 2001
Prime Minister's Office
Economic Planning Agency
Okinawa Development Agency
Prime Minister's Office
ıce Jan 2007
istry of Defence
Defence Agency
Defence Agency
National Public Safety Commission
National Public Safety Commission
Financial Reconstruction Commission
stry of Agriculture, Forestry and Fisheries
Ministry of Agriculture, Forestry and Fisheries
inistry of Economy, Trade and Industry
Ministry of International Trade and Industry
/inistry of Education, Culture, Sports, Science and Technology
Science and Technology Agency
Ministry of Education
Ministry of Environment
Environment Agency
Ministry of Finance ("Zaimushō")
Ministry of Finance ("Ōkurashō")
Ministry of Foreign Affairs
Ministry of Foreign Affairs
linistry of Health, Labour and Welfare
Ministry of Health and Welfare
Ministry of Labour
Ministry of Justice
Ministry of Justice
Ministry of Transport
Ministry of Construction
stry of Land, Infrastructure and Transport
National Land Agency
Hokkaidō Development Agency
Ministry of Post and Telecommunications
linistry of Public Management, Home ffairs, Posts and Telecommunications
Ministry of Home Affairs
Management and Coordination Agency

argues that so long as administrative vice-ministers continue to meet in committee with the Chief Cabinet Secretary the day before Cabinet meetings to review the agenda, their powers will be hard to curtail (Neary, 2002: 128).

The lower house has the upper hand in the legislative process: a bill rejected by the upper house can still become law if it is approved by the lower house for a second time with a two-thirds majority. However, most legislation (especially important legislation) originates with the bureaucracy rather than with the legislature itself (Bingham, 1989: 11–12). Even major bills such as the annual budget bill are generally rubber-stamped by the Cabinet and the Diet; for example, from 1955 to 1977, the Diet made only one substantive revision of the budget (Bingham, 1989: 15).

If the power and effectiveness of the Cabinet and the Diet has often been questioned, there is one Japanese institution which is universally seen as extremely important: the Ministry of Finance. The vast range of powers it wields (in effect, wielded mostly by its senior bureaucrats) makes the Ministry of Finance a virtual 'super-ministry', with an extraordinary degree of control over the financial sector, and over public-sector revenues and expenditure. Through its *de facto* control of the budget, the Finance Ministry has been able to exert considerable influence over the policies and priorities of other ministries, as well as over those of prefectures and municipalities which receive substantial funding from central government. The Ministry designs and operates the national tax system (though the actual collection of taxes is carried out by a separate agency), plans and operates the national financial system, regulates the banking system (including supervising the Bank of Japan), regulates securities trading, sets and collects customs and shipping duties, plays a strategic role in international economic trade, and plans and implements the national government budget system, including preparing the budget bill for Cabinet and Diet approval. For understandable reasons, the post of Finance Minister is highly coveted, yet few politicians are really able fully to comprehend, let alone direct, the Ministry's vast range of activities and operations. The change of the Ministry's Japanese name in January 2001 was highly symbolic and deeply resented by bureaucrats, since the old name alluded to a thousand-year-old history (Neary, 2002: 123). The renamed Ministry had fewer functions, as some of its budgetary powers were transferred to the Cabinet Office.

## Local government

Whereas prior to the Second World War Japan had a highly centralized political order, the Occupation reforms sought to introduce a system of local government which would check the overweening dominance of the central state, instituting a system of prefectural and municipal governments. Nevertheless, national legislation always takes precedence over local legislation and, in practice, Tokyo bureaucrats often exercise considerable control over the activities of local government. Bingham notes that while the Local Autonomy Act of 1947 makes governors and mayors responsible for a wide range of public services, these elected local officials often have little power over the services they are legally obliged to deliver (Bingham, 1989: 53–4). Detailed policy and budget programmes prepared by local governments have to be approved by Tokyo. Ministers actually have the power to remove elected governors and mayors who fail to comply with their orders. The very title of the Local Autonomy Act calls attention to a core problem in Japanese politics: the degree to which real local autonomy can be said to exist in local government. To a large extent, local administration is dominated by the central Japanese state. At the same time, local governments are continually seeking to carve out greater autonomy from Tokyo, leading to considerable creative tensions in their relations with national-level politicians and bureaucrats.

Japan has 47 prefectures; four of these are not prefectures in the regular sense, but three cities (Tokyo – whose City Hall complex is illustrated in Illustration 5.2 – Osaka and Kyoto) and one region (Hokkaido), which have been given legal status equivalent to prefectures. Each prefecture has a prefectural assembly with an elected membership. Governors, who are elected, are the chief executives of prefectures, and have a wide range of powers; they preside over a considerable number of public programmes, notably public law and order (including local courts and police), health and welfare (including hospitals, social services and environmental protection), infrastructure (including roads, transport, land development, utilities and parks) and education and culture (including schools, libraries and art galleries). Because many of these programmes come under the jurisdiction of national ministries, governors are obliged to work closely with the relevant bureaucracies in all manner of budgetary and regulatory matters. Around 60 per cent of local government revenues

**Illustration 5.2 Tokyo Metropolitan Hall building**

derive from central government funds of one sort or another (Abe *et al.*, 1994: 66). Many prefectures and large cities maintain sizeable offices in Tokyo; rather like foreign embassies, these offices have the task of maintaining close contact with the relevant national-level officials, and monitoring the latest developments concerning budgetary or policy issues (Steiner, 1965: 321–3). Officials of the Ministry of Home Affairs (part of a new, larger Ministry since 2001) have long exercised significant budgetary and other controls over local and prefectural government in Japan.

Municipalities in Japan have various different forms: large cities (with a population over 500,000), cities, towns, villages, and 23 'special wards' in Tokyo. Mayors are elected; like prefectural governors, they have strong executive powers and are nominally accountable to weak assemblies. Nevertheless, the 1960s and 1970s saw an increasing trend towards more open and effective local government, as community groups and citizens' movements moved into the political arena and sought to break the dominance of cosy old-boy networks which had previously characterized prefectural and municipal politics. Most local politicians are not formal members of national parties, though they often have close personal links with these parties.

Positive evaluations of Japanese local government tend to stress the successes of prefectures and municipalities in initiating policies and carving out greater autonomy. Local governments have played a significant role in areas such as welfare and environmental policy, but negative evaluations of Japanese local government emphasize the subordination of local politics to national control. Reed cautions that local autonomy and centralization are value-laden terms, and that social scientists should be wary of idealizing the local and deprecating the central (Reed, 1986: 3–4). He points out that both central and local government have plural, multiple identities rather than unitary connotations. Based on a very detailed study of relations between central and prefectural governments in Japan, Reed concludes that although the inter-governmental system is not very good in Japan, it is generally good enough to be reasonably effective. At the same time, he observes that despite the low quality of most local politics in Japan:

> Mayoral and gubernatorial elections are a major source of flexibility and responsiveness in the Japanese political system even under these seemingly adverse circumstances. (Reed, 1986: 170)

Despite its generally lacklustre performance, local government in Japan does contain the potential to act decisively and to great effect, as was the case when pollution problems threatened Japan's economic miracle in the 1970s.

During the 1980s and 1990s, a number of new trends emerged in local elections. Many 1980s elections were 'non-competitive', in that outcomes were largely brokered by deals between leaders of local parties (Neary, 2002: 153–8), and this led to growing voter apathy, and sometimes to a backlash by the electorate. When the LDP was challenged nationally from 1994 onwards by a curious alliance of parties, voters refused to support leading candidates endorsed by *ad hoc* anti-LDP groupings. The 1995 Tokyo and Osaka gubernatorial elections were won by celebrity entertainers, and in 1999 they were again won by independents rather than by mainstream party candidates. Nevertheless, active and dynamic prefectural governors could make a difference; in prefectures ranging from Kanagawa to Oita and Okinawa, effective leadership has produced significant results.

Reform of local government in Japan is now long overdue; the aftermath of the 2011 Tohoku earthquake clearly illustrated the need to empower the regions to take urgent action to address pressing socioeconomic issues, without the need to refer all key decisions back to the bureaucrats and politicians in Tokyo. The DPJ had long laid stress in the need to decentralize power in Japan, but made little headway with this agenda after taking office in 2009. Yoichi Funabashi provocatively proposed that the seat of the Imperial Palace should be now be transferred back to Kyoto, as a symbol of the commitment to decentralization – followed by a wholesale transfer of government operations from Tokyo to the regions (Funabashi, 2011: 13). So far, such radical proposals have met only a lukewarm response.

## The judiciary

The constitution states that the judiciary must be independent, and in theory it could play an important role in shaping the interpretation of legislation, and make decisive interventions over controversial matters. Nevertheless, the Supreme Court has generally played a very low-profile role in Japan. Some important judicial decisions have influenced government policy; for example, decisions by courts in the 1960s that found major companies guilty of causing hazardous pollution helped precipitate new legislation and the setting up of an environment agency. But Upham argues that following important judgments, the bureaucracy steps in to take control of the situation, refusing to recognize an institutional role for the judiciary in shaping social change (Upham, 1987: 27).

The judiciary often makes decisions favouring government positions, and the Supreme Court is more conservative than lower-level courts. The Supreme Court has 15 members, all appointed by the prime minister; although in theory they are subject to regular re-election, no sitting member has ever failed to be reconfirmed (Ramseyer and Nakazato, 1999: 17). All judges have previously spent some time working as prosecutors, experience which may socialize them into seeing cases from the perspective of the state. According to some scholars, the problem is not that conservative politicians (such as the long-ruling LDP) interfere directly in the judicial process, but rather that senior judges have often shared LDP policy positions. Judges who join left-wing legal organizations or pass verdicts against the government are far less likely to be promoted than more conservative judges (Ramseyer and Nakazato, 1999: 18–20). A more positive view of the Japanese judiciary may be found in the work of John Haley, who argues that Japanese judges enjoy considerable judicial independence (Haley, 2006: 90–122). A middle path is steered by David O'Brien and Yasuo Ohkoshi, who demonstrate the need for a very nuanced and well-informed view of these issues (O'Brien and Ohkoshi, 2001: 37–61). Japanese judges tend to be cautiously conservative in their decisions, partly because their promotion is based on a points system, and they lose points if their decisions are overturned by a higher court.

The lengthy, drawn-out nature of Japan's legal procedures limits the capacity of the judiciary to act swiftly and effectively. In criminal cases, virtually all those brought to trial are convicted; partly in response to domestic and international criticism of the high conviction rate, Japan introduced a quasi-jury system of 'lay judges' in 2009 (Johnson, 2009). Jury trials require judges to prepare extensively and then to write up very quick judgments. Although in theory lay judges (in effect, jurors) are supposed to speak first and play a crucial role in deciding verdicts, in practice they often defer to the views of their professional counterparts. The quasi-jury system is something of a messy compromise and has yet to be institutionalized fully, but it has already increased the accountability of the judiciary.

## Bureaucracy and the bureaucratic-dominance debate

Although extremely powerful and prestigious, the Japanese bureaucracy is relatively small and inexpensive. While there were over a million civil servants in 2011, this figure included large numbers of postal workers and members of the Self-Defence Forces. The core of the 'civil service' as commonly understood is Administrative Service I, which includes the managerial and clerical staff of the ministries and most agencies, and numbers less than a quarter of a million. The higher echelons of the civil service, entered through high competitive examinations, constitute a tiny elite within this larger group. Fast-stream bureaucrats (who are drawn largely from top universities such as Tokyo University and Kyoto University) are traditionally highly respected; they used to be seen as an extremely dedicated and competent elite, and as far more trustworthy than the majority of elected politicians. At the same time, these bureaucrats are also regarded as somewhat arrogant, rule-bound and inflexible. Public distrust for bureaucrats increased greatly during the 1990s, as a result of scandals such as a Health Ministry cover-up over HIV-infected blood, and growing evidence that ministerial inspection teams were treated with disgracefully lavish hospitality on their travels around Japan (Neary, 2002: 119–21). The economic woes of Japan from the early 1990s onwards also undermined the standing of bureaucrats, exploding the myth that Japan was bound to flourish under their omniscient administrative guidance. Despite the prestige enjoyed by senior bureaucrats, Japanese government offices are generally cramped and rather seedy: the corridors of power are often stacked with cardboard boxes containing old documents.

A central question is: who holds power in Japan? Where does the power reside? In short – who runs Japan? In general, most people might assume that power rests in the hands of the government of the day, but in the Japanese case many scholars have disputed the extent to which politicians are really in effective control of the country. According to van Wolferen:

> The Japanese prime minister is not expected to show much leadership; labour unions organize strikes to be held during lunch breaks; the legislature does not in fact legislate; stockholders never demand dividends; consumer interest groups advocate protectionism; laws are enforced only if they don't conflict too much with the interests of the powerful; and the ruling Liberal Democratic Party is, if anything, conservative and authoritarian, is not really a party, and does not in fact rule. (van Wolferen, 1989: 25)

He goes on to argue that most outsiders have been deceived by appearances: although Japan has the outward trappings of a liberal democratic state, sovereignty does not rest with the people – whatever the 1947 constitution may say. Power in Japan belongs to a political, bureaucratic and corporate elite, but the precise location of the power is difficult to establish: power is somewhat diffuse in what van Wolferen terms 'the elusive state'.

There is, naturally, an alternative perspective. Albrecht Rothacher has argued that while power is not so clearly focused in Japan as in countries with presidential systems (USA, France), or other countries where the government is commonly formed by a single party (Britain), Japan is quite comparable with countries which have complex coalition arrangements, and where five or six key individuals are the principal power-brokers – countries such as Italy, Belgium, the Netherlands, Italy and Israel (1993: xi). Essentially, Rothacher regards leaders of the LDP's various factions as the equivalent of party leaders in other systems.

He views the Japanese power structure as a pyramid (Rothacher, 1993: 2–4), with the LDP's faction leaders at the top, then the LDP's parliamentary party below, along with the senior bureaucrats of the main ministries and the heads of the *keiretsu* conglomerates. Together they comprise around 350 people. Below them is a third tier which he calls the 'elite at large', comprising around 1,600 people. This includes around 250 who cannot be readily classified in terms of bureaucracy, business or politics – people such as journalists, prominent *yakuza,* academics and representatives of different interest groups. The fourth tier consists of around 10,000 'elite aspirants', up-and-coming managers from the business sector, provincial politicians and middle-ranking civil servants.

Rothacher's central argument is that a distinct Japanese power elite does exist and can be identified: power is not so diffuse as van Wolferen claims. However, Rothacher does not concentrate much on the decision-making process itself: he is concerned with who holds power, rather than who exercises it. Most legislation is drafted not by politicians, but by bureaucrats. LDP cabinet ministers rotate their jobs on average about once a year, and are rarely in post long enough to stamp their ideas on a particular ministry, even if they were minded to do so. Van Wolferen points out that Cabinet meetings in Japan often last only 10–15 minutes, and almost invariably rubber-stamp the decisions already made by the top civil servants in the various ministries (van Wolferen, 1989: 32). In other words, even if we accept the composition of Rothacher's pyramid, LDP faction bosses are only nominally at the top. Real power is not always wielded by elected politicians accountable to parliament, whatever the external structure may suggest.

At the core of the problem is the simple fact that, although Japan has a multi-party parliamentary system, a single party held the reins of power from 1955 to 1993, and again formed the core of the government from mid-1994 to 2009. The Liberal Democratic Party was produced by a merger between two conservative parties, a merger supported and even promoted by big business. Apart from a brief period of socialist rule (1947–8), the Japanese government was in the hands of the conservatives from the time the 1947 constitution was enacted until 1993. For academics sympathetic to Japan, this political stability was often cited as evidence of a smooth-running, relatively conflict-free political order, and to the national genius for cooperation. It is frequently argued that Japan's phenomenal success in post-war economic reconstruction could never have been achieved without the political continuity provided by the LDP and its forebears.

One problem in approaching this issue is that the education and background of many LDP politicians closely resembled that of many Japanese civil servants. During the 1990s, around 25 per cent of LDP Diet members were ex-bureaucrats, and around half the post-war prime ministers of Japan have come through this route. Senior civil servants commonly receive plum retirement jobs when they leave ministerial service (usually early), either in business, politics, or with other public-sector agencies – a process known as *amakudari,* or 'descent from heaven'. Some commentators have suggested that 'ascent to heaven' might be more appropriate as a description, since these superannuated bureaucrats typically receive salaries and benefits well in excess of their former civil-service renumeration.

Civil servants are hired annually straight from university, and therefore belong to a cohort based on year of graduation. When one of their cohort becomes vice-minister (the highest position within a ministry), the remainder promptly retire to allow him to assume unchallenged seniority within the organization. The new vice-minister is obliged to help his colleagues find re-employment outside the ministry (Johnson, 1995: 149–50).

The upper echelons of the civil service are dominated by graduates of Tokyo and Kyoto Universities, along with a few other elite national and private universities. Senior Japanese bureaucrats invariably had strong personal ties with LDP politicians, with whom they worked closely on the drafting of policies and legislation. Around 60 per cent of these civil servants are law graduates, and a large proportion are graduates of the Tokyo University Law Faculty. These elite bureaucrats, many of whom attended a small group of 'high-level' feeder high schools in Tokyo, constitute a self-reproducing group drawn mainly from the middle class. The LDP had a number of 'policy research council divisions', which worked closely with one or more ministries in the preparation of legislation. The process by which drafts are developed is a complex one, which is open to contrasting interpretations.

Critics of the system argue that it is characterized by 'bureaucratic dominance'; the civil servants are in effective control of the process.

During the American Occupation, it was decided to govern Japan through the existing civil service, and in consequence much of the pre-war bureaucratic power was retained. The distrust felt by many Japanese people towards their politicians – and the lack of legitimacy enjoyed by those politicians – led them to give more esteem to 'neutral' bureaucrats. Even recently, 80 per cent of all legislation passed was originally drawn up by bureaucrats rather than politicians. Furthermore, legislation gives extensive powers to the bureaucracy to pass official ordinances which are effectively new laws; these ordinances outnumber actual laws by around 9:1. The bureaucracy therefore has quasi-legislative powers in its own right. Chalmers Johnson argues bluntly: 'Who governs is Japan's elite state bureaucracy' (1995: 13; for a full account, see 115–40). Johnson argues that bureaucratic influence is not confined to initiating legislation, but also includes direct meddling in the Diet's deliberative process (Johnson, 1995: 124).

An alternative view is that of party dominance, the argument that the LDP has the upper hand in the power relationship. This view has gained currency since the late 1970s, and it is partly borne out by figures which show that Japanese senior bureaucrats themselves believe – by a narrow margin – that ministers have more power than they do. Overall, however, the general picture is of two groups that are quite finely balanced, rather than a clear-cut superiority of one over the other. Koh notes that according to Chalmers Johnson, the recent period has seen an increase in bureaucratic 'sectionalism' and 'infighting' – the bureaucrats, in other words, have experienced similar problems to those traditionally experienced by the politicians.

Koh (1989) offers a third alternative: he regards the LDP and the bureaucrats as two evenly matched competing forces, with neither able to dominate the other: despite an apparent shift towards the party politicians, there is no overall dominant group. Keehn similarly argues that there is a 'symbiotic relationship' between the two sides: 'for the most part, a powerful bureaucracy has served LDP interests' (1990: 1037). Haley claims that the image of a 'ruling triumvirate' of politicians, bureaucrats and business leaders is a 'false model' which obscures the limited capacity of the Japanese government to control the private sector (Haley, 1987: 357). He characterizes the Japanese policy process as one of 'governance by negotiation'.

Yet whether or not the bureaucracy ever really did run Japan, the cosy relationship between politicians and civil servants was never quite the same following the LDP's loss of monopoly political authority in 1993. Rosenbluth and Thies argue that whereas in earlier decades it had often suited the LDP to delegate day-to-day policy making to the bureaucracy, in the higher stakes political environment after the electoral reforms of 1994, elected politicians of all parties became much more closely engaged in policy issues (Rosenbluth and Thies, 2010: 115–16). As a result, both the LDP and DPJ developed a strong interest in public-sector reform. The LDP pushed through major administrative reforms in 2001, while in 2008, the Basic Act for National Civil Service Reform was passed in the Diet. Detailed legislation to implement the reform process was lost when the LDP dissolved the lower house in mid-2009. But the incoming DPJ was elected on a mandate of further curbing bureaucratic power. The new administration viewed some senior bureaucrats with outright suspicion, regarding them as natural allies of the LDP rather than as politically neutral technocrats. However, in practice, the DPJ struggled to bypass the civil service, and arguably failed to make proper use of the highly experienced bureaucratic elite when faced with major calamities such as the Fukushima nuclear crisis.

## The policy process

A weakness of most analyses cited above is that they neglect the role of the business sector – especially that of major companies – in Japan's high-level decision making. Some scholars argue that Japan is actually ruled by an 'iron triangle' of politicians, bureaucrats and businessmen. According to Krauss and Muramatsu (1988: 208–10), Japan operates a system of 'patterned pluralism', which has the following features: a strong government and bureaucracy; blurred boundaries between state and society; the integration of social groups into government; political parties which mediate between government and interest groups; government which has been thoroughly penetrated by mediating organizations such as political parties; and interest groups which form alliances with political parties and bureaucratic agencies.

In short, the main feature of governance in Japan under the 1955 system was the remarkable degree to which the functions and goals of government, the ruling party, the bureaucracy and interest groups have been merged together. Importantly, the Japanese elite is rather homogeneous; most of its members are graduates of a small number of well-known universities, such as Tokyo, Kyoto, Waseda and Keio.

Certain faculties of these universities, especially the Tokyo University Law Faculty, have produced a remarkable proportion of the country's leaders. In 1986, for example, there were 22 administrative vice-ministers (the top-ranking civil-service post) in Japan: 16 were alumni of the Tokyo University Law Faculty, three had attended other Tokyo University faculties, two were Kyoto University graduates, and only one had attended neither university (Koh, 1989: 141).

How does the process of policy formulation work? Nakano (1997) views the Japanese policy-making process as very complicated; terms such as 'bureaucratic dominance' and 'party dominance' serve to obfuscate what are very elaborate interactions between different players. According to the circumstances of each case, a variety of decision-making processes are employed, reflecting attempts by the various components of the dominant order to accommodate their respective interests. Nakano argues that 'policies cause politics' (1997: 14–16). By this he means that where a policy agenda initiated by bureaucrats will require legislation, this has the effect of activating a range of interest groups from both the government and non-governmental sectors. Each stage of the legislative process causes further ripples, as consultation takes place with different government departments. Meetings are held between politicians and parties, and with consultative councils and commissions of inquiry. Proceedings in the Diet begin with a committee stage, and negotiations concerning possible amendments are held with opposition parties. Later, the legislation is approved by the full Diet.

Parliamentary legislation does not lie at the heart of all policy making; important decisions often involve business leaders, in addition to bureaucrats and politicians. Nakano sees two main modes of governance here: elite accommodation politics, in which big business is a key player, and client-oriented politics, where small businesses and other interest groups share *in* the allocation of benefits (Nakano, 1997: 65).

Elite accommodation politics brought together the three elements of the so-called 'iron triangle': prominent government politicians, the leaders of the Keidanren (Federation of Economic Organizations), and senior officials of the economic ministries and agencies. The Keidanren principally represented the core industries which benefited from state-led initiatives to rebuild Japan's economy after the war: iron, steel, banking and electricity. Following the 1960 Security Treaty riots which gave rise to a political crisis in Japan, industry leaders joined forces with bureaucrats and politicians to present a united front in facing down the leftist challenges to the capitalist order (Nakano, 1997: 90). Just as Prime Minister Ikeda set out to buy off public dissent through the 'income-doubling plan', so Japan's big companies backed the strategy of rapid economic growth, which led to strong ties with the ruling political and bureaucratic elites (Illustration 5.3). Corporations accepted increased regulation in exchange for more involvement in policy formation. The strategy of rapid economic growth was effectively an elite pact, formed in the interests of mutual preservation. Thus the present-day form of patterned pluralism emerged over time, as a result of shared political and economic imperatives.

There are multiple connections between the three elements of the triple alliance. In the past, politicians from the LDP influenced bureaucrats via their control of appointments, and by recruiting former bureaucrats to become LDP Diet members. Bureaucrats were able to influence business through their powers of 'administrative guidance', and their authority to devise secondary legislation of a regulatory nature. In return, business provided most of the funding on which the LDP's political machine relied. However, the economic

**Illustration 5.3 Rightist protestors in a sound truck protesting in front of the Diet**

downturn of the 1970s helped produce more flexible, less monolithic relationships between the three components. The Keidanren's influence declined significantly, leaving individual industries and companies more freedom to create direct bilateral ties with politicians via campaign contributions and the emergence of *zoku*. Nakano (1997: 91) argues that the iron triangle has now become much less iron and rather more angular than before, with a less pervasive influence on politics and policy making.

The patterns of governance described by Nakano typically exclude or limit popular participation in the decision-making process. Closed circles of politicians, administrators and interest groups are often the sole parties to important decisions, and there is little reference to considerations of public interest. The LDP had an impressive track-record in converting opposition groups (such as environmental protesters) into loyal supporters, by offering them benefits in exchange for their cooperation. In a similar fashion, Calder (1993: 246) described the inter-relationship of the Japanese industrial sector and the bureaucracy as based upon 'circles of compensation', circles including both regulators and the regulated. Supported by state-provided benefits, members of these circles offered various kinds of support to the bureaucracy in return. For both newcomers and outsiders, penetrating these charmed circles is difficult. Japanese elite governance is, paradoxically, both inclusionary and exclusionary. While efforts are made to include as many voices as possible in the policy-making process, this strategy has the effect of excluding dissident interest and minority views, as well as downplaying considerations of public interest. A fascinating example of the new forms of policy process seen in the early twenty-first century was Koizumi's successful railroading through of postal privatization legislation in 2005; despite opposition to the proposals from vested interests and lobbies with strong political links inside the then-ruling LDP, the prime minister was able to call a general election and invoke the results to claim a popular mandate for his policy (see Maclachlan, 2006).

The 2009 end of LDP rule means that previous studies of the policy process and the inter-relationship between the three components of the 'iron triangle', already surpassed by the Hashimoto reforms, now look extremely dated. New research is urgently needed on these topics. Mainstream perspectives such as that of Rosenbluth and Thies suggest that politicians are now firmly in the policy driving seat, and the collusive relationships between the private and public sector no longer function as before; instead, there has been an 'unravelling of institutional complementarities' (2010: 124–6). Sherry Martin argues that there has been a general movement away from elite dominated power politics and towards grassroots empowerment and democratic activism, often led by women (2011: 6–7). However, observers of the debacle over the Fukushima nuclear crisis, from which neither power plant owners TEPCO nor the bureaucrats charged with regulating them emerged with any credit, are more sceptical that there has really been such a fundamental break with the past.

## Conclusion

In terms of formal structures, Japan's political order closely resembles those of western liberal democracies. The academic debate is concerned less with the formal order than with how power is held and exercised in practice. For mainstream scholars, the Diet has become increasingly powerful during the post-war period, and party politicians are in a dominant position *vis-à-vis* bureaucrats. For revisionist scholars, Japan has been a 'facade democracy', in which elected politicians were largely the captives of bureaucratic and business interests. For scholars using culturalist approaches, Japan has its own distinctive form of political institutions and processes; these should be understood as indigenous adaptations of western models, which cannot readily be understood using conventional social science categories and criteria.

# 6

# Political Society: Parties and Opposition

Few aspects of contemporary Japan inspire as much controversy as its party-political order. For mainstream scholars, Japan is a working liberal democracy similar to those of western Europe or the United States. For revisionists, Japanese electoral politics are a travesty that has little to do with popular representation, and everything to do with structural corruption and special interests. For culturalist scholars, Japan's politics reflect the distinctive nature of the country's history and culture, and attempts to draw comparisons with other nations are therefore often inappropriate. Revisionist critiques of the Japanese political system were based partly on the fact that the Liberal Democratic Party (LDP) was able to govern almost continuously from 1955 to 2009 – with the exception of a brief interlude between 1993 and 1994, followed by a spell during which the LDP formed the largest party in a coalition administration. However, the decisive defeat of the LDP by the Democratic Party of Japan (DPJ) in 2009 had the effect of 'normalizing' Japanese politics, demonstrating that power could change hands from one major party to another.

Nevertheless, some interesting and potentially awkward questions remain. Central among these would be how far Japan's parties have policy platforms, organizational structures and patterns of support that resemble parties in western liberal democracies. Many scholars emphasize the distinctive features of Japanese parties, particularly their factionalism and the importance of political patronage. Is there a real difference between the LDP and DPJ, or are they barely distinguishable both in the ways they operate and the policies they propose? Are party leaders becoming stronger, more powerful and more electorally significant? Another key question concerns the nature of the party system itself: is Japan in the process of adopting a two-party system, rather than the multi-party system that operated for many decades?

During the 1950s and early 1960s, many commentators expected the Japan Socialist Party eventually to displace the Liberal Democratic Party from power. In the early 1990s, a seven-party coalition did briefly oust the LDP, and subsequently anti-LDP forces coalesced into a major second party, the Democratic Party of Japan, established in 1998. Underlying the debate about Japan's party system have been calls for reform: reform of the electoral system (enacted in 1994), reform of electoral funding, reform of the faction system, and reforms aimed at creating an Anglo-American style two-party system. These reformist agendas met with varying degrees of success. Revisionists see reform of electoral politics since 1993 as broadly unsuccessful, an argument which reinforces their criticisms of the political order. Mainstream scholars are inclined to see more evidence of reformist successes, exemplifying gradual Japanese convergence with western liberal democratic models and practices. Culturalist scholars argue that Japanese politics is simply different from the politics of other countries, and can only be understood in culturally specific ways.

## The rise of the Democratic Party of Japan

The Liberal Democratic Party of Japan was an electoral anomaly for decades: returned to office almost continuously since 1955, yet operating in an open and competitive political system, the LDP was a byword for one-party dominance. Only briefly (1993–4) was the LDP out of power. Yet on 30 August 2009, the opposition DPJ swept to power in lower-house elections which saw a near-reversal of the vote four years earlier. How did this happen, and what did it signify?

The LDP was famously created through the merger of the old Liberal and Democratic parties, two conservative, pro-business and pro-American parties, in 1955. For the next four decades the main opposition was the Japan Socialist Party (later renamed the Social Democratic Party of Japan). In 1993, the LDP was ousted from power, temporarily thwarted by a fractious seven-party coalition, which was united only by a shared opposition to LDP rule. In effect, the LDP had been removed from power primarily by prominent defectors (led by 'shadow shogun' Ichiro Ozawa) who had formed new, 'reformist' rival parties; but in 1994 the LDP was able to return to power by forming a pragmatic and implausible alliance with the Socialists. By 2003, however, the Socialists had virtually collapsed, while most leading anti-LDP figures had united to join the catch-all DPJ. Yet this more coherent DPJ opposition faced a strong challenge from Junichiro Koizumi, one of the LDP's most popular and visionary post-war premiers. In 2005, Koizumi led the LDP to its strongest lower-house election result since 1986, winning 304 seats versus the DPJ's 113. Just four years later, the tables were turned: the DPJ took 308 seats compared with the LDP's 119.

The 2005 and 2009 election results testified to a fundamental volatility in the Japanese electorate: neither the LDP nor the DPJ have a particularly solid core vote, and the outcome on both occasions was decided by a large number of swing voters. The lower house is divided into two components, comprising 300 constituency seats, and 180 party-list seats. The DPJ won 221 constituency seats but only 87 party-list seats, while the LDP won 64 constituency seats, yet still secured 55 party-list seats. In other words, without their party-list seats, the LDP would have been completely routed. The remaining party-list seats were distributed among a number of smaller parties, some of whom gained no constituency seats at all.

At the same time, as Manuel Alvarez-Rivera argues, the first-past-the-post system had the effect of exaggerating the size of the DPJ win (Alvarez-Rivera 2009). The party gained 73.7 per cent of the constituency seats with only 47.4 per cent of the vote in single-member districts, whereas the LDP gained a mere 21.3 per cent of these seats despite winning 38.7 per cent of the constituency votes (see McCargo 2010 for detailed sources). In many constituencies, races between LDP and DPJ candidates were very close run; the LDP was helped by the fact that its coalition partner, New Komeito, refrained from fielding candidates in most constituencies (and lost in the eight seats where they put up candidates). Nevertheless, the DPJ secured the largest share of the popular vote in all eleven party-list regions of Japan, gaining 48.3 per cent overall, and securing over 40 per cent in all except Chugoku and Kyushu; by contrast, the LDP only topped 30 per cent in two regions. LDP performance in the party-list seats was lamentable, and the party gained only 26.7 per cent of the vote overall, an historic low, despite the fact that voter turnout was over 69 per cent, the highest for almost two decades. In the party-list vote, the DPJ received 29,844,799 votes, up almost nine million compared with the 2005 elections, while the LDP was down over seven million votes to 18,810,217. In the constituency votes, DPJ received a total of 33,475,334, an increase of nearly 8.7 million on 2005; while the LDP secured 27,301,982, a fall of just over five million votes. What these figures illustrate is how well the LDP vote held up; the party received eight and half million more party-list votes than it did constituency votes, suggesting that many voters cast their party lists for the LDP even when voting for other candidates at the constituency level.

Nevertheless, while the DPJ secured a convincing overall majority (308 out of 480 seats), despite some over-optimistic polling, their final numbers fell short of the 320 votes required to over-rule any legislative veto from the upper house, where the DPJ lacked a majority. To avoid this possibility, the DPJ was obliged to form a coalition with two minor parties, the Social Democratic Party and the People's New Party. In this respect the DSP election victory was less spectacular than it first appeared; though tiny, the coalition partners sought to hold the government hostage, leaving the DPJ with very limited freedom of manoeuvre on sensitive issues such as the future of American military bases on Okinawa.

## The significance of the DPJ victory

To a large extent, the 2009 lower-house elections were a referendum on the performance of the long-dominant LDP, in which the DPJ's primary appeal lay in the simple fact that it was not the LDP. Many voters were casting their ballots to express their frustrations with the complacency of the incumbents, their long-standing, cosy and collusive relations with the bureaucracy and leaders of big business (the so-called 'iron triangle'), their disappointment with the growing gap between haves and have-nots, perceptions about an uncertain economic future, and fears that Japan was declining in regional and global significance, especially given the rise of China. While the contrast between the LDP's strong showing in 2005 and weak performance in 2009 might seem to suggest a dramatic reversal in LDP fortunes, this would be misleading. Koizumi was a maverick leader who repeatedly declared his determination to 'smash' the LDP and slaughter its 'sacred cows'. Though mistrusted and disliked by many prominent figures in his own party, Koizumi was able to appeal to the voting public over the heads of the LDP machine, projecting a highly personalized form of leadership through the use of media such as daytime TV programmes (see McCargo 2003: 69–76). In other words, the LDP performed so well in 2005 because Koizumi was able to present himself as an 'anti-LDP' candidate. But when Koizumi was eased out by his own party soon after delivering the 2005 election victory, the LDP proved singularly unable to repeat his electoral prestidigitation by again persuading the public that the best way to rein in the party's excesses was actually to vote for it.

Koizumi was followed by three hapless, one-year premiers: Shinzo Abe (2006–7), Yasuo Fukuda (2007–8) and Taro Aso (2008–9). Each was a blueblood member of Japan's hereditary political elite: the grandson, son and grandson respectively of a former prime minister. During Japan's long post-war economic rise, the emergence of what amounted to an elected LDP aristocracy, among which Diet seats were passed from father to son, had gone relatively unnoticed. But following the decade-long economic slump of the 1990s, Japanese voters, who saw the erosion of lifetime employment and other benefits, began to question the wealth and privilege of the political class. While old ideological divides now largely lacked salience, opposition politicians converged around ill-defined notions of 'reform' (for which read 'anything but the LDP') to form the DPJ. The problem in a nutshell: the very same voters who felt alienated by the LDP's failings had also grown up during the long, safe decades of LDP rule, were quietly comfortable with the dominant party, and were nervous about trusting the running of Japan to anyone else. Hence the phenomenon of the anti-LDP LDP voter, for whom Koizumi was the standard-bearer. Exit Koizumi, and the anti-LDP voters finally crossed the rubicon and voted against the LDP.

## The nature of the DPJ

The DPJ is a hybrid party, founded in an earlier incarnation in 1996 before assuming its present form in 1998 when the original DPJ merged with three other parties. The DPJ was further boosted by a merger with the Liberal Party in 2003. The party claims to adhere to an ideology of 'democratic centrism', enshrined in five rather vague principles. The most substantive of these is the third principle, which calls for a 'decentralized and participatory society' – an implicit critique of the 'iron triangle' and the LDP's intimate connections with the bureaucracy. The party loftily claims as its political standpoint:

'We stand for those who have been excluded by the structure of vested interests' (DPJ, 2011)

The DPJ was a catch-all party, containing a number of prominent defectors from the LDP, along with others who had made their careers in the Japan Socialist Party or smaller opposition parties. During the early years of the DPJ, leadership alternated between two dominant figures: Yukio Hatoyama, a blue-blooded right-winger with roots in the LDP, and Naoto Kan, a moderate leftist who had cut his political teeth in the citizens' movements of the 1970s (Stockwin, 2008 195–7). However, the internal politics of the DPJ became more complicated when Ichiro Ozawa joined the party in 2003. Ozawa, a political heavyweight who had masterminded the short-lived end of LDP rule in 1993–4, assumed the DPJ leadership in 2006 after a long journey from the LDP (1969–94), via the New Frontier Party (1994–8) to the Liberal Party (1998–2003) and finally to the DPJ. But Ozawa's political career had been marred by controversy; he had gained a reputation as an opportunistic 'fixer', closely associated with the heady mix of money and politics that many Japanese voters saw as a major problem with their political system. Ozawa had withdrawn his candidacy for the DPJ leadership in 2004 because of a pensions scandal, and was forced to resign as DPJ leader in May 2009 because of a fundraising scandal.

It might seem logical to assume that the remarkable 2009 swing to the DPJ illustrated a wave of popular support for the party. Yet such a reading would be simplistic: the DPJ was not in particularly good shape even in 2009. Yukio Hatoyama, who replaced Ozawa and led the DPJ into the August 2009 campaign with Ozawa's backing, had been party leader for only four months when he was appointed prime minister. The controversy surrounding Ozawa significantly undermined the DPJ's credibility. Like his three immediate LDP predecessors as prime minister, Hatoyama was the scion of a prominent political family. Hatoyama's grandfather Ichiro was prime minister from 1954 to 1956, while his brother Kunio was a minister in the Taro Aso cabinet until mid-2009. The Hatoyama family have been facetiously dubbed 'Japan's Kennedys'. Under Hatoyama, the DPJ leadership was closely associated with the same troublesome issues that had dogged the LDP: a hint of financial scandal and a pervasive elitism. In many respects, the LDP and DPJ were rather alike.

Despite these shortcomings, the DPJ was highly successful during the 2009 election campaign in building a positive image among voters, especially swing voters. Key to this success was the party's much-praised manifesto, a glossy 23-page document which was extensively circulated in both hard copy and electronic versions. This was the first time an election manifesto attracted major attention in Japan. The document featured images of Hatoyama showing his concern for children, the elderly and the disadvantaged, so tapping into the popular perception of Aso as uncaring and aloof. The manifesto also contained a number of specific campaign promises, notably a pledge to provide every family with a monthly subsidy of 26,000 yen (around $260 per child). In times of austerity and financial uncertainty, such commitments offered a strong incentive to vote DPJ. The DPJ also succeeded in recruiting a good number of 'new look' candidates, including many women (dubbed the 'Princess Corps') who were calculated to appeal more to younger voters than the greying, male dominated ranks of the LDP. A record number of women, 54, were elected to the Diet in 2009.

Not all DPJ messages were positive. Frustration with the LDP was a theme which was highlighted in Hatoyama's first press conference as prime minister:

> During this election, we often heard all around the country numerous expressions of anger, dissatisfaction and sorrow from the public. How did Japan turn out like this, why did my hometown become like this – these thoughts we must keep firmly in mind. And we must assume the heavy mantle of squarely meeting those concerns. (Hatoyama, 2009)

The election results reflected popular irritation with the LDP as much as the strengths of the DPJ. DPJ Diet member Ikuo Yamahana argued that his party successfully capitalized on public perceptions about the failed leadership of the LDP, including the rotating premierships of the post-Koizumi period (interview, 7 December 2009). Yamahana suggested that if the LDP had handled their image and presentation a little better, their defeat would have been much narrower. The DPJ was able to crystallize its campaign around a single, catchy message, a rallying-cry for 'regime change' (*seiken kotai*). At the heart of this message was the claim that bureaucrats had become too powerful, and too removed from the concerns of ordinary people. Assessments of the DPJ's media strategy during the election vary, but the party did receive a lot of favourable coverage from electronic media and a couple of leading newspaper groups. New media played little role in mobilizing voters, however; while Japan abounds in bloggers, political blogs have yet to be mainstreamed as an influence on the electorate (McCargo and Lee, 2010).

Former LDP financial services minister Tastuya Ito (who lost his seat in the elections) concurred, claiming that the 2009 defeat testified to widespread feelings of repulsion towards the LDP, rather than genuine support for the DPJ (interview, 4 December 2009). Ito also attributed the LDP's poor performance to Taro Aso's 'hoody', aggressive manner, which women voters found particularly offensive. Aso had lost public credibility early on in his prime ministerial term, when it emerged that he had no idea about the real price of instant noodles. Ironically, the DPJ campaign in 2009 closely resembled the style of Koizumi's very successful LDP campaign in 2005 – making a direct appeal to the voters, so by-passing discredited old-style politicians (Shin-kun Haku interview, 11 December 2011). The result reflected public anger with the LDP's privileged hereditary politicians (*seshu giin*). Of the LDP members of the 2005–9 lower house, 112 (37.8 per cent) were blood relatives of other or former politicians. This included eleven out of the seventeen ministers in Aso's cabinet (Nagata, 2009). Though not immune from the problem, the DPJ scored rather better, with only twenty bluebloods in the lower house during the same period. Nevertheless, the bluebloods were disproportionately influential, including both party leader Hatoyama and kingmaker Ozawa. The 2009 elections saw the number of hereditary politicians fall from around 25 per cent of the lower house to roughly 15 per cent (ABC Radio, 2009). In part, this change reflected a backlash against the practice; on another level, it simply reflected the poor performance of the LDP overall, given that the former ruling party had a larger proportion of 'hereditaries' than any other.

## Signs of long-term change?

Debate has rumbled in the Japanese elections literature for years about the extent to which 'traditional' values and forms of organization have been gradually displaced by more 'modern' phenomena. In his classic 1971 study, Gerald Curtis argued that in urban areas successful election candidates won by creating their own personal support organizations, known as *koenkai* (Curtis, 1971). These organizations were loyal to candidates rather than to parties, and were more redolent of patron–client relationships than western-style constituency associations. Nevertheless, Curtis ended his book by arguing that *koenkai* were already in the process of being displaced by more modern forms of campaigning, which were not based on direct personal connections (1971: 252). In fact, *koenkai* turned out to have a much longer shelf-life than Curtis anticipated, and formed a key element in the LDP's electoral success during the post-1955 period. Scott Flanagan and a team of colleagues published *The Japanese Voter* in 1991 (Flanagan *et al.*, 1991), a deliberate attempt to produce a study comparable with the classic texts *Political Change in Britain* (Butler and Stokes, 1974) and *The American Voter* (Campbell *et al.*, 1960). *The Japanese Voter* identified a long-term decline in the LDP vote, seen in the rise of 'modern values' which could favour opposition parties. Almost twenty years before the 2009 DPJ victory, Flanagan was arguing that voters faced an 'empty choice' between a ruling party they disliked and an opposition they did not trust in office (1991: 446). It took another two decades for the (small 'c') conservative Japanese electorate to steel itself to oust the ruling party, despite long-standing and extremely high levels of popular mistrust of politicians and the political system.

This view is borne out by 2007 survey research conducted as part of the Asian Barometer Project, which found considerable generational differences in political attitudes:

> those who are in, and over, their seventies value authoritarianism and collectivism, and at the same time appreciate contemporary Japanese democracy. The *dankai* [post-war baby boomer] generation, who experienced the student movement in their youth, have the most active and autonomous views toward politics. Those in their thirties are pessimistic about politics. Those in their twenties tend to value the government's exercise of power; except for this, they seem to have negative attitudes. The younger generation does not appear to have a clear awareness of democracy. (Ikeda *et al.*, 2007: 12)

Broadly speaking, these survey results suggest that younger Japanese people have much more sceptical and critical attitudes concerning politics. While 'modern' political values typically include a greater openness to new ideas and to opposition parties, in the Japanese context, such values also correspond to feelings of disillusionment and dissatisfaction. Such voters may be easily swayed by valence issues and negative campaign themes, and may also have the potential to become deeply apathetic or alienated. While this attitudinal context helps explain the LDP's loss of power and the 2009 swing to the DPJ, it may not augur well for the future. Such a volatile and disenchanted younger electorate could easily revert to supporting the LDP, so as to punish the DPJ for any sins of omission or commission.

## A messy aftermath

In the months immediately following the 2009 election, support for the DPJ ebbed rapidly. The DPJ made various attempts to retain public support, including the creation of a Government Revitalization Unit that summoned officials to budget screening sessions which were broadcast live online from a Tokyo gymnasium. Bureaucrats were challenged to account for pork-barrel projects and forced to slash unnecessary public works projects, under the slogan 'From concrete to humans' – a crude dig at the LDP's murky ties to the construction industry (*Daily Yomiuri*, 13 November 2009). But such populist posturing failed to stem declining support for the DPJ, reflecting public concern over the financial scandals that continued to plague DPJ secretary-general Ichiro Ozawa, who was questioned by prosecutors in January 2010 following the arrest of three of his former or current aides. The high hopes raised by the end of LDP rule in 2009 proved short-lived. Hatoyama's weak leadership became an increasingly serious potential electoral liability for his party. He was haunted by his flip-flopping over the future of the Futenma US military base in Okinawa, an emotive issue that deeply divided the voting public. In June 2010, Hatoyama stepped down, after only nine months in office. DPJ secretary-general and power-broker Ichiro Ozawa resigned alongside him. But while Hatoyama was now political history, Ozawa, believed to control a faction of around 150 Diet members, remained a troubling force to be reckoned with. While lacking the popular credibility to return as leader, Ozawa nevertheless retained the capacity to make life extremely difficult for any DPJ prime minister.

The DPJ quickly elected finance minister Naoto Kan to serve as party leader and premier. A former social activist, and the first Japanese premier for 14 years not to come from a blueblood political family, Kan faced an early baptism of fire in the form of the 11 July 2010 House of Councillor elections. Overall, the DPJ remained the largest party in the House of Councillors, with 106 (down from 116) seats to the LDP's 84 (up from 71). Yet the election left the DPJ well short of the overall majority, which had previously seemed well within the party's grasp. One of the most interesting developments of the 2010 election was the emergence of the fledgling Your Party, which took eleven seats and won a surprising 13.6 per cent of the party-list vote. This modernizing conservative party made a strong appeal to yuppie voters, and has the potential to woo disenchanted ex-supporters from both the DPJ and LDP.

Yet the primary reason for the DPJ's reversal of fortunes was public disappointment with the party's performance in office: the failure of the party to live up to extravagant 2009 manifesto promises, the government's apparent inability to balance the books, and its persistent reluctance to adopt a clear stance over the US–Japan security relationship. Two years after the remarkable electoral successes of August 2009, Naoto Kan was also gone, after taking the rap for his government's inept handling of the March 2011 earthquake, tsunami and the ensuing Fukushima nuclear crisis. Kan was effectively ousted from power by his old adversary Ozawa, who had mobilized opposition with the DPJ to make Kan's survival as party leader untenable. However, this was a dangerous game to play: the DPJ's hold on power looked terribly fragile, and the party now enjoyed very little public support. When Yoshihiko Noda became Japan's sixth prime minister in five years in September 2011, the country's future political direction was very unclear. Like Kan, Noda came from a non-elite background; unlike the rather haughty Kan, he appeared humble and self-deprecating, referring to himself unflatteringly as a 'dojo loach' a shy, eel-like scavenger fish that feeds on the bottom of river banks.

## Explaining the LDP

For many decades, studying the politics of Japan meant studying the politics of one leading party, the Liberal Democratic Party (LDP). For better or worse, factions (known in Japanese as *habatsu*) played a central role in keeping the LDP in power for 38 years, from 1955 to 1993. In recent decades, the LDP has usually had about five factions, each led by a faction boss who provided financial patronage (amounting to the equivalent of millions of pounds) to his parliamentary associates in exchange for their support during the post-election horse-trading sessions which determined the allocation of ministerial portfolios. Jobs were assigned in the proverbial smoke-filled rooms. As Hrebenar and Nakamura explain, the faction system means that

'LDP cabinet members are selected by "illogical" criteria that have no direct relation to the individual abilities of the politicians themselves' (Hrebenar and Nakamura, 2000: 125). This means that faction leaders and long-serving Diet members attain high political office, including the post of prime minister, more or less regardless of aptitude. In 1998, the popular Ryutaro Hashimoto was replaced as prime minister by lacklustre Keizo Obuchi, simply because Obuchi controlled a large faction – despite the fact that many younger Diet members tried to block his election (Hrebenar *et al.*, 2000: 110). When Obuchi died suddenly in 2000, Yoshiro Mori, widely regarded as completely unsuitable, became prime minister for exactly the same reason. This was a system born out of what Curtis terms 'the politics of complacency' (1999: 28); party leaders were picked for purely internal reasons, irrespective of their ability to secure electoral support.

Junichiro Koizumi, who succeeded Mori as prime minister in 2001, was an outspoken critic of the LDP's faction system (despite being also a product of the same system), and selected his first cabinet without reference to factional quotas. For his first cabinet reshuffle in September 2002, he again refused to consult faction leaders in selecting his ministers, and broke with tradition by asking most incumbent ministers (11 out of 17) to stay on in office for the sake of continuity. One commentator noted that: 'This new-style reshuffle made the faction leaders feel endangered and powerless, darkening the mood inside the LDP' (Suzuki, 2002: 33). If future LDP leaders had followed Koizumi's example, the faction system might have been doomed. In the event, factions reasserted themselves once Koizumi left office in 2006, vindicating revisionist scepticism that they had ever gone away.

The pre-eminent position of the LDP during the 1955–93 period partly derived from the Public Offices Elections Law. The multimember constituency system, used until electoral reform was implemented in 1995, tended broadly to favour the LDP, which alone had the financial resources to put up several candidates in a single constituency. This resulted in low levels of electoral competition, since around 80 per cent of seats were regarded as 'safe'; in the 1989 lower house elections, for example, a mere 838 candidates stood for 512 seats – a ratio of 1.64 candidates per seat. Another important reason for the LDP's formidable electoral strength was the underrepresentation of Japan's urban population in the constituencies of the House of Representatives. The result was a problem of malapportionment: the number of voters per Diet member ranged from around 106,000 to 336,000. LDP strength was concentrated in conservative rural areas, where the party assiduously cultivated Japan's small but disproportionately influential farming lobby. As a result, urban voters lost out – they had to pay for the heavy rice production subsidies to Japanese farmers, and for the protectionist policies which limited foreign imports of beef, for example. The smaller opposition parties had little chance of winning seats in rural areas, and were forced into competing with each other in a limited number of urban constituencies, instead of challenging the LDP on a more equal footing across the country. At the same time, some scholars (such as Curtis, 1988: 49–52) have stressed that the rural vote was not a complete explanation for LDP success: by the late 1980s, only about a quarter of LDP voters lived in villages and small towns; 46 per cent lived in cities with a population of more than 100,000. Nevertheless, the rural bias in the electoral boundaries was historically important in building up LDP strength.

In western countries, political scientists tend to analyse voters in terms of their economic and social status, but some writers have argued that Japanese party politics are not strongly connected to sociocultural divisions in society. Whilst it is true that there is no direct equivalent of, say, the Jewish or Hispanic vote in the United States, a major study of the Japanese voter by Scott Flanagan *et al*. has argued that 'value cleavages' and 'social networks' play a vital part in determining voter choice. As Flanagan notes:

> Community bloc voting, which is often based on the exchange of community votes for government funding of local projects and the rounding up of personally obligated votes, favors the ruling party and helps explain its uninterrupted majority control of the Diet for over thirty years. (Flanagan, 1991a: 196–7)

Clearly, social networks which allow candidates to acquire votes en bloc rather than through individual choice operate far more effectively in rural areas than in, say, Tokyo, Osaka or Nagoya. The LDP could easily do well in the countryside, but faced difficulty in large cities, which have a more complex social structure. Theoretically, gradual changes in the values held by the Japanese, coupled with changes in the make-up of society, ought eventually to have harmed the fortunes of the LDP. However, the party showed itself to be remarkably resilient in weathering changes in wider society until

1993. Curtis has argued that the debate about voters' changing values was flawed:

> But as the Japanese developed their economy, they showed that 'traditional' and 'modern' were not antithetical but more compatible concepts than many people had assumed . . . Japan successfully modernized on Japanese terms. (Curtis, 1999: 32–3)

## Reforming party funding

The growing demands for political reform voiced in Japan during the 1990s centred on two main issues: reforming the electoral system (discussed in Chapter 5), and reforming the system of party funding. In response to concerns about political fundraising, legislation passed in 1994 introduced a system of subsidies for political parties which was intended to obviate the need for improper relationships between politicians and business. The subsidies involved were extremely generous, but there were serious concerns about how these funds were used, especially since corporate donations were not outlawed when the subsidy system was established (Foreign Press Center, 1995: 86–8). All major parties were entitled to government funding, based on a formula calculated according to the number of Diet seats held by parties, and the number of votes they gained in the most recent elections (Hrebenar *et al.,* 2000: 79–80). However, only parties with at least five Diet seats, or 2 per cent of the popular vote, were eligible. In the first year of operation this new system generated the equivalent of $272 million for Japan's political parties. At the same time, the rules on declaring donations were changed; whereas before parties did not need to declare donations of less than ¥1 million, the ceiling was now lowered to ¥50,000. Corporate and personal donations were also restricted to a maximum amount, though the sale of 'party tickets' – a long-standing loophole – remained permissible, and provided invaluable income even for the 'reformist' Democratic Party, which gained ¥2.6 million from this source in 1997 (Hrebenar *et al.,* 2000: 80). The Japan Communist Party was the only party to take a stand on principle, refusing to accept government subsidies. Penalties for financial and electoral irregularities were greatly increased, and corporate donations were supposed eventually to be completely abolished.

## Opposition politics

It is tempting to look upon Japanese party politics under the 1955 system as essentially stagnant, lacking a real adversarial dimension. But to do so would be to grossly over-simplify. Over 50 per cent of Japanese voters were voting for non-LDP parliamentary candidates in lower house elections from 1967 onwards. There was far more support for opposition parties than has often been realized. But the LDP was not destined to be ousted by its main opposition counterpart from 1955 to 1993, the Japan Socialist Party, later renamed the Social Democratic Party of Japan (SDPJ). The party's performance in the 1992 upper house elections was distinctly disappointing, marking the beginning of a terminal decline for the SDPJ. When the end of LDP rule finally came in 1993, the SDPJ was the largest party in the seven-party coalition that formed the new government. But the party was also a major loser in that election, gaining a mere 70 lower house seats – just over half of the 136 it won in 1990. The plot thickened in July 1994, when the demise of two successive anti-LDP coalitions led to a bizarre, and once unthinkable, coalition between the Socialists and the LDP, with SDPJ leader Tomiichi Murayama as prime minister. Instead of an ideological stand-off between the two main parties, Japan was ruled by an alliance of the old adversaries, which lasted until 1998. Lower house elections in 2000 saw the SDPJ reduced to just nineteen seats; the ill-conceived coalition with the LDP effectively killed off the party.

## The labour movement

Despite the weakness of most Japanese unions, there is a close relationship between union membership and voting preference. In fact, union membership is a more useful variable than the white-collar/blue-collar distinction: union members are far more likely to support left-wing parties than their non-unionized counterparts (Watanuki, 1991: 70). The Americans built up the power of unions during the Occupation period in order to create a wider range of political forces in the country, though later they outlawed a proposed general strike, and banned public servants from striking. There were numerous serious labour disputes in post-war Japan: Toyota was almost brought to its knees at one point in the 1950s, and Japan

National Railways was infamous for its regular and crippling strikes. But as with the opposition parties, trade unions in Japan have a history of division and failure to mount an effective challenge to the dominant conservative order. About 24 per cent of workers were unionized in 1995 (Japan Institute of Labour, 1997: 48), a decline from 35 per cent in 1970, and 31 per cent in 1980. Whereas previously different union federations were affiliated with different parties (the DSP with Domei, which was dominated by private-sector unions, and the SDPJ with Sohyo, dominated by public-sector unions), in 1987 the majority of unions joined a single national federation called Shin Rengo, which had 7.7 million members in 1995. The creation of this federation weakened the traditional support base of the SDPJ, which had already been undermined by the privatization of public-sector enterprises which had traditionally formed the backbone of Sohyo.

About 94 per cent of labour organizations are so-called 'enterprise unions', which are specific to a particular company rather than representing occupational categories across a range of employers. This tends to lead to a cosy relationship between union leaders and company management, producing smooth labour relations characterized by such phenomena as strikes held during lunch hours. These unions have been widely praised by economists and management consultant types, who have seen them as one of the secrets of Japan's post-war success; they are held to have encouraged innovation and reform and to have helped Japanese workers achieve high wage levels. They are also sometimes seen as promoting a greater say for workers concerning their jobs and conditions. Critical analyses view most of these unions as mere fronts for employer interests.

Much more radical than the enterprise unions were public-sector unions such as that of the old Japan National Railways (until privatization in 1987), and the Japan Teachers' Union. These unions had well-established records of opposing the LDP, but their particular grievances made their tradition of support for the SDPJ a mixed blessing: the close association between the Socialists and public-sector unions limited the popular appeal of the SDPJ. But unions provided SDPJ candidates with considerable support at election times, and have also provided financial support to the party. In addition, many SDPJ Diet members (at times up to half) have been ex-union officials. With the decline of many progressive public-sector unions, as a result of falling membership and the privatizations of the 1980s, one of the main sources of traditional support for left-wing parties was eroded; this decline was one factor in the electoral weakening of the SDPJ during the early 1990s. Rengo is now closely linked to the Democratic Party of Japan and has directly backed many DPJ electoral candidates.

## The end of LDP rule in 1993

The LDP, continuously in office for 38 years since 1955, was briefly ousted from power in the general election of July 1993. Had the old order collapsed, or had it metamorphosed itself into some new form? To understand the end of LDP dominance in 1993 requires looking further back, first to the series of scandals which dogged the LDP through the late 1980s and early 1990s, and then to May 1992. In that month Morihoro Hosokawa, a former LDP MP and prefectural governor from a distinguished aristocratic family, established the Japan New Party, which had a rather vague platform of political reform. Hosokawa explicitly set out to bring about a realignment in the existing political order, breaking the LDP's long stranglehold on power. When Prime Minister Kiichi Miyazawa lost a crucial no-confidence vote moved by members of his own party on 18 June 1993, more than 50 MPs deserted the LDP. Two new parties were formed by the deserters, parties emerging out of political groupings which had been some months in the making: the Japan Renewal Party, and the New Harbinger Party. The Japan Renewal Party (which began with 36 MPs) was the more important of these, since its two key figures Tsutomo Hata and Ichiro Ozawa (see Box 6.1) had been prominent leaders of the LDP'S younger generation, forming their own faction the previous year. The New Harbinger Party consisted of younger LDP MPs of only one to two terms' standing. Like the JNP, these parties trumpeted support for reform, and claimed to favour cleaning up politics, ridding it of its systemic corruption.

A general election was called on 18 July 1993, and the three new parties together won over 100 seats in the 512-seat lower house. Although the LDP remained by far the largest party with over 220 seats, the new parties were able to block the formation of an LDP minority government by joining forces with four of the old opposition parties (including the Socialists and Komeito), creating a seven-party coalition. A number of features of the new political order were striking. The first is that the LDP was very little weakened by the election results themselves. The party had been weakened primarily by the defections to new conservative parties, rather than by the actual outcome of the election. Since LDP Diet members had their own private *koenkai,* or constituency organizations, the defectors were able to take the great bulk of their support with them when they joined new parties. The old Japan Socialist Party, by contrast, lost heavily in the elections, dropping from 134 seats to 70. It seemed that many voters who wished to express their dissatisfaction with the LDP were very happy to do so by switching their allegiance to new conservative parties. In some ways, the fact that these new parties contained many seasoned ex-LDP politicians actually made it easier for voters to shift their support, secure in the knowledge that they were choosing people with extensive experience in government who could continue to run the country in the time-honoured post-war fashion.

Another element in the demands of reformers was a desire to see the emergence of an effective two-party system. As Curtis notes, the creation of a two-party system had long been a kind of holy grail for many analysts and practitioners of Japanese politics, who seemed to believe that if Japan emulated the British electoral system of single-member constituencies 'policy-oriented, party-controlled, inexpen-

**Box 6.1 Ichiro Ozawa (born 1942)**

Ozawa is from Iwate prefecture; his father was an LDP politician and minister. He attended Keio University and studied unsuccessfully for the bar before inheriting his father's Diet seat in 1969. Long a key member of the Tanaka faction, Ozawa became secretary-general of the LDP in 1989. In 1993 he broke away from the LDP, formed the Japan Renewal Party (JRP), and so precipitated the end of 38 years of LDP rule.

The key figure behind the Hosokawa and Hata administrations, Ozawa was for a while the darling of the American media. In his bestselling 1993 book Blueprint for a New Japan, he advocated a more assertive international role for Japan. But Ozawa's unpopularity and his controversial reputation contributed to the collapse of the anti-LDP coalition in 1994. The JRP subsequently merged into the New Frontier Party, which was renamed the Liberal Party. Ozawa became leader of the Liberal Party in 1997. After a spell in coalition with the LDP (end of 1998 to 2000), Ozawa's Liberal Party rejoined the opposition. He was the president of the Democratic Party of Japan (DPJ), from 2006 until May 2009, when he resigned over a funding scandal, and secretary general of the party from 2009 until 2010, when he was again forced to resign due to a financial scandal. Ozawa ran for the DPJ leadership in 2010 once more, but was defeated by Naoto Kan. He nevertheless remains a very powerful figure in the DPJ.

sive campaigns and [a] two-party format' would automatically follow (1999: 162). In reality, however, the advocates of electoral reform settled for the lowest common denominator in 1994: a hybrid system of single-member districts and proportional representation, which ended up pleasing no one. There was a continuing current of support for a second round of electoral reform, but little consensus on how to achieve it.

A further feature of the new generation of conservative politicians which emerged in the 1993 election was their desire for Japan to assume a more prominent political role in the international community, and be more outspoken in its foreign policy objectives. In other words, whilst the new parties might have seemed less conservative than the LDP in their desire to weed out corruption, the realignment was actually part of a neo-conservative project to revitalize and reinvigorate a Japan that would then be able to play a more assertive global role, placing Japan and the USA on much more equal terms than had previously been the case.

## Japanese politics after 1993: the second party system?

Hrebenar *et al*. (2000: 4–7) has argued that after 1993 Japan adopted a new party system, fundamentally different from the 1955 system which had been characterized by LDP dominance under a 'one and a half party' political order. He argues that the 1955 system was best described as a 'predominant party system' (a term derived from the work of Giovanni Sartori – see Hrebenar *et al*., 2000: 9). By contrast, the new Japanese party system that emerged after 1993 was a multiparty one; while the LDP remained the largest single party, it did not consistently command a majority of parliamentary seats in both houses of the Diet. Accordingly, the LDP was obliged to rely upon formal coalitions or close working relationships with other parties. While under the 1955 system the Socialists had formed the main opposition, the new party system saw the emergence of conservative opposition parties which simultaneously both emulated and challenged the LDP. These parties underwent a bewildering series of splits, transformations and reincarnations during the post-1993 period; different factions of 'reformists', led by prominent political figures, kept reinventing themselves in slightly different guises. Most of these factions and parties were led by, and composed largely of, former LDP politicians. The underlying problem for these parties has been neatly summarized by Gerald Curtis: 'If a new party talked like the LDP and walked like the LDP, then there seemed to be little reason for voters not to continue to support the LDP' (Curtis, 1999: 36). New parties could score points off the LDP during times of crisis, could lure some Diet members to defect to the opposition, and could make bold claims about their commitment to reform, without having to account to the electorate for their achievements. While serving as a constant insurgent irritation to the LDP, parties of this kind were not well-positioned to replace the largest party unless they could somehow replicate the LDP'S broad base of support.

In April 1994, Hosokawa was forced out of the premiership, partly as a result of an old corruption scandal; partly because his position had become virtually untenable as he struggled to deliver on a political reform package which he had trouble selling to many of his coalition partners; and partly as a result of pressure on him from hostile bureaucrats in the Finance Ministry. Following Hosokawa's resignation, Hata took over as premier, but the SDPJ deserted him, leaving the ruling coalition with a minority of the parliamentary seats. This desertion arose from Ozawa's attempts to create a new parliamentary caucus, an alliance of the main anti-LDP forces which excluded the Socialists. Ozawa was determined to lay the foundations of a new 'catch-all' party, and believed that the SDPJ could not be accommodated within such a grouping (Curtis, 1999: 173–83). Yet in fact, on this occasion Ozawa was out-manoeuvred by his political rivals. In developments which took most analysts by surprise, at the end of June 1994 the SDPJ formed an extraordinary new coalition government with the LDP and the small Sakigake Party. This coalition was led by Tomiichi Murayama, the first socialist premier since the 1940s. Murayama proceeded to renounce most of the key tenets of SDPJ belief, including opposition to the existence of the self-defence forces and to the Japanese flag. Murayama proved rather a popular prime minister on a personal level, but thereafter his party was unable to make any credible electoral showing.

At the end of 1994, the Japan New Party, the JRP and the DSP merged to form the New Frontier Party (NFP), later renamed the Liberal Party, which included some elements of Komeito. Ichiro Ozawa enjoyed close relations with Komeito chairman Yuichi Ichikawa, popularly known as the ichi-ichi alliance (Curtis, 1999: 122). This alliance was a mixed blessing, given widespread public distrust of Komeito. New Frontier represented the culmination of Ozawa's ambitions: always mistrustful of the Socialists, he sought to replace them with a 'catch-all' opposition party of a conservative, reformist persuasion.

The LDP regained the premiership at the beginning of 1996, though the party remained reliant on support from the SDPJ and Sakigake. For a while it seemed that a new order was emerging, dominated by the LDP and New Frontier: in effect, a two-party system of identical twins. The LDP was able to consolidate its position in the October 1996 lower-house elections, coming close to regaining an overall majority. But the limited electoral appeal of the NFP, especially under the leadership of the increasingly unpopular Ozawa, helped open the way for the rise of another reform party, the Democratic Party, which won impressive gains in the 1998 upper-house elections. Democratic Party leader Naoto Kan (previously of Sakigake) was a former health minister who became a public hero after he exposed the complicity of the ministry in allowing the use of HIV-contaminated blood. For a time Japan's most popular politician, his standing was undermined by news of a sexual affair. Meanwhile the Socialists were in terminal decline and Komeito re-emerged as a political force as New Komeito, now allied with the LDP. The Communists performed well for a time by presenting themselves as the only alternative to competing conservative factions, but their successes proved short-lived.

By the end of 1998, developments had turned full circle: Ozawa's Liberal Party joined a coalition with the LDP, which was now led by the lacklustre machine politician Keizo Obuchi. The old guard and the 'reformers' were back together again, confirming what many had long suspected: there were no substantive differences between the LDP and its supposed opponents. The hopes and promises of 1993 had apparently ended in failure. As Stockwin notes, post-1993 developments abundantly demonstrated that 'the natural condition of Japanese party politics is fragmentation' (Stockwin, 1996: 274–5); Japanese political parties, like the Japanese public, have rather lost the plot. In this fluid situation, no certainties remain: though the LDP can no longer rely on assuming a dominant position, new forces have also failed conclusively to displace its predominance. Curtis noted ironically that when he visited Tokyo in 1998, he was struck by the number of Diet members who no longer included the name of their party on their business cards; some had changed party five times in the previous five years (1999: 25–6).

By sabotaging the grand old party of Japanese politics, the new generation of conservatives may have weakened the relative position of politicians *vis-à-vis* bureaucrats, as bureaucrats are more able to play off bickering coalition partners against one another. Van Wolferen speculated:

> It is conceivable that future coalitions composed of the existing splitters of the LDP, new splitters, what is left of the LDP and the older, minor parties could become indistinguishable from what the LDP has been – a passive and secondary player in Japan's government. (van Wolferen, 1993: 60)

In other words, given the resilience of 'the System' and its capacity to neutralize challenges (whether from within or without), the ambi-

*Figure* 6.1 House of Representatives election results for the LDP and JSP/SDP(J), 1958–2009

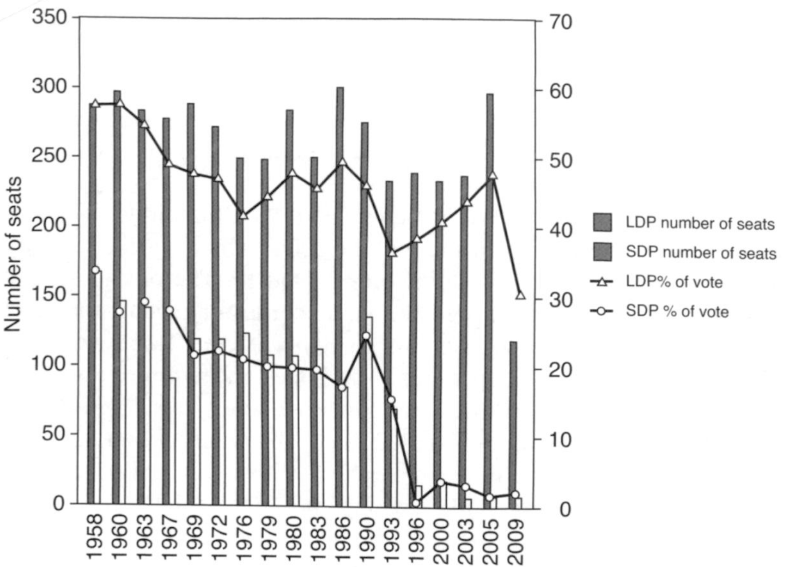


*Notes*: 1955–1991:The Japanese Socialist Party; 1991–1996:The Social Democratic Party of Japan (SDPJ); since 1996:Social Democratic Party (SDP). Percentage of vote from 1996 is the figure for single-seat constituencies.

*Sources*: *Japan Almanac*; Statistic Bureau, Ministry of Public Maangement, Home Affairs, Posts and Telecommunications, Japan, *Japan Statistical Yearbook 2000*, *2002*, *2003*. Election results, Ministry of Public Management, Home Affairs, Posts and Telecommunications, Japan, available at http://www.soumu.go.jp/senkyo/senkyo_s/data/index.html.

tion and even hubris of the ex-LDP rebels could actually undermine the very reformist causes which they profess to espouse. Developments in the years that followed certainly lent some support to revisionist views that the post-1993 upheavals were much less far-reaching than they appeared.

## Is there a new Japanese politics?

In the first years of the twenty-first century, another view was also gaining currency: a fundamental realignment was really now unfolding. Two parallel developments underpinned this view: the LDP's revival under Koizumi, and the emergence of the DPJ as a serious challenger to LDP dominance (for a summary of election results from 1958 to 2009, see Figure 6.1).

Junichiro Koizumi became LDP leader and prime minister in April 2001. Coming to power after the uninspiring Keizo Obuchi – nicknamed 'cold pizza' because of his dull personality and performance – who died in office, and Obuchi's inept right-wing successor, Yoshio Mori, Koizumi had two very easy acts to follow. Koizumi successfully appropriated most of the reformist rhetoric of his opponents, proclaiming himself determined to undertake structural changes without fear of sacred cows or 'hidden sanctuaries'. With his striking hairstyle and telegenic way of speaking, he achieved extraordinary personal approval ratings of over 80 per cent soon after taking office, and proved extremely popular with ordinary voters, especially women. Partly because of his lack of a strong support base in the LDP itself, Koizumi was forced to take his message directly to the public, using media techniques ranging from a weekly e-mail newsletter to frequent appearances on daytime television (McCargo, 2003: 69–74).

While Koizumi's popularity gradually declined – especially after he expressed strong support for the March 2003 US-led invasion of Iraq – he successfully pioneered a new mode of Japanese politics, one that called into question the emphasis of 'mainstream' political scientists upon supposedly decisive factors such as social cleavages and coherent policy programmes. Rather like Britain's Tony Blair, he seemed to demonstrate that an attractive leader could repackage a political brand that had been losing traditional support. Some analysts argued that Koizumi's emergence was a major setback for substantive political reform, helping to shore up LDP support just when the party was poised on the brink of crisis. Given Koizumi's weak position within the LDP, it was widely assumed that he had little chance of implementing any major structural changes; yet his public pledges to carry out far-reaching reforms undercut the *raison d'être* of the DPJ. The surprisingly early November 2003 election saw such a two-party system emerging more explicitly. Yet after delivering another election victory for the LDP in 2005, Koizumi left office the following year, after a controversial premiership rather bigger on style than substance.

By 2003, all the most impressive political figures from earlier 'new' parties had now assembled in the Democratic Party. The demise of the SDPJ and the rise of the DPJ led many commentators to argue that the political reforms of 1994 had contributed to the emergence of a two-party system. Steven Reed and Kay Shimizu have argued – following French political scientist Maurice Duverger – that the creation of an electoral system dominated by single-member districts leads inexorably to a two-party system (Reed and Shimizu 2009: 29). Frances McCall Rosenbluth and Michael Thies go even further, arguing that new electoral rules of the game have helped create conditions for the emergence of a 'New Japanese Politics' (Rosenbluth and Thies 2010: 95–122). Features of this new politics include 'parties that are more programmatic and centralized than the personalistic and fragmented LDP during its era of dominance' (2010: 96), leading to greater emphasis on 'explicit party manifestos, on the personalities and abilities of party leaders, and campaigns that are national in scope' (2010: 97). At the same time, 'district-level personalism' has declined in salience, and ordinary voters have been empowered at the expense of special interests.

Rosenbluth and Thies go on to argue that although a pure two-party system remains unlikely, only a couple of small parties – Komeito and the Japanese Communist Party – remain afloat, and they are sustained only by their party-list vote. Single-member districts have a 'winner takes all' logic that militates against thriving smaller parties. 'We expect alternation in power to become a regular feature of Japanese politics' (2010: 104). They also note that all Japanese governments since 1993 have been coalitions: even where dominant parties had sufficient Diet votes to go it alone, they chose not to do so. According to Rosenbluth and Thies, LDP factions, though still operating, are no longer so powerful as previously: a larger number of small groups has replaced the 'big 5' *habatsu* that dominated the LDP from the 1960s to the 1980s (2010: 110–11). The decline of factions has been accompanied by greater centralization of power

*Table* 6.1 Strength of political groups in the House of Representatives, 2002–10

| | Number of Representatives | | | | | |
|---|---|---|---|---|---|---|
| | *Dec. 2002* | % | *Jan. 2003* | % | *Oct. 2010* | % |
| Liberal Democratic Party | 240 | 50 | 243 | 50.63 | 116 | 24.16 |
| Social Democratic Party | 18 | 3.75 | 18 | 3.75 | 6 | 1.25 |
| New Komeito | 31 | 6.46 | 31 | 6.46 | 21 | 4.37 |
| Japanese Communist Party | 20 | 4.17 | 20 | 4.17 | 9 | 1.87 |
| New Conservative Party | 7 | 1.46 | 10 | 2.08 | – | – |
| Democratic Party of Japan | 125 | 26.04 | 118 | 24.58 | 307 | 63.95 |
| Liberal Party | 22 | 4.58 | 22 | 4.58 | – | – |
| Liberal League | | | | | – | – |
| Your Party | | | | | 5 | 1.04 |
| People's New Party | | | | | 4 | 0.83 |
| The Sunrise Party of Japan | | | | | 3 | 0.62 |
| Group for upholding the interest and life of the nation | | | | | 2 | 0.41 |
| | | | | | – | – |
| Group of Independents | | | | | – | – |
| Other Independents | 15 | 3.13 | 15 | 3.13 | 5 | 1.04 |
| Vacancies | 2 | 0.42 | 3 | 0.63 | 2 | 0.41 |
| Total | 480 | 100 | 480 | 100 | 480 | 100 |

*Sources*: Ministry of Home Affairs, Japan House of Representatives, *Japan, Strength of Political Groups in the House of Representatives*, http://www.shugiin.go.jp/itdb_main.nsf/html/index_e.htm; Statistics Bureau, Ministry of Public Management, Home Affairs, Posts and Telecommunications, Japan, *Japan Statistical Yearbook 2003*; Japan Information Network, http://jin.jcic.or.jp/stat/index.html; House of Representative, Japan, Strength of Political Groups in the House of Representative (accessed 6 October, 2010) available: http://www.shugiin.go.jp/index.nsf/html/index_e_strength.htm.

within the LDP, including more authority for the party president who doubled as prime minister. Strong leadership has become more important, both internally – to manage the party – and externally, to present a positive and dynamic image to the electorate in a more competitive political environment (2010: 116).

According to Rosenbluth and Thies, there is a 'new logic' (2010: 122) which makes Japanese politics in the second decade of the twenty-first century dramatically different from the mode of politics that obtained in the final decades of the twentieth century (for a summary of the strength of different political groups in the first decade of the twenty-first century see Table 6.1). According to this logic, 'The new majoritarian electoral rules produced incentives for politicians to align themselves into two large, majority-seeking parties aimed at the large swath of voters in the political middle' (2010: 186). This logic was clearly seen in the 2009 election results, which saw high levels of turnover in urban areas where old-style *koenkai* politics was weakest. Rosenbluth and Thies suggest that the DPJ is emerging as a more coherent centre-left party that offers an ideological alternative to the LDP, though both parties will need to stick 'close to the political middle' (2010: 192).

The arguments of Reed, Shimuzu, Rosenbluth and Thies appear heavily influenced by their readings of the Koizumi period. Since 2006, Japan has not been characterized by strong prime ministers whose bold public images and policy initiatives have shaped the national political agenda. Under both LDP and DPJ rule, premiers have come and gone on an annual basis. Most have quickly proved to be inept communicators who lacked the popular touch. They have also been undermined by protracted factional infighting within their parties. Accordingly, other commentators are much more critical of the current political order. Stockwin suggests that the DPJ is effectively 'a second conservative party', and on some economic issues may be to the right of the LDP (2008: 196). Richard Samuels sees the DPJ as characterized by deep and intractable divisions:

> One often speaks of 'centre-left' as a single position on an ideological spectrum, but in the case of the DPJ, the hyphen should be read as a plus sign. Those who came to it from the centre and those from the left have never really found common ground on many important issues. So, while some say that the DPJ has always been a 'mutt,' I think a 'menagerie' of cats and dogs may be more apt. Internal leadership challenges are common in political parties in

every competitive democracy, but the DPJ must be among the most fractious of the world's ruling parties. (Samuels, 2011)

Such readings cast doubt on the rosy picture of Japanese politics as presented by mainstream authors, converging on a British-style two-party system characterized by strong leaders and vote-winning policy manifestos. Samuels goes on to argue that neither the LDP nor the DPJ has much core electoral support, leaving both parties extremely vulnerable to voter whims and valence issues. The more the DPJ has to compromise with the LDP to secure passage of measures through the Diet, the more the DPJ risks losing what remains of its distinctive electoral identity. DPJ kingmaker Ichiro Ozawa enabled Hatoyama to become prime minister, forced Naoto Kan out of office, and secured patronage power over key appointments made by Noda – so perpetuating a divisive, LDP-style factionalism that undermines the party's electoral credibility. Whereas the Rosenbluth and Thies mainstream reading projects a stable dream scenario for Japanese politics, Samuels' revisionist critique suggests the real possibility of further meltdown. Gerald Curtis, a mainstream scholar typically known for his positive assessments, has argued that Japanese politics is currently engaged in a process of 'creative destruction' – one apparently more destructive than creative. Unless Japanese politicians can demonstrate leadership in the wake of the Fukushima crisis, he suggests, 'the public will be alienated from the political system in a much more profound way than at any time since the Second World War and Japan's decline will be inexorable (Curtis, 2011a: 182).

On 2 July 2012, Ichiro Ozawa left the DPJ to form a new breakaway party, taking around 50 members of the Diet with him. Although numerically the losses were a blow to the Noda government, they potentially offered the ruling party a new lease of life, free at last from Ozawa's overbearing influence and endless grandstanding. Ozawa's departure removed a major source of DPJ instability at a stroke, and was a great boost to Noda's position.

## Conclusion

For mainstream analysts, developments in Japanese politics since 1993 vindicate their central arguments. Japan does have a pluralist system, power can change hands, and factions are waning. The Democratic Party had proved it could defeat the LDP, while the LDP under Koizumi had cast off the negative features of factionalism, and reached out directly to the voters through the mass media. Revisionists were much more sceptical, seeing the fragmentation of recent years as evidence of chaos and collapse in the Japanese order, rather than pluralism. For them, Japanese parties had become indistinguishable sectional interest groups with no genuine public support, and the electorate was increasingly detached from active engagement with the world of politics. Those who view Japanese party politics from a political-economy perspective often see the entire political order as fatally vitiated by structural corruption, and hopelessly distorted by special interests. Culturalist analyses viewed Japanese politics as highly distinctive, failing to conform to the tenets of western political science, but nonetheless functioning successfully according to a logic of its own.

# 7

# Socialization and Civil Society

How are Japanese people socialized into the prevailing political order? To what extent do different elements of Japanese society act as checks and balances on the power of the state, and the ruling elite? This chapter examines two aspects of Japanese society: sources of socialization (such as education and policing), and the nature of civil society, as manifested in the media, community organizations and protest movements. Most mainstream scholars would argue that Japanese institutions are highly successful in producing good citizens, and that the majority of Japanese people play a constructive role in the political and civic order. Revisionists are generally more sceptical, believing that the Japanese state in some way compels or coerces its citizens into compliance and outward conformity. Those analysts who use culturalist approaches view Japanese society as primarily shaped by cultural norms and traditions, rather than by state-led social forces and institutions.

## Sources of socialization and social control

### *The education system*

The history of Japanese education is a complex subject of study. The most important episodes in this history are the Meiji period, and the post-war Occupation. During the Meiji period, in the second half of the nineteenth century, Japan was preoccupied with the task of 'catching up' with the West by engaging in an extremely rapid process of industrialization and modernization. Part of that modernization was the establishment of a system of education, a system inspired by French, German, British and American models. It was a highly centralized system based around tightly disciplined state-run schools, and a few elite public universities (see Goodman, 1989: 32–3). By 1905, 95 per cent of children were receiving primary education. The school system was designed to inculcate nationalist principles, principles that were incorporated into the Imperial Rescript on Education of 1890 (see Passin, 1982: 151–2). This official statement stressed the nationalistic aims of Japanese education, emphasizing filial piety and loyalty to the Emperor, including a militaristic injunction to bear arms for the state in times of emergency.

During the American Occupation, the pre-war education system was seen as one of the main factors that had led to the rise of militarism in Japan. The Occupation authorities undertook a purge of teachers and education officials, had 'militaristic' textbooks rewritten, and imposed limits on central government control over schools. Schools and teachers were given power to decide their curriculum and textbooks, and elected local school boards were established based on the American model. The 1947 Fundamental Law on Education had parallels with the constitution, and placed an emphasis on equal opportunities. It reflected ideals of egalitarianism and democratization, and contained a provision that 'Education shall not be subject to improper control, but it shall be directly responsible to the whole people' (Schoppa, 1991: 32–4). Since the war, two alternative visions of what education is all about have been in strong competition with one another: a vision of education as a centralized system directed by the state for national objectives, and as a decentralized system run on democratic lines.

After the end of the Occupation, conservatives sought to make changes in the education system, especially with regard to the powers of the Ministry of Education over textbooks and the curriculum. Despite the strong resistance of the Japan Teachers' Union, there were several key conservative successes in the immediate post-Occupation period. In 1956, the elected local school boards were abolished; in 1958, the Ministry of Education curriculum was made compulsory; and, in 1963, it was decided that local authorities rather than teachers were to select textbooks. By the 1970s, the uniformity being fostered by a system based on entrance exams for academic generalists was increasingly seen as a problem, and there was growing pressure for diversification of the system (Schoppa, 1991: 34–48).

### *The education system today*

Japan's schools are widely praised for their successes in teaching core skills, and Japanese pupils generally perform very well in international league tables for their levels of literacy, numeracy and scientific knowledge. These impressive skill levels reflect a highly demanding school system, which is organized around the preparation for entrance examinations. There are entrance examinations even for some kindergartens and elementary schools, as well as for middle schools, but the most important are usually those for senior high schools and universities. Many – though not all – entrance examinations use a standardized format of multiple choice questions; they typically test rote learning and powers of memorization, rather than creativity or critical thinking.

Since passing or failing entrance examinations really does largely determine a child's future (many companies and other organizations recruit more or less directly from particular vocational schools, colleges and universities, and there is little concept of 'lifelong learning' and little scope for 'late developers' in Japan), the pressure to succeed in them is enormous. The tyranny of entrance examinations leads to highly structured and often extremely boring lessons, in which a teacher works through an approved textbook mechanically (usually covering one page per class hour). The contents of textbooks are a matter of intense controversy, since the Ministry of Education compels teachers to use approved textbooks, and the approval process is intensely political, especially for subjects such as history and social studies. Critical academics and teachers have accused the Ministry of censoring textbooks, especially by playing down Japanese aggression before and during the Second World War (see Herzog, 1993: 196–217). But others have argued that the widely reported 1982 textbook issue was unduly politicized by leftist groups and by the Chinese government (Ijiri, 1996: 64–5). However, Yoneyama argues that textbook censorship is not confined to politically sensitive topics. She cites the example of a new school textbook by a Nobel prize-winning Japanese physicist, which failed to win Ministry approval because it sought to promote critical thinking rather than to offer students clear-cut answers (Yoneyama, 1999: 148–9).

Pressure to succeed in the education system comes primarily from parents. Like many other Asian societies, Japan is characterized by a special breed of mothers facetiously known as 'education mothers' (*kyoiku mama*), mothers who will stop at nothing to advance their children educationally. 'Education mothers' typically visit their childrens' schools regularly, become active figures in the PTA (parent–teacher association), and ingratiate themselves with the principal and other teachers, as well as seeking out the best *juku* schools (private cram schools) for their children to attend during evenings and at weekends. *Juku* are a huge industry, and are considered enormously important for examination preparation; a common complaint of high-school teachers is that students are too tired to study properly, because they spend long hours attending *juku* after the end of the school day.

Whereas secondary-school students in many countries typically move from classroom to classroom between lessons, in Japan pupils have virtually all their classes (apart from science lab classes and sports periods) in their own 'home-rooms', staying in the same group throughout the day. They are rarely divided into different sets or streams for different subjects. Student participation in classes is often limited to copying from the board and answering occasional questions based on homework exercises. A typical 'home-room' class might have 48 or 50 pupils. Secondary-school teachers use various techniques (such as calling on pupils by their class numbers, or row by row) to make sure that all students take turns in answering questions, since older children and teenagers rarely volunteer information in class. Each class has its own home-room teacher who carries a considerable degree of responsibility for the welfare of its members, even outside school hours. In the event of a pupil having any particular problem, the home-room teacher will often visit the family at home. Despite the pressures of homework and cram schools, many pupils devote considerable time and energy to club activities, particularly sports activities ranging from traditional Japanese sports such as *kendo,* to baseball, swimming and volleyball. Some clubs meet at 7 am to spend an hour and a half practising each morning before the beginning of classes, then stay on for a further two hours after lessons end.

Discipline is strictly observed in most Japanese schools. Pupils stand up when the teacher enters the room, and bow on an order from the class captain before sitting down; a similar ritual takes place at the end of each class. Pupils are responsible for cleaning the board after each lesson, they wear uniforms (in most local authority schools, the boys' uniforms are modelled, bizarrely, on nineteenth-century Prussian uniforms) and they are closely monitored for infringement of uniform rules. Cleaning the school (including the public areas) is the responsibility of the pupils, and is done after lessons have finished. While many Japanese schools are immaculate, in schools with a more liberal regime cleaning is less meticulous: the cleaner the school, the stricter the school discipline. The dark side of Japanese education includes widespread problems of bullying, refusal to attend school, and illegal use of corporal punishment (Okano and Tsuchiya, 1999: 195–210; Yoneyama, 1999: 147–241). Some students are so alienated by the school system that they withdraw into modes of silence and resistance.

During the early post-Occupation period, the Japan Teachers' Union (Nikkyoso) was a powerful force, with a huge membership and a successful track record of campaigning for improved pay and conditions for teachers (Thurston, 1973: 40–79). Nikkyoso was closely connected with the Japan Socialist Party; in effect, the Cold War bipolar national politics in Japan was mirrored in schools across the country, as unionized leftist teachers struggled for power with conservative school principals and boards of education. However, as Schoppa notes, this ideological standoff became increasingly empty, and less and less related to real problems in the education system: 'Conditioned by years of hard fought ideological combat, these actors show few signs of noticing the shift in subject matter' (Schoppa, 1991: 22). While in theory unionized teachers favoured a more open education system with a more liberal disciplinary regime, and the freedom to use non-authorized textbooks, in reality they were major beneficiaries of orderly school regimes and mechanical teaching methods. Despite long working hours and excessive paperwork, teaching in most Japanese schools is a relatively straightforward business; negligible class preparation is needed, the same textbooks can be assigned year after year, pupils rarely ask questions, and teachers receive good salaries and long vacations. In effect, leftist teachers and rightist education authorities established a cosy and collusive understanding, a practical *modus vivendi*.

Despite this shared vested interest in the educational status quo, there was a growing awareness that the school system was failing to produce more creativity. Prime Minister Nakasone (1982–7) was vocal in his advocacy of educational reform, arguing that violence and bullying in schools meant the need for better teaching, more internationalization of education, and reform of the entrance examination system (Schoppa, 1991: 211–50). Similar arguments have been made by successive governments. As Japan embarked on the painful transition from an industrial to a post-industrial society, the workforce was ill-prepared to adapt to the new global information economy. Japan might be able to produce hardware – such as computers – but the software was increasingly coming from the West, from more flexible societies, such as, the United States and Europe. Neither the over-centralized educational bureaucracy, nor teachers with a declining union movement (see Thurston, 1989: 186–205), who had little incentive to increase their own workloads or improve their own skills, proved remotely capable of responding to the challenge. In the abstract, bureaucrats, teachers and parents all favour far-reaching educational reforms, but in reality all are locked into the existing system focused on examination cramming. As Goodman explains:

> Parents want a more liberal system but are afraid of how their own children's chances might be affected; employers want more creativity in production, but do not want to lose the conformity, instilled by education, that goes into that production; politicians publicly support the liberalisation of the system in their search for votes, but often tacitly approve of a system that seems to have led directly to the Japanese 'economic miracle'; bureaucrats are only 'servants of the people', and yet the Ministry of Education will fight to prevent even the slightest loss of its centralized power. (Goodman, 1989: 34)

In 1998, the Education Ministry announced a significant shift in policy, popularly known as the *yutori* (low pressure or no cramming) reforms. These reforms, supported by the Japan Teachers' Union, introduced reduced class hours, more student-centred, interdisciplinary and problem-based learning, in line with international trends that placed a reduced emphasis on rote learning. At the heart of the reforms was a desire to produce students with a 'zest for living'. But the publication of the 2003 PISA international educational performance league tables – coordinated by the OECD - produced considerable shock in Japan, which was ranked sixth in terms of mathematical literacy, fourteenth in reading literacy, second in scientific literacy, and fourth in problem-solving literacy. While most countries would have been delighted with such results, they represented an apparent drop from the 2000 figures – which had placed Japan as number one for mathematical literacy – and formed part of a downward trend in Japan's performances in such international tests since the early 1980s

(Takayama 2008: 395). The somewhat hysterical media and national reaction to the 2003 PISA scores played into the hands of critics of the controversial *yutori* reforms – which had as yet barely been implemented. Conservatives argued that the reforms represented an ill-conceived dumbing-down of standards that was undermining Japan's international competitiveness. As a result, conservative educationalists were able to push through changes to the *yutori* policy, including the introduction of a national standardized testing regime in 2007. The DPJ came to power in 2009 promising a new round of reforms. Further changes introduced in 2011 and 2012 placed an increased emphasis on the study of Japanese language and mathematics.

### *Higher education*

The higher-education sector is much less impressive than the school sector. University and college students typically regard their years in higher education as a reward for hard work at high school, and a period of rest and recuperation before entering the workplace. University students commonly sleep in lectures, examinations are not taken seriously, and almost everyone graduates. Arch-revisionist McVeigh argues that little education actually takes place in Japanese higher-educational institutions: 'students perform student roles in a sort of ritualized rhetorical reality which lacks educational substance' (McVeigh, 1997: 219). In another book, he suggests that Japanese higher education has basically failed, and that many Japanese students do not really study in order to obtain their degrees (McVeigh, 2002: 14, 239). McVeigh's very critical view of Japanese higher education is contested by other scholars, who argue that the tertiary sector in Japan performs relatively well, and is indeed improving. McVeigh argues that his perspective reflects his own experiences of teaching in 'typical' private colleges and universities, rather than the elite national universities that have attracted greater scholarly attention. McVeigh's arguments apply with greater force to social sciences and humanities, than to natural and applied sciences.

In Japan, there is a fiercely hierarchical league table of universities and colleges, and many university students have a 'complex' about their failure to gain admission to better institutions. While there are several highly regarded private universities (such as Waseda and Keio), students at second or third-tier private universities typically wish they had gained admission to more prestigious public universities. Even students at leading national universities such as Nagoya University or Osaka University are often bitter that they failed to enter the more prestigious Tokyo University. The Japanese higher-education system is so pervaded by a sense of hierarchy that many university graduates consider themselves to be failures. Since there have been no substantive attempts to reform Japanese higher education, it could be assumed that the prevailing emphasis on socialization rather than education in colleges and universities is a deliberate policy, supported by elite policy makers in both the public and private sectors (McVeigh, 1997: 219).

Declining numbers of 18-year olds as a result of the falling birth-rate means that many of Japanese more than 500 private universities – especially less prestigious ones – face possible bankruptcy over the next few years. While there has been much talk of internationalizing the higher education system, the number of Japanese students opting to study abroad is in freefall; Japanese enrolments in British universities fell by a third between 2003 and 2008 (Fitzpatrick, 2011). The government hopes to attract more foreign students to attend Japanese universities, but language and cultural barriers coupled with poor teaching standards mean that Japan typically mainly attracts those international students who are unable to access higher education in western countries.

### *Education and politics*

In theory, the Japanese education system is highly meritocratic. Those who succeed in passing the right entrance examinations will be admitted to the best elementary schools, junior high schools, senior high schools, and then to top colleges or universities. Many excellent schools are public rather than private, though there has been a growing preference for private high schools in recent years. Yet, in practice, the degree of social mobility in Japan is very similar to that of Britain and the United States (see Ishida, 1993). Prestigious universities such as Tokyo University receive most of their students from a small number of 'feeder' high schools, the majority of which are in the Kanto (greater Tokyo) area. These schools in turn have close relationships with a few junior high schools that supply most of their students; and these junior high schools tend to draw most of their students from a limited pool of elementary schools. Indeed, even some kindergartens have entrance examinations. Many of the successful entrants to Tokyo University will have attended the same well-known *juku,* where they crammed together for the entrance examination. Some families send children to stay with relatives, or even move house, in order to enter the right school catchment area. Access to the best schools and universities therefore remains largely the prerogative of the middle classes, and especially of upper-echelon families whose parents (usually fathers) command high salaries.

Rohlen argues that Japan's high schools:

> are best understood as shaping generations of disciplined workers for a technomeritocratic system that requires highly socialized individuals capable of performing reliably in a rigorous, hierarchical, and finely tuned organizational environment. (Rohlen, 1983: 209)

From a political perspective, this view of education has potentially disturbing implications. McVeigh argues that Japan's education system is designed to serve the interests of the ruling elite, placing emphasis on the need to create a docile workforce in the interests of economic growth and social order. In other words, the education system is supposed to help suppress dissent and limit the parameters of political participation, 'maintaining an orderly, predictable and controlled environment that is conducive to elite goals and economic pursuits' (McVeigh, 1998: 179). According to McVeigh, the Japanese education system does not teach values of democracy, individual rights and grassroots initiative as commonly understood in western countries: Japanese education is not 'converging' with an Anglo-American model, but derives from a completely different set of assumptions about the relationship between state, society and the individual.

## Policing and the criminal justice system

This book has discussed alternative interpretations of Japanese society, including one which views Japan as based upon the group and ruled by principles of harmony and consensus, and another which views Japan as based upon principles of social control, the state imposing order upon the population through a range of mechanisms. How far does the nature of Japanese society, with its characteristic emphasis on the group, produce Japanese politics? Or how far is the Japanese political order itself producing a high degree of conformity to group norms? The whole problem can be examined from two alternative perspectives.

One important factor in shaping Japanese society is the mechanisms of social control which exist in Japan. In particular, how can we explain the very low rates of crime and other 'deviant behaviour' in Japan? As with the impressive literacy rates and high standards of numeracy achieved in Japanese education, statistical evidence seems to suggest a model system. Is this testimony to the Japanese national character, or does it reflect an oppressive set of government policies which have the effect of limiting personal freedom?

Mouer and Sugimoto (1989: 234–71) suggest that the issue may be considered in the light of what they call two 'illustrative analogies', cormorant fishing and falconry. In the Japanese art of cormorant fishing, the cormorants are kept on long leashes and trained to respond to instructions, even handing over everything they catch to their master. In the western art of falconry, the falcon is free to fly around in search of prey, but is also trained to return to the hand of its keeper. They compare this with two alternative images of Japanese society: the organized society, with its tight discipline imposed from above, and the associative society, characterized by more fluid structures which nevertheless preserve a general cohesion. Whilst these are metaphors rather than exact descriptions, Mouer and Sugimoto argue that the former corresponds broadly with Japanese society, and the latter with western society. However, it could be argued that both images imply that individual Japanese citizens (the birds) are subject to the overarching guidance and control of a master, in the form of the state. The group model would deny the existence of such an authority, seeing the coordination of collective activity as an inherent, almost an instinctive, phenomenon.

Whatever the nature of the control mechanisms which underpin Japanese society, the results in terms of crime statistics are impressive. David Bayley, a Los Angeles police officer who studied the Japanese police at first hand, entitled the first chapter of his book 'Heaven for a Cop' (Bayley, 1991: 1–10). According to UNODC figures for 1998–2001, there were nine times as many murders in the USA and three times as many in Britain than in Japan (UNODC 2001). Levels of less serious offences are also proportionally lower. Guns are tightly controlled in Japan, and play a very small part in the crime picture. How are these low levels of crime achieved? Explanations focus on two areas: policing practices, and wider social behaviour. In practice the distinction is not hard-and-fast, since the kind of policing practices adopted in Japan would not be readily acceptable in western societies.

These practices include the use of small 'police boxes' (*koban*) in every neighbourhood (see Illustration 7.1), which entails keeping the police very close to the goings-on of the community (a practice which has been successfully emulated by the Singaporean police); and, rather more insidiously, the 'residential survey', when police officers visit every Japanese home twice a year. They ask a long list of questions, including who lives at the property, how they are related, how old they are, whether they work and if so where, and what motor vehicles they own (see Bayley, 1991: 79–82). All this material is recorded on special forms, along with lists of valuable items owned

**Illustration 7.1 Kyoto station police koban**

by the household, and more general information about what is going on in the neighbourhood, whether there are any suspicious people around, and similar questions. They also visit commercial premises and collect similar sorts of information. The average patrol officer in Tokyo makes about 450 of these visits each year. The information gathered does not go onto a central computer or even a central filing system, but remains in the police box for use by the local officers. The data is not used by other government bodies, though it may be used by detectives, or by members of special police agencies concerned with monitoring political dissidents.

Often middle-aged police officers with considerable experience and well-developed social skills carry out these visits, rather than younger officers. Not everyone cooperates, though most do. A list of good topics of local conversation is posted up in each police box and frequently updated; the police use these topics to strike up rapport with people and persuade them to fill in the forms. Some leftists refuse, and it is harder to elicit interest in community matters from apartment dwellers than from house dwellers. For this reason, many forces have put extra resources and assigned more experienced officers to conduct residential surveys in apartment buildings, which are seen as more likely to house criminals and subversives. Not all local police forces are able to gather sufficient in-depth information about their neighbourhoods, however, especially in large cities, and there is some evidence that the *koban* system is becoming less effective. In 2004, there were about 6,500 police boxes (*koban*) and 7,600 residential rural police boxes (*chuzaisho*) in Japan (Police Policy Research Center 2005: 3–4). These small police stations cover a wider area than the urban *koban*.

One striking feature of the Japanese system is that crime prevention is a core activity, accorded a status (and resources) comparable with that of crime investigation. All Japanese neighbourhoods have crime prevention associations (Ames, 1981: 41–6), and volunteers may patrol wearing special armbands. More conservative elements in the community, especially local businesses such as shops, often provide the core of support for these associations, since they stand to gain most from low crime rates (Parker, 1984: 68). Special patrols may be established when serious crimes have been committed, such as those organized by parent groups in Kobe following a brutal child murder case in 1997.

Apart from the practices of the police themselves, socioeconomic factors may play some part in the low crime rates; given that unemployment is relatively low, there are few ethnic tensions and few slums or ghettoes (though all three of these points are somewhat contentious). While the prison population is only 20 per cent of that of the United States, there have been regular executions in recent years: seven in 2009, fifteen in 2008 and nine in 2007 (Matsutani, 2010). The social stigma and attendant consequences associated with punishment are strong deterrents in themselves; for example, a Japanese schoolteacher convicted of drink driving would almost certainly lose her or his job, being considered a person unfit to take responsibility for teaching children.

More difficult to correlate with the low incidence of violent crime is the fact that violence pervades popular Japanese culture – especially in *manga,* or comic books. These comic books, widely available and often read by children, contain many horrific scenes and frequently feature violence against women, such as the gang rape of schoolgirls. Does this fictional violence actually offer a release for dangerous emotions which would otherwise manifest themselves in disturbed behaviour? Well-publicized criminal cases involving violence committed by juveniles – such as the beheading of a Kobe boy by a 14-year-old in 1997 – seem to suggest that *manga* could play a role in encouraging brutal criminal behaviour. Concerns about juvenile crime were further exacerbated by other high-profile cases, including a 2008 case where a teenager randomly killed a man by pushing him into the path of an oncoming train (*Japan Times,* 2008). But although crime rates in Japan did rise somewhat between 1996 and 2002, they have declined in recent years and hit a 23-year low in 2010 (*Mainichi Daily News*, 2010). Greater public anxiety about crime was not reflected in numbers of actual incidents.

According to Bayley, there are three key factors which account for the control of 'deviant behaviour': propriety, presumption, and pride. By propriety, he means the innumerable rules about what is proper behaviour, which so characterize all forms of life in Japan. Bayley makes the provocative contention that 'Japanese orderliness in large matters, such as crime, seems to be related to orderliness in small things' (1991: 177). This is an argument on the general principle that if you take care of the pennies, the pounds will take care of themselves: if you train people not to drop litter and to tie their dressing gowns the proper way, then they won't do anything criminal.

Goold has criticized Bayley for presenting 'a picture of Japan and the Japanese criminal justice system that is ultimately marred by oversimplification and Orientalism' (2004: 20). A very different view of the Japanese police, unsurprisingly, is expressed by revisionist scholars. Gavan McCormack is extremely critical of the use of confessions by the criminal justice system in Japan, pointing out that 86 per cent of criminal convictions in Japan were handed down on the basis of confessions, and that defendants were convicted in over 99 per cent of cases sent to trial (McCormack, 1986b: 187). The latter statistic is especially disturbing. Although Japanese prosecutors and Justice Ministry officials argue that this high conviction rate reflects the fact that doubtful cases are not brought to court (Parker, 1984: 107), this argument seems rather unpersuasive. Public prosecutors have considerable powers which give them the upper hand in criminal trials. McCormack points out that before the Second World War, political deviance was regarded as criminal, and that the criminal justice system has frequently been used to defeat or to neutralize political protest. He also cites political cases in which suspects have been held on remand for very lengthy periods without trial – as long as ten years, in one case – in violation of basic principles laid down by the United Nations. The system of so-called 'substitute imprisonment' (limited to 28 days in total) is described by McCormack as 'a relic of Japan's authoritarian past' (1986b: 193). He explicitly questions Bayley's favourable appraisal of the standards of behaviour maintained by the Japanese police. As Parker quotes one Japanese police officer as saying when asked why suspects confess so readily: 'It is no use to protest against power' (1984: 110). Nevertheless, David Johnson concludes his fieldwork-based comparative study of Japanese prosecutors with the remarkable claims that 'the Japanese way of justice is uncommonly just' (2002: 280) and in many respects superior to the American system.

While Bayley argues that substitute prison is used rarely, he notes that in recent years 90–100,000 people had been held in this way annually. In 1985, 62.5 per cent were held for less than 10 days, which means that 37.5 per cent (or somewhere around 37,500 people) were held without charge for more than 10 days. Those held in this form of detention have no automatic access to lawyers and are not eligible for bail, which means that (in Bayley's words) 'confession becomes in effect a condition for bail' (1991: 145). He also notes:

> Precharge detention is an opportunity for moral suasion to be applied to erring individuals. Pressure to confess is only partly to obtain convictions. More important, it is applied to teach, to humble, to extract contrition and repentance. Arrest is tantamount

> to conviction . . . The primary purpose of Japanese criminal justice, unlike American, is not to exact punishment. Its actions are symbolic, indicating social exclusion . . . An analogue of what the Japanese police want the offender to feel is the tearful relief of a child when confession of wrongdoing to parents results in an understanding laugh and a warm hug. (Bayley, 1991: 149)

Yoshio Sugimoto sees matters rather differently, claiming with regard to the 'residential survey' that:

> In this situation, ideological control – in Gramsci's term, hegemony – is in full swing. The agencies of social control promote a worldview supportive of the established order in every area of life until it becomes part of the 'world-taken-for-granted'. With successful implementation of this process, self-policing becomes a daily reality. (Sugimoto, 1986: 70)

In other words, the appearance of popular consensus is in fact simply a manifestation of 'self-policing', the outcome of direct and indirect forms of state-imposed social control.

### *Crime and deviant behaviour*

The generally positive image of law and order in Japan is severely tarnished by the ubiquitous presence of mafia-style organized crime, in the form of *yakuza,* or gangsters. These gangsters, conspicuously dressed in tasteless suits and white shoes, and often driving large Mercedes cars, control illegal businesses such as drugs and prostitution, and appear to operate with virtual impunity. Many *yakuza* bosses enjoy close relations with prominent conservative politicians, and are effectively immune from prosecution. Numbers of *yakuza* in the late 1980s stood at around 90,000, organized into around 1,400 gangs, located within a number of larger organizations. The largest of these is the Tokyo-based Yamaguchi-gumi, which has gained in power and prominence in recent decades. *Yakuza* gangs are extremely hierarchical, but are also characterized by fictive kinship ties that cut across formal structures (Hill, 2003: 67–8).

New anti-*yakuza* legislation was introduced in the early 1990s, but Hill suggests that these laws were rather symbolic and inadequate seriously to counter gang activity (2003: 176). The existence of *yakuza* gangs remains a serious indictment of the effectiveness of the

Japanese police, with whom they enjoy cordial, even jocular relations (Ames, 1981: 105–29). As Ames notes, that there are many parallels between the police and the *yakuza,* from political perspectives to sartorial preferences (Ames, 1981: 120–1).

Another problem area is that of juvenile delinquency, especially in the field of auto crime. As with the *yakuza,* criminal activity of this kind is collective and group-oriented. Teenagers form gangs known as *bosozoku,* or reckless driving tribes (Ames, 1981: 84–5). In fact, much of their driving is not so much reckless as infuriating: they typically ride flotillas of large and extremely noisy motorcycles at slow speeds through urban and residential areas, in the evening, or at night. Later on, they move up to racing around in cars. Sometimes rival *bosozoku* engage in fighting and their members may become involved in other more serious criminal activities such as theft. Despite their superficially anti-social, quasi-anarchistic pose, the behaviour of gang members is in fact highly ritualized, there is a strict group hierarchy and tight internal discipline, and most 'graduate' or 'settle down' when they become legal adults at the age of 20 (see Sato, 1991, especially 72–104). Sato concludes that '*Bosozoku* was a symbolic rebellion which was born and nurtured partly by the mass media and producers of consumer goods' (1991: 101). Like the *yakuza, bosozoku* mirror the structures and hierarchies of the mainstream Japanese society from which they appear to deviate.

Some similar characteristics can be seen in *yankii*, punky Japanese youths renowned for their rudeness and bad behaviour. They typically engage in deviant or criminal behaviour including under-age drinking, theft and mugging or blackmailing older men – known as *oyaji gari* ('elderly men hunting'). These youth phenomena are widely depicted in popular culture, including Flunk Punk Rumble (*Yankii-kun to megane-chan*) a long-running television drama derived from comic books.

It is difficult to establish the extent to which the social conformity manifested in Japan's low crime rate was related directly to the promotion of support for 'established order' in the form of votes for the LDP. May it be argued that people who were socialized into obeying laws were more likely to hold conservative political attitudes, and were therefore more likely to vote for conservative parties such as the LDP? This would seem on the face of it logical, but it is very difficult to prove. There is, not surprisingly, evidence that Japanese voters who support increased police powers tend to be conservative politically, but that is something rather different. What we would need to establish here is whether the Japanese were more inclined to vote for conservative parties (like the LDP) than voters in other countries (such as Britain or the USA) who had not been subjected to the same mechanisms of political and social control; and we would also have to establish that the conservative voting behaviour was a direct manifestation of social control rather than, say, approval of LDP economic performance. On balance, the jury remains out.

An alternative view, which may be equally critical both of the ideal-type group model approach and of Sugimoto's theory of Japan as a 'control state', could draw on the idea of the distinction between *honne* and *tatamae,* the difference between the external face of Japanese behaviour and the true feelings of the individual. It could be argued that whilst control mechanisms such as the rather oppressive policing techniques practised by local *koban* officers are effective for the most part in modifying outward behaviour (*tatemae*), the *honne* may nevertheless remain non-conformist and continues to cherish subversive, rebellious or aggressive thoughts. In other words, we need to distinguish between thoughts and actions which are expressed, and those which remain unexpressed or repressed. Outward conformity with the system may hide inner rebellion, which manifests itself at election times. This explains why outwardly demure Japanese housewives and nondescript bank clerks sometimes took immense pleasure in sending anonymous donations to anti-Narita Airport protestors, or casting their votes for the Japan Communist Party. Many Japanese people have a well-developed capacity for working on two levels of reality, and this extends beyond the niceties of daily life and into the political sphere. For all the socialization processes, individual life is still going on beneath the façade. Japanese people may often appear to think and behave very conventionally, but appearances are deceptive, and do not begin to tell the whole story.

## Forms of social organization and participation

### *The role of the mass media*

For mainstream scholars, the Japanese media functions as an important 'watchdog', monitoring and criticizing the actions of government along liberal democratic lines. Revisionist scholars, by contrast, have argued that Japan is not a functioning democracy in the western sense; a critical assessment of the workings of media is an important element in the revisionist case. Karel van Wolferen, for example, portrays Japan's media as the 'lapdogs' of the country's political establishment (van Wolferen, 1989: 93–100).

Japan's national-level media output is dominated by a small number of organizations: NHK, a public broadcasting body somewhat similar to the BBC, and five large newspaper groups affiliated to private television stations. The market leader is the Yomiuri group, linked to NTV, closely followed by the Asahi group and TV Asahi (Table 7.1). The Mainichi group (TBS) once rivalled Yomiuri and Asahi, but fell on harder times and now trails them in circulation. Two specialist financial newspapers occupy the same sort of position as the *Wall Street Journal* and the *Financial Times: Nihon Keizai Shimbun* (or Nikkei), linked to TV Tokyo, and *Sankei Shimbun* (Fuji TV). While in the 1960s, the Yomiuri, Asahi and Mainichi newspapers all adhered to a left-wing political line, during the 1970s, Yomiuri shifted to a more conservative stance and usurped the long-standing lead of the Asahi group. Despite the greater prestige of the 'big-five' dailies, much of the more interesting and critical reporting appears in weekly and monthly magazines which range from muck-raking to serious political analysis, many of them owned by the same companies as the major papers. And while the 'Big 5' boast formidable circulation figures, critics argue that these numbers are artificially boosted by some dubious distribution practices (Alford and McNeill, 2010); though still very high by international standards, newspaper circulations are now falling.

While press freedom is guaranteed under the constitution, successive LDP governments sought to coopt the media through measures such as providing newspaper groups with prime office locations in central Tokyo at bargain-basement prices. There is also a controversial system of *kisha* (press) clubs operating in political circles and at government departments. Approximately 15 reporters from the major news groups, wire services and NHK gain exclusive access to press clubs at party offices, offices of political factions, ministries, and even the Prime Minister's Office. Facilities provided at these clubs may be quite extensive, including meals and places to sleep as well as phone and fax lines. In effect, club members become 'insiders' at the organizations they are assigned to cover; by contrast, reporters from local, weekly and monthly publications are excluded from information – as are foreign correspondents.

*Table* 7.1 Circulation of Japan's major national newspapers (2009 estimates, morning editions)

| | *Total* |
|---|---|
| *Yomiuri Shimbun* | 10,018,117 |
| *Asahi Shimbun* | 8,031,579 |
| *Mainichi Shimbun* | c. 3,800,000 |
| *Nihon Keizai Shimbun* | 3,052,929 |
| *Sankei Shimbun* | 1,846,591 |

*Sources*: ABC statistics cited in Alford and McNeill, 2010.

*Kisha* club members are not restricted to contacting politicians through their offices. Groups of reporters regularly begin the day with early morning visits to the homes of key sources such as the Cabinet Secretary, and tail them almost constantly on a rota basis. These reporters stage 'night attacks' on the homes of important figures, sometimes playing mah jong with them until the small hours. Under these circumstances, journalists and their sources inevitably build up a very close rapport, leading to a loss of objectivity and decline of standards. The internal discipline of the clubs – in which a common line is determined by the club captain – makes it impossible for members to secure any 'scoops', with ostracism the punishment for anyone going it alone. While politicians benefited from positive coverage provided by the club reporters, the reporters would jealously defend their sources from the prying eyes of rivals outside the charmed circle.

Typically, major political scandals in Japan have been broken by non-press club journalists. Kakuei Tanaka, for example, was exposed in the 1970s only when a weekly magazine ran corruption allegations that were followed up by foreign correspondents and investigated by the US Senate. The Recruit-Cosmos scandal was actually exposed by *Asahi Shimbun* reporters, but they were working for the Yokohama bureau, not the Tokyo parliamentary beat (Farley, 1996: 148–9). In effect, the *kisha* club system was not itself the root of the problem, but was a reflection of the internal structures of Japanese news organizations. These organizations were not dedicated to a critical quest for information, but to a hierarchical and cartelized model of news-gathering that did not challenge the privileged position of power-holders (Hall, 1998: 46–7; Freeman, 2000: 160–79). Nevertheless, Jake

Adelstein, one of the few foreigners ever to work as a Japanese *kisha* club reporter argues that his colleagues at the *Yomiuri* believed they were 'the final guardians of this fragile democracy we have in Japan' (2009: 33). He concluded: 'The Japanese press is often characterized by the foreign media as a bunch of sycophantic lapdog office workers, but this isn't exactly the case' (2009: 34). The Democratic Party of Japan came to office in 2009 pledging to abolish the *kisha* clubs, but soon found this was easier said than done (Fackler, 2009). Former *New York Times* journalist Takashi Uesugi (2008) has published a provocative book in Japanese entitled *The Collapse of Journalism* . Nevertheless, the oppositional stance adopted to the DPJ by the Yomiuri and other media groups meant that relations between journalists and power-holders became much less cosy than before.

In recent years, much of the most energetic and challenging political coverage has been found in the private television sector, rather than in worthy-but-dull NHK, or the lumbering flagship newspapers (Illustration 7.2). Traditionally, Japanese TV journalists adopted a highly respectful style of interviewing, providing questions in advance, and not pressing politicians to offer proper answers. The result was dull television and little effective media scrutiny of the political process. During the mid-1980s, TV Asahi led the way with new programming featuring more rigorous interview formats. The

**Illustration 7.2 A live TV broadcast from the streets of Tokyo**

most important programmes were the 10 pm late evening show *News Station,* and the morning weekly *Sunday Project,* which included a regular extended interview slot. Programmes such as these helped to increase public interest in political issues, especially a series of corruption scandals in 1992–3, and may have contributed marginally to the brief demise of LDP rule which began in mid-1993 (McCargo, 2003: 56–61).

By the beginning of the twenty-first century, a new mode of media presentation was in vogue among politicians, epitomized by Junichiro Koizumi's premiership. The good-looking Koizumi was a master of the 'wide-show', building his popularity with female voters by appearing on down-market television programmes featuring celebrity gossip and sensational crimes. While some commentators saw this as a more open and accessible mode of politics, others despaired at its superficiality, arguing that substantive issues had been replaced by a cult of political personality. Koizumi sought to base his demands for often vague 'reforms' on a direct media tie-up with voters, thereby bypassing formal political structures. Yet in reality he had little control over his own party, let alone his government. Media became increasingly important, yet serious debate and analysis was giving way to a preoccupation with trivia. When Koizumi left office in 2006, he had raised the bar in terms of public expectations concerning the ability of Japan's leaders to communicate with voters. None of his three LDP successors was able to achieve anything resembling Koizumi's rapport with the public; rather, just as the smooth-talking Tony Blair made the tongue-tied premiership of his successor Gordon Brown almost intolerable to the British public ear, so Japanese voters accustomed to Koizumi became increasingly alienated by the gaffes of successive LDP prime ministers.

Koizumi certainly created an appetite for a more open style of political communication, yet ironically the DPJ won office in 2009 without a particularly impressive media strategy, and in the face of very critical coverage from at least three of the Big 5 newspaper groups (McCargo and Lee 2010: 240–1). The DPJ ousted the LDP partly through the use of mainstream media, especially television. Partly because of long commutes and cramped apartments, many young voters access technologies from their cell phones rather than laptops or PCs. Mobile phone news web sites mainly report information from mainstream news organizations; newspapers are still the most authoritative news sources, and television the most popular. So far, there is no well-established cadre of political bloggers who have gained credibility and public acceptance. As a result, blogging and the Internet played relatively little role in the LDP's defeat. Despite its image as a high-tech nation, Japan remains attached to some very analogue, hierarchical thinking about what constitutes credible information.

### *Voluntary and professional associations*

Japan is rich in associational life, possessing a great abundance of social capital in the form of neighbourhood associations (*chonaikai*), public safety committees, police support groups, voluntary organizations, volunteer social workers and probation officers, parent–teacher associations, and interest groups of all kinds. An impressive range of collective activities exists in Japan: although this is now declining, on Sunday mornings in some residential districts, teams of residents can still be seen weeding paths, clearing gulleys and gathering up rubbish. Community networks of this kind can be very effective in helping Japanese politicians to create support groups, and to mobilize community bloc-voting (Flanagan, 1991a: 196–7). Curtis explained how neighbourhood associations were a key element in one successful LDP candidate's campaign organization and strategy (Curtis, 1971: 87–125). While there is an ever-present tendency for Japanese social capital to be enlisted in the service of politicians, this rich community organization can also give rise to independent political life, when circumstances so require.

The prominent role played by women in many community groups partly reflects the limited career choices available to Japanese women. Sugimoto suggests (1997: 153–4) that becoming a 'networker' is considered by many Japanese women a reasonable alternative to paid employment or full-time home-making. Networkers engage in a wide range of activities, from running workers' collectives or recycling shops to engaging in protest movements concerning environmental or other issues. Volunteerism is a very important phenomenon in post-war and contemporary Japan, yet the state has been centrally involved in mobilizing many volunteers and voluntary organizations for its own purposes (Avenell, 2010: 85–91). As Avenell argues, voluntary organizations in Japan constitute 'a sphere of activity institutionally and ideationally shaped by a pervasive state vision wherein volunteers are expected to be selfless, apolitical subjects engaged in social issues (*kadai*) formulated, sanctioned and nurtured by the state' (2010: 91).

## *Modes of civil society*

Keiko Hirata argues that there are several reasons why the citizens' movements of the 1960s and 1970s failed to generate a strong civil society. Many of the movements were preoccupied with single issues – once a specific grievance was addressed, the organization would collapse. Leadership of the groups was often weak; but most importantly, she argues that Japan's developmental state 'imposed structural constraints on citizens' activism and fostered passivity, thus hindering the growth of long-lasting movements or coalitions' (Hirata, 2002: 17). She invokes culturalist arguments to explain the way Japanese people accepted bureaucratic pressures to over-concentrate on economic development. However, she argues that globalization and the attainment of 'mature' industrial status, have recently weakened the developmental state, creating more space for civil society and for the emergence of non-governmental organizations (NGOs). She sees the Kobe earthquake of 1995 as a 'watershed event', helping to discredit state-centred approaches to solving problems, and encouraging the growth of voluntary associations (2002: 33–4). The earthquake helped stimulate the voluntary sector: volunteers who sought to assist earthquake victims established new non-profit organizations in Kobe to manage the emerging 'volunteer work boom'. While the phenomenon of the 'citizens' movements' as understood in the 1970s did not endure, new manifestations of similar political tendencies have continued to emerge.

Hirata's particular interest is the way in which Japanese NGOs have assumed considerable importance in lobbying the government to influence overseas development aid policies; this is a relatively narrow focus. In the most detailed and wide-ranging study of Japanese civil society yet published in English, editors Pharr and Schwartz argue that post-war Japan had an activist state with carefully targeted policies. While economic interest groups have flourished, other non-state organizations have encountered widely differing degrees of success (Pharr and Schwartz, 2003). Ducke argues that compared to similar organizations in other developed countries, most Japanese NGOs are amateurish, attached to simplistic ideas of developmentalism, and present themselves as non-political (Ducke, 2007: 42). Avenell concludes that:

> Corporate actors have fostered social capital-type activism, with targeted support for prominent civic groups and the creation of

> civic networks. Influential activists have crafted a powerful logic of proposal which tends to reinforce the vision of state and corporate elites at the expense of a more pluralistic conceptualization of social activism and civil society more generally. (2009: 283)

Pekkanen argues that 'Japan's dual civil society supports democracy through social capital generation and community building, but largely lacks sizable professional groups that influence the public sphere or policy making (Pekkanen, 2006: 3).

Protest politics assumed new forms in Japan following the US invasion of Iraq in 2003. Urban groups, with young people assuming leading roles, staged demonstrations that appropriated elements of popular culture – including the use of rave music and huge sound systems – for anti-war causes (Hayashi and McKnight, 2005). Their rejection of the Iraq war was linked to frustration with neo-liberal economic policies that left many young people unable to access secure employment, apparently condemned to live as impecunious *fureeter* – temporary contract workers. While criticized by an older generation of activists for their lack of ideological clarity or clearly articulated demands, these forms of protest were clear testimony to a new and less hierarchical form of political participation in Japan. In the wake of the 2011 earthquake, tsunami and nuclear crisis, similar forms of protest re-emerged. Some of these are captured in a German/Japanese documentary entitled *Radioactivists* (www.radioactivists.org).

## Contrasting perspectives on Japanese civil society

For mainstream scholars, there are innumerable parallels between Japanese civil society and the civil societies of western democracies. For all its shortcomings, the Japanese education system is seen as highly effective in producing a literate and numerate population, and Japanese police and criminal justice system offer an outstanding model of crime prevention which other countries should study. The media provides Japanese people with detailed information about politics and current events, and alerts them to scandals and abuses of power when necessary. At the same time, the rich community structures of Japanese cities, towns and villages make for a high degree of associational life, and these structures can form the basis for various forms of social and political participation, ranging from electoral mobilization to environmental protests.

For revisionist scholars, the picture is much more bleak. The Japanese education system strives to produce unthinking citizens who will dedicate themselves to diligent consumerism, and will be deeply reluctant to challenge the prevailing order. This conformity is reinforced by an anodyne and largely uncritical media that constantly fails in its duties as a watchdog, and by a quietly repressive police and justice system. Although community groups can form the basis of protest movements and grassroots resistance, the establishment is highly skilled in co-opting them, neutralizing their dissent, and turning them into support organizations for conservative politicians.

For those scholars who emphasize culturalist perspectives, the education system is an important source of socialization into values – such as harmony and hierarchy – which are central to Japanese society. These values are reinforced by other social institutions, such as the media and the police. Japanese communities reflect a group model of organization that is quite distinctive, and although groups may sometimes adopt collective stances which challenge the interests of political power-holders (as in protest movements), both sides then typically seek to find ways of solving their differences, through compromise and the sharing of benefits.

# 8

# Japan's External Relations

In 2010, China decisively overtook Japan as the world's second largest economy. While this shift had been long in the making – China was already ahead using a number of standard indicators – the downgrade to number three was an important symbolic moment for Japan, reflecting changing dynamics of political influence as well as financial and industrial clout. Since the end of the Pacific War, Japan had been the most important nation in Asia, and the primary ally of the United States. In the wake of the spectacular 2008 Beijing Olympic Games, China had claimed a front row seat on the international stage – rather as had Japan in 1964, and South Korea in 1988.

Yet for all Japan's economic clout, two main factors had long militated against a global role for Japan, both of them legacies of the Second World War. The first was a lingering distrust of Japan, felt especially by China, Korea and other victims of Japanese aggression. The second factor was hesitancy on the part of Japan to assert itself internationally, a reluctance, which reflected the formal 'self-disarmament' implied in the 1947 Constitution. By permanently renouncing the right to wage war, Japan had sidelined itself. As such, Japan was described as an 'incomplete superpower', combining a giant economy with much smaller global clout. At the same time, Japan's lack of natural resources means that the country remains heavily reliant on imports of oil (especially from the Middle East) and raw materials (especially from Asia). This reliance meant that Japan needed to maintain friendly relations with much of the world, and could ill afford to antagonize key suppliers. In other words, Japan has a huge stake in the maintenance of international order, yet lacks conventional mechanisms for helping preserve or establish such order.

*Map* 8.1 Japan in Pacific Asia

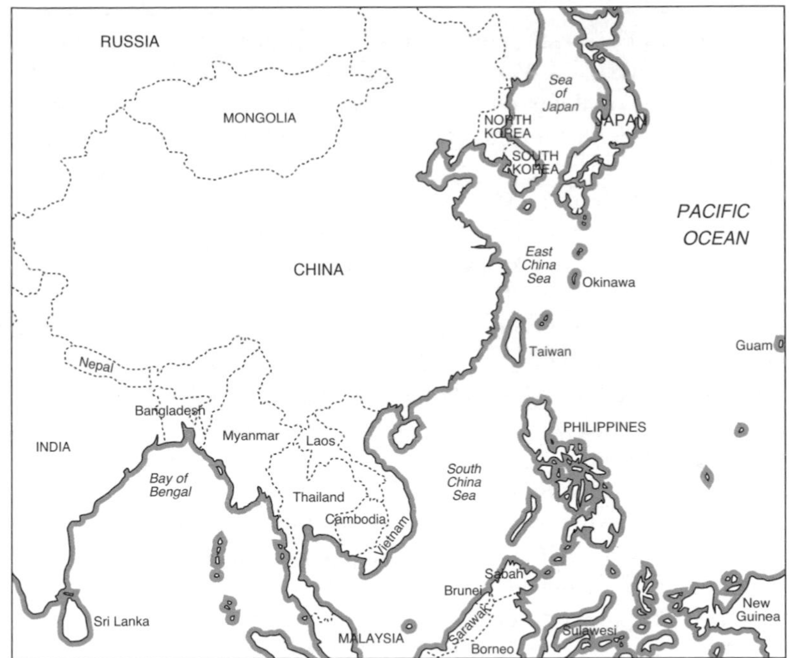


One obvious symbol of this relative impotence is the composition of the UN Security Council: Japan has a much larger economy than the UK (or France), yet does not have a permanent seat on the Council. To some extent, this paradox reflects the determination of the Second World War allies to retain their seats at the world's top table: but it also derives from domestic opposition to Japan claiming an international status commensurate with its economic standing. Japan has long enjoyed a senior status among the world's industrialized nations (as evidenced by membership of the G8), but this is not matched by a clear role as a regional leader in Asia, let alone globally. Revisionist perspectives on Japan have emphasized the contradictions inherent in Japan's relations with the rest of the world, whereas mainstream accounts offer a more sympathetic view, and culturalist perspectives emphasize the distinctive historical nature of Japan's international position.

## Japan's Self-Defence Forces

Since the 1947 Constitution banned the Japanese from re-arming, at the onset of the Cold War, the Americans were obliged to take on the main burden of defending both Japan and the wider Asia-Pacific region from the threat of attack by either the Soviet Union or China. Whilst these commitments have been scaled down over time in accordance with the Nixon doctrine, notably with the US withdrawal from Vietnam in 1975, at their height they included huge military forces in the Philippines and Okinawa, as well as in Korea and mainland Japan.

The Japanese position on defence is unique, not only because of the special nature of the Japanese Constitution, but also because of the domestic political and psychological sensitivity of the issue. The humiliating defeat of the country at the end of the Pacific War left a whole generation of Japanese people deeply uneasy about the pursuit of militarism, and highly suspicious both of their own political leaders and of American interests and intentions. It is not enough to see Article 9 of the Constitution simply as a proscription imposed upon Japan from outside; it also struck a chord with many of the Japanese people, particularly those with left-wing or liberal views. The full text of the article reads as follows:

> Aspiring sincerely to an international peace based on justice and order, the Japanese people forever renounce war as a sovereign right of the nation and the threat or use of force as means of settling international disputes. 2) In order to accomplish the aim of the preceding paragraph, land, sea, and air forces, as well as other war potential, will never be maintained. The right of belligerency of the state will not be recognized.

Right-wingers have always been uncomfortable with a constitutional stipulation which seemed to them to violate the sovereignty of Japan. On numerous occasions, conservatives (many of them senior politicians in the ruling LDP) have sought in various ways to expand Japan's military role. Unlike in many countries, where foreign policy issues are often perceived as separate from the normal domestic political agenda, the question of Japan's defence posture has always been of the utmost political importance. As a result of the creative way in which Article 9 has been reinterpreted, Japan's Self-Defence Forces

(SDF) enjoy a curiously ambiguous status. The SDF are 'exclusively defence-oriented', which means that they:

- can only act if attacked;
- must take only minimum actions required for defence; and
- the size of their capability must be limited to the minimum necessary for defence - that is, there should be no offensive or strategic weapons.

In international law, 'self-defence' covers both individual and collective defence, but clause 9 is usually viewed as meaning that only acts of individual defence are permissible. It is not clear how this definition would hold up in the event of a military crisis. The self-defence forces are also under civilian control, answerable to the prime minister and the cabinet, members of which must all be civilians according to the Constitution. Conscription is banned, and so is overseas despatch of the self-defence forces. This last stipulation was not a legal ban, though, but a resolution passed by the upper house in 1954.

In 1976, Japanese defence policy was clarified in the National Defence Programme Outline (NDPO) (see George, 1988: 239–45). This included the principle of a gradual, progressive improvement in Japan's defence capability up to specific force levels which would allow the SDF to carry out two main tasks: full surveillance during peacetime, and the capacity to deal with limited acts of aggression. To reassure the public, the NDPO was linked to a maximum ceiling on military expenditure of 1 per cent of Japan's GNP (this ceiling was officially exceeded in 1988 and 1989, and questions have been raised about the accounting procedures used in meeting the 1 per cent target). Successive annual white papers on Japan's defence policy published since 1976 have emphasized four central points:

- an 'exclusively defence-oriented policy' (in other words, force cannot be used until an attack takes place);
- a pledge never to become a military power which will threaten other countries;
- the adherence to three non-nuclear principles, which are not possessing, manufacturing or harbouring nuclear weapons; and
- a commitment that the military will remain under civilian control. (Defence Agency, 1997: 103–4)

The irony of the situation has been that although the LDP (1955–93, 1994–2009) was repeatedly re-elected on the strength of policies which promoted economic growth, the majority of the Japanese public has broadly supported the views of the opposition and media 'peace coalition' on defence questions. While public support for more explicit defence policies has been growing in recent years, the LDP has generally been quite cagey about defining Japanese defence policy. Areas of controversy include:

- What is meant by 'the principle of self-defence'?
- What is meant by 'minimum necessary defence capability'?
- What is meant by 'limited and small-scale' military aggression?
- What is the area to be defended under the self-defence provisions?

For this reason, Japan has always been reluctant to provide the United States with any clear commitment to take over particular defence functions, or play a specific defensive role. Rather, Japan has quietly but steadily increased the size and capability of the SDF. One important symbolic change in the direction of 'normalization' was made in 2007, when the Defence Agency was officially upgraded to become the Ministry of Defence, a policy pushed strongly by the then Abe government.

In 1992, the Diet approved the International Peace Cooperation Law, which made it possible, in principle, for members of the self-defence forces to be deployed in international peace-keeping operations. The SDF were subsequently despatched in support of a number of PKOs, primarily under UN auspices – notably in Cambodia, East Timor, Angola, Mozambique and Golan Heights – was well as undertaking various humanitarian operations and supporting election monitoring. It was rather tricky for left-wingers and liberals to oppose SDF activity that was branded with the word 'peace' and conducted under a UN umbrella. Nevertheless, for conservative politicians this was a calculated move, designed to create precedents for the overseas deployment of the SDF and assert the notion that Japan was now functioning as a normal country.

The success of this conservative strategy was nicely illustrated by the contrasting responses of Japan to the first and second Gulf wars. In 1990, domestic opposition and LDP weakness meant that it did not support the US-led war to drive Iraq out of Kuwait. Instead, the Japanese government provided $13 billion for post-war reconstruction. The United States expressed considerable displeasure at the failure of the Japanese to offer any material assistance. However, in 2004, following the US-led invasion of Iraq by a 'coalition of the willing', Japan sent 600 members of the SDF to the Southern Iraqi city of Samara to engage in reconstruction work. Because of their ambiguous legal position, Dutch and later British and American troops provided security for the SDF forces – so avoiding the risk that they might be forced to open fire in self-defence. Japan paid only $5 billion as a financial contribution for reconstruction projects on this occasion, the symbolism of the SDF deployment counting for much more than chequebook diplomacy. The Iraq deployment, made possible through the passage of the 2003 Iraq Special Measures Law, was not carried out under UN auspices and was not, strictly speaking, a peace-keeping operation. In effect, it amounted to the first deployment of Japanese troops in wartime since 1945. Japan has not sent ground forces to Afghanistan, but did provide maritime support for the refuelling of the US Navy for a time, and despatched a 10-member SDF medical team to the country in early 2011.

Conservative law-makers hoped that the Iraq precedent could pave the way for constitutional reform, centring on the revision of Article 9. Calls for revision of the Constitution – a shorthand for amending or abolishing Article 9 – were a major theme of political debate during the 1990s, supported by the *Yomiuri Shimbun* newspaper group and a range of other actors (Boyd and Samuels, 2005: 27–34). In 2007, at the initiative of hawkish premier Shinzo Abe, the Diet passed a bill allowing for a national referendum on Constitution reform. But Abe left office shortly thereafter, public support waned, and the three-year moratorium on holding a referendum subsequently lapsed.

## The US–Japan alliance

The US–Japanese security relationship has been evolving since the Occupation period, as the Americans have put increasing pressure on Japan to expand their defence forces and capabilities. A wide range of views has been expressed about the nature of the relationship, ranging from former US Ambassador to Japan Mike Mansfield's claim that: 'US–Japan relations is the most important bilateral relationship – bar none' (Mansfield, 1989); to more pessimistic American views, which see Japan as a potentially dangerous force to be 'contained' by foreign policy initiatives; and left-wing Japanese criticisms of the security alliance as a militaristic continuation of the Occupation.

As early as 1950, the Americans ordered the Japanese to establish a substantial police reserve of 75,000 men to replace US troops who were being moved to Korea (George, 1988: 245–6). The year 1951 saw the signing of the US–Japan Security Treaty, which stated that the USA would maintain forces in Japan, but with the proviso that Japan would increasingly take over responsibility for its own defence provisions. The worst year for US–Japanese relations since the Pacific War was 1960, when the Mutual Security Treaty was revised. The new 'Treaty of Mutual Cooperation and Security' met with widespread opposition and was greeted by angry street demonstrations that mobilized millions of protestors. Yet in one sense the treaty was highly favourable to Japan: although the USA promised to defend Japan, Japan made no such pledge to come to the aid of the United States. The supposedly 'mutual' treaty was entirely one-sided. But this very lack of equality left Japan in a firmly subordinate position to the United States, dependent upon continuing good relations with the Americans. As Japan gained in economic power, this relationship of political subordination to the United States became increasingly problematic.

Partly in recognition of the changing economic status of Japan, the American 'Nixon doctrine' of 1969 called upon US allies in Asia to assume more of the financial burden for their defence. The Vietnam debacle was reducing American enthusiasm for military entanglements in the Asia-Pacific region; and, increasingly, Japan was expected to pay a larger share of the American defence costs. By the mid-1980s, the Japanese were paying around $21,000 a year for each American serviceperson on their shores, and in 1990 the Japanese government agreed to pay 50 per cent of the entire cost of the American defence establishment. The USA was unhappy about the nominal 1 per cent of GNP limit on defence spending set by the Japanese, pressing them repeatedly to raise the proportion to 2 or 3 per cent. Their ever-increasing trade deficits with Japan did nothing to placate American unease. In the wake of the 1979 Iranian Revolution, the Americans began to believe that their own capacity to respond to potential military threats was severely stretched, and that Japan needed to assume greater responsibility for regional security around its immediate territorial waters and airspace.

Japan's first response to American pressure was directed at rebutting the charge that Japan was enjoying a 'free ride' in defence terms. The Japanese government emphasized what it called its 'Comprehensive Security' policy, which involved counting development aid and efforts to ensure supplies of food and energy as part of an overall security strategy (George, 1988: 257–9). In other words, though the Japanese might not be making a substantial direct military contribution, they were supporting international political and economic stability in innumerable different ways. This argument did little to impress the Americans, but the phrase has continued to have currency as part of the arguments of those who favour only moderate, incremental increases in defence spending and activities.

During Yasuhiro Nakasone's term as prime minister (1982–7) there was a distinct change in the direction of Japanese foreign policy. Nakasone took a hawkish line on defence matters. (George, 1988: 261). Under his premiership, the Defence Agency issued a statement saying that the concept of 'self-defence' need not apply only on Japanese soil, territorial waters or airspace, but could extend beyond the immediate area of Japan itself. This was a significant change in previous interpretations of the concept of self-defence, and came much closer to satisfying American demands. Nakasone also sought to break through the 1 per cent GNP ceiling, and made a couple of attempts to do so by appealing directly to public opinion. Whilst more Japanese people began to be reconciled to the *fait accompli* of the SDF and the Security Treaty, this did not mean that they supported an expanded defence role for Japan such as his government advocated.

How powerful are the self-defence forces today? On the one hand, Japan possesses sizeable military assets, and now ranks as the number four defence spender in the world, topped only by the USA, China and the UK, and ahead of France, Germany, Saudi Arabia and Russia (ISS 2011: 33). Expenditure in 2009 was slightly less than in 2001, at around ¥4.77 trillion, or roughly US$51.1 billion (ISS 2011: 245–8). In 2009, the strength of the forces stood at 247,746, including 151,641 in ground self-defence forces, 47,123 in maritime self-defence forces, and 45,600 in air self-defence forces. The SDF has 374 ground-based combat aircraft, 95 maritime-based combat aircraft, 49 major combat vessels and 18 submarines.

Yet, quite recently, independent analysts have suggested that the Japanese forces could only hold up a serious attack for a couple of days; their defensive posture meant that they possessed only a narrow range of capabilities. According to Hanami, 'a substantial military budget does not easily translate into a substantial fighting force' (Hanami, 1993: 595). Roger Buckley suggests that despite its sizeable defence establishment, 'Japan appears most unlikely to deploy its so-called Self-Defence Forces for much beyond the rescue of its own citizens in emergency situations abroad' (2002: 223).

Aurelia George, by contrast, argues that the traditional view of Japan as a 'free-rider' in defence terms is now in need of re-examination: from a weak and dependent American ally in the early post-war period, Japan has evolved into a powerful regional lieutenant with a military role that is edging beyond the boundaries of self-defence. Although it remains dependent on the US security umbrella, Japan has begun the transition to a collective security state with some degree of regional force projection (George, 1988: 237). Takashi Inoguchi has argued that there is a 'functional disparity' between the USA and Japan which clouds relations between the two (Inoguchi, 1993: 58–60). Both countries have considerable vested interests that incline towards protectionism, and a tendency to put domestic political considerations before foreign policy priorities. According to Inoguchi:

> what appears to one side as the adversary's lack of transparency and over reliance on foreign pressure (the American view of Japanese politics), or to the other side as unpredictability, arbitrariness and a self-congratulatory system (the Japanese view of American politics), seems to disturb and irritate the other nation immensely. (Inoguchi, 1993: 59)

One important debate concerns the extent to which Japan's policy changes are driven by external pressures: is Japan simply a reactive state? Japan tends to be seen in this way by outsiders, but Inoguchi argues that this does not do justice to the complexities of Japanese politics, where even the LDP had to build up a consensus before effecting a policy shift. Thus the security policy which successive LDP governments wanted to pursue was frequently at variance with its actual policy.

Japan and the USA issued new 'Guidelines for US-Japan Security Defense Cooperation' in September 1997 (see Katahara, 1998: 70–3). This was not a revision of the 1960 Security Treaty, and did not directly address specific regional tensions such as the North Korean situation. However, the new guidelines did contain several important points, including greater sharing of intelligence information (Japan was now receiving 'real-time' defence intelligence direct from US agencies), collaboration between US and Japanese forces when taking part in UN peace-keeping operations or international humanitarian operations, and an increased emphasis on bilateral defence planning and exercises. Significantly, the guidelines noted that 'Japan will have primary responsibility to take action and repel an armed attack as soon as possible'; the main US role would be a supporting one, such as providing strike power in the event of an airborne attack on Japan. The US–Japan security relationship continues to attract criticism. Analysts such as Shunji Taoka of the *Asahi Shimbun* argued that the changes seen in the new guidelines were an example of 'making the house heavier when it is already located on soft ground' (Taoka, 1997).

In 2007, Japan signed a security pact with Australia, and made overtures towards greater cooperation with India, envisaging a 'values based' arc of Pacific alliances that would include, yet move beyond, the core security relationship with the United States. But the rumbling controversy over American bases in Japan has been a constant reminder of the centrality of that relationship.

## Okinawa and the issue of American bases

The presence of substantial US bases in Japan has become increasingly problematic in the post-Cold War world. Japan is home to around 36,000 American military personnel and dozens of bases, including the headquarters of the Seventh Fleet and the Third Marine Expeditionary Force. The Japanese government pays a substantial proportion of the costs associated with the bases, despite the fact that they serve just as much as an 'unsinkable aircraft carrier' in the Pacific, as to protect Japan itself. The Americans withdrew from their bases in the Philippines in 1992, and some in Japan hoped this would a precedent for a reduced US military presence there. Prominent politicians, including former Prime Minister Hosokawa, have called for a new policy of a 'US–Japan alliance without bases'. Some supporters of this argument suggest that bases should revert to the formal control of the Japanese government, but could still be used by US forces. Critics, however, argue that a reduction in the size or status of US forces in Japan would give the wrong signal, perhaps encouraging assertive or aggressive moves by China or North Korea.

The USA later proposed a gradual scaling back of its Japan-based deployments. These plans would include moving around 8,600 marines from Okinawa to the American territory of Guam. Nearly three quarters of the American military personnel in Japan are based in Okinawa, part of a chain of islands lying between Kyushu and Taiwan. Okinawa only formally reverted to Japanese control in 1972, having remained officially occupied for more than twenty years after the end of the Occupation. Many Okinawans are vocal critics of the American bases which have been focus of regular mass protests. A series of troubling incidents, ranging from the rape of a young Japanese schoolgirl by three marines in 1995 to the crash of a military helicopter onto a local university in 2004, has fuelled public anger against bases that occupy a huge geographical footprint and have considerable negative social impact. In 1996, the American and Japanese governments agreed in principle to relocate Futenma, the most contentious Okinawa airbase, to a new coastal site in the north-east of the island. But building a huge new airbase on Okinawa has become virtually impossible in political terms, and successive Japanese administrations have been unable to deliver on the deal (Curtis, 2011b: 2). Following the change of government from LDP to DPJ in 2009, Prime Minister Hatoyama called for Futenma to be closed, and for any new base to be located outside Okinawa, and preferably outside Japan. Although he later changed his mind and agreed to support the original relocation plan, Hatoyama was quickly ousted from the premiership, in part at least because he had dared to query Japanese subordination to American defence priorities, and so blotted his copybook in Washington (Wright, 2010: 459). Wright argues that it would be perfectly possible to move the Marines at Futenma to the nearby Kadena Air Force base, an option resisted by vested interests in the American defence establishment.

Okinawa epitomizes the contradictions of the Mutual Security Treaty, continuing to function in many respects as a de facto American military colony where local views and democratic principles count for very little. Successive American and Japanese administrations have failed to produce creative solutions which would support the demilitarization of Okinawa and the re-balancing of the US–Japan security relationship. Gavan McCormack has argued that the level of popular resistance to any new base construction in Okinawa was so high by the end of 2011 that no Japanese government would be able to proceed with such plans (McCormack *et al*., 2012).

## Japan and Asia

Is Japan best seen as a source of inspiration for Asia, an ally in the economic and political development of the region? Or is Japan actually seeking to play on the idea of a shared Asian identity for the purpose of dominating and exploiting Asia? This was an ambiguity clearly apparent during the 1931–45 period, when the Japanese invaded and occupied much of Southeast and East Asia, claiming that they had come to liberate Asia for the Asians, but in practice setting up puppet governments to do their bidding in the region.

One paradox that must be addressed at the outset is Japan's own ambivalence about its Asian identity. From an external perspective, Japan is clearly an Asian country; yet this is not a view with which all Japanese people would find themselves in sympathy. Japan has long regarded itself as an honorary member of the western club of industrialized nations. Yet as an island country not directly connected with the continent of Asia, Japan tends to regard itself as a distinct and separate entity. In 1885, the Japanese intellectual Yukichi Fukuzawa wrote a book called *The Break Free from Asia Theory,* in which he said:

> Although Japan lies close to the eastern edge of Asia, the spirit of its people has transcended Asian conservatism and moved towards western civilisation . . . Japan cannot afford to wait for the enlightenment of its neighbours, in the hope of working with them for the betterment of all Asia. It should break formation and move forward along with the civilised countries of the West. (Quoted in Rowley and do Rosario, 1991: 17)

In practice, this emulation of the West and sense of superiority to Asia was to lead to Japanese imperialism in the region, as Japan first annexed Korea, then Manchuria, and eventually invaded Southeast Asia.

Once Japan had succeeded in 'moving forward' to the extent of overtaking many western powers economically, there was a general recognition, at least in theory, that Japan needed to rejoin Asia in order to play a global role commensurate with its position. But negative stereotypes of Asia remain common in Japanese thinking and behaviour, as evidenced by the poor treatment received by some guest workers in Japan. There is a tendency for the Japanese to see the rest of Asia simply as a ready source of raw materials, despite the considerable changes in the nature of Japan's trade with the region as industrialization spreads from the original NICs (newly industrialized countries) to the new dragons of Southeast Asia.

In part, the Japanese leaning towards the West was a direct outcome of the international conditions following the Pacific War.

Japanese adventurism in Southeast Asia and elsewhere had left a lasting legacy of distrust, whilst the American Occupation marked the beginning of a close political and economic relationship with the United States which was to take precedence over any Asian entanglements. One Japanese scholar, Masahide Shibusawa, has gone so far as to argue that:

> In fact, after the war, Japan was literally banished from continental Asia, and had to survive virtually on its own resources, with little prospect of being able to take part in any regional system that might develop. With wartime memories still fresh, few countries in either Northeast or Southeast Asia wanted its involvement in the region in any form or context. (Shibusawa, 1984: 158)

He contrasts this with the situation of post-war Germany, which was incorporated into a new European order by its western neighbours in the post-war period. During the 1950s and 1960s, Japan was preoccupied with the pursuit of economic reconstruction, and sought to protect and subsidize its agriculture. The only major Japanese investment in the Southeast Asian region was in securing supplies of raw materials, primarily oil supplies from Indonesia. In the early 1960s, Prime Minister Ikeda called for Japan to establish its international status through economic development, setting the tone for the 'economism' which followed.

By the late 1960s, Japan had become the primary trading partner for most Southeast Asian countries, and during the 1970s Japan began making substantial investments in the newly industrializing countries (South Korea, Taiwan, Hong Kong and Singapore) as it sought to enter their markets and transfer some production there. Yet in the early 1970s there were virulent anti-Japanese protests in Thailand and Indonesia, demonstrating that economic success does not necessarily lead to a more positive international image. Japanese premier Tanaka had a disastrous visit to Southeast Asia in 1974, when he was widely heckled by hostile crowds.

When the Association of Southeast Asian Nations (ASEAN) was first formed in 1967, the Japanese were not terribly impressed. Indonesia had been a prime mover in the formation of the Association, but at the time was in a parlous economic condition. Japan's attitude towards ASEAN changed after the fall of Saigon in 1975. The Japanese realized that they could no longer rely upon the Americans to take charge of the Southeast Asia connection, and Japanese markets and sources of raw materials would have to be secured by a new diplomatic line. There was a significant change of tone by Japan, which began to talk in terms of mutual understanding and *nemawashi* (consensus-building), laying the groundwork for business and trade deals. The ASEAN countries also recognized the importance of Japan; now that the Americans had been defeated over Vietnam, they started to look elsewhere for models of success and development.

In 1977, Japanese premier Fukuda visited Southeast Asia, promising $1.55 billion in economic assistance, and calling for a new framework of Japan–Southeast Asian relations. He promised a 'heart-to-heart' relationship based on mutual understanding, and pledged that Japan had no intention of remilitarizing. This became known as the Fukuda doctrine, and remains substantially intact today. Although a good rapport between Japan and the ASEAN countries was central to the Fukuda doctrine, it was also true that the Japanese sought good trading relations with the countries of Indochina, and indeed with Burma. Japan hoped to promote cooperation between ASEAN and communist Indochina. The aim was to use economic means to ensure the stability of Southeast Asia, thereby obviating the need for military power to be used. The contrast between Tanaka's failed visit to the region in 1974 and Fukuda's very successful visit of 1977 was abundantly clear.

Thai political scientist Chaiwat Khamchoo has quoted one Japanese scholar as saying that the Fukuda doctrine was 'a trader's diplomacy: of the economy, by the economy and for the economy' (Khamchoo, 1991: 8). There was nothing inherently new about the Fukuda doctrine; it was essentially a restatement of the position Japan already held. He saw Japanese policy towards Southeast Asia as a 'declaration of enlightened self-interest' (Khamchoo, 1991: 10); the idea was to forge a link between Japan's economic interests and the development of Southeast Asia in such a way as to make sure that such development depended upon Japan. The Fukuda doctrine was part-and-parcel of an 'omnidirectional foreign policy' that reached out to each side of any potential conflict. Richard Cronin is one of many scholars who disagrees, seeing the Fukuda doctrine as a turning point when: 'For the first time since World War II, Japan began to consciously articulate its interests in Southeast Asia' (Cronin, 1991: 60). One example of this change was that Japan did not remain impartial over vexed matters such as the Cambodia conflict during the 1980s. Despite some pressure from the business sector, the Japanese did act to suspend aid to Vietnam following the Vietnamese invasion of Cambodia. In doing so, Japan supported the position taken by the ASEAN countries.

In the 1980s, the Japanese began investing heavily in ASEAN countries, particularly Thailand, Indonesia and Malaysia. Despite the high levels of Japanese investment in Asia, investment in the USA and Europe was even higher. There was also a certain caution about Japanese investment strategies in Southeast Asia. Japanese companies were believed to have an informal understanding among themselves that they should not try to gain more than a 30–40 per cent market share in any one local industry. Nevertheless, this has proved difficult in certain sectors: in the car industry, for example, Japanese models some became very dominant throughout the region. The range and pre-eminence of Japanese products in Southeast Asia has to be seen to be believed; not only manufactured goods, but also cultural products such as video games and cartoons are extremely pervasive in the region.

One source of resentment against Japanese has been their reluctance to devolve management responsibility to local staff. In this area they are regarded as decades behind many American and European companies. Many Japanese companies have virtually no locals in key positions other than a token personnel manager. The most severe critics of Japan in Southeast Asia have accused the Japanese of a form of neo-colonialism, what the Filipino nationalist writer Renato Constantino (1989) calls *The Second Invasion*. He notes that the early emphasis of Japanese investment in the Philippines was on 'pollution-causing, extractive, raw-material producing and labor-intensive industries' (1989: 45). He cited as an example a plant built by Kawasaki Steel. Whilst at first glance this looked like the beginnings of a Philippine steel industry, initial impressions were misleading; the plant concentrated on 'sintering' – the most pollution-creating phase of the steel-making process – and all other stages would continue to be carried out in Japan. By moving the sintering out of Japan, the company could escape from environmental protests at home.

Japan's failure to produce a clearly articulated response to the Asian financial crisis which beset the region from mid-1997 was a source of great disappointment in Southeast Asia; a golden opportunity to assert more explicit leadership in the region was squandered, partly because of Japanese reluctance to make any independent initiatives that might antagonize the United States. The idea of a Japanese-backed 'Asian' crisis fund, briefly mooted in September 1997, was vetoed by Washington. The United States feared that such an initiative would undermine the role of the IMF and the World Bank. Nevertheless, the 1998 US$30 billion 'New Miyazawa Initiative', involving substantial financial support for crisis-hit countries, helped to shore up Japan's economic centrality to the region. The emphasis was on reinvigorating existing models rather than promoting substantial reforms (Hook *et al.*, 2001: 205–6). In retrospect, the turn of the millennium probably saw the high-water mark for Japanese investment and influence in the region; South Korea had become a serious rival both in terms of manufacturing and cultural industries, while China's rise to the position of the pre-eminent regional power was now inexorable. But Japan had yet to make hard choices between Asia and the West, especially on the question of a new trading bloc, the Trans-Pacific Partnership, which the Japanese government expressed interest in joining during 2011 (Pilling, 2011).

## Japan and China

The relationship between Japan and China is an extremely important one. There are numerous parallels between the two civilizations, and many supposedly 'distinctive' features of Japanese culture – such as the tea ceremony, the use of chopsticks, and writing with ideogramatic characters – were actually imported and adapted from Chinese culture. Both China and Japan have exalted notions of their place in the world: while Japan sees itself as the first Asian society to challenge western hegemony in modern times, China regards itself as the 'middle kingdom', the ancient civilization around which the world has long revolved. In other words, both China and Japan regard themselves at least as the world's pre-eminent non-western power, if not simply as the world's pre-eminent civilization. Although most western scholars regarded the main global struggle of the twentieth century as one between the USA and the USSR, for China and Japan their own long-standing rivalry has often loomed much larger.

As Caroline Rose notes, the Chinese leadership believes that Japan owes China a huge cultural debt, since so many features of Japanese civilization are borrowings from the Chinese (Rose, 1998: 8–10). Japan was for a time a tributary state of China, but in due course the tables were turned: Japan relegated China to a lowly status in the world order, a status that was confirmed by the obvious military and political decline of China in the nineteenth century. From 1894 to 1945 ('fifty years that overshadow two thousand'), Japan pursued a policy of imperialist aggression towards China. Chinese incompetence and corruption allowed for an easy victory in the 1894 Sino-Japanese War, and from then on Japan represented a role model for China to emulate. Beginning with the Manchuria Incident of 1931, Japan sought to subjugate and colonize China, committing numerous atrocities in the process (see Rose, 1998: 14–16).

Following the Chinese Revolution of 1949, Sino-Japanese political relations were largely frozen until 1972, when Prime Minister Kakuei Tanaka (following the lead of the United States under Nixon) initiated steps to normalize diplomatic relations between the two countries (see Mendl, 1995: 80–1). In the period that followed, economic relations between China and Japan began to flourish, and the two countries signed a formal peace treaty in 1978. Some outstanding issues remained unresolved, however, such as the status of the disputed Senkaku Islands. Sino-Japanese relations received a major setback in 1982 when an intense conflict broke out concerning the way in which Japanese school textbooks dealt with Japan's wartime role in China (for a definitive account, see Rose, 1998). China issued a formal diplomatic protest over the issue, which has clouded relations between the two countries ever since, despite what Mendl refers to as the 'thickening network of ties between the two countries' during the 1980s (Mendl, 1995: 83).

Following the end of the Cold War in 1989, relations became even closer as Japanese investment poured into business ventures in a China now committed to operating a marketized economy within a totalitarian political order ('one country, two systems'). Compared with western countries, Japan adopted a 'soft' response to China's bloody repression at Tiananmen Square in June 1989; conscious of Chinese sensitivities concerning the war, Japan has always been reluctant to voice open criticisms of China's human-rights record. For example, Japan's national public broadcasting agency NHK is well-known for its low-key treatment of controversial issues such as China's Tibet policy.

High-level visits by Chinese and Japanese leaders helped secure improved relations between the two countries in the 1990s. One particularly symbolic visit was that of the new Japanese Emperor to China in 1992. During this visit – the first ever by a Japanese monarch – he made a partial apology for Japan's wartime actions, a statement which did not fully satisfy the Chinese but was regarded as excessive by many conservative Japanese politicians. Conflicting views of the past are likely to remain a source of tension between

China and Japan. The gradual decline of a pro-China 'old guard' in the LDP and the bureaucracy (especially the Foreign Ministry) allowed tensions between the two countries on a range of bilateral issues to become more apparent. As Japan stumbled economically at the end of the twentieth century, fast-growing China was presented with a real opportunity to gain the upper hand in the China–Japan relationship for the first time in centuries. In Tokyo, the fear was now of 'Japan-passing' rather than Japan-bashing – in other words, the declining importance of Japanese concerns *vis-à-vis* an overarching American and global preoccupation with China (Hook *et al.,* 2001: 171–2). The Japanese have had to come to terms with a newly downgraded status as only the second most powerful player in the Asia–Pacific. This status was heralded by the extremely successful Beijing Olympics in 2008, an event which echoed and arguably surpassed earlier 'coming of age' Asian Olympiads in Tokyo (1964) and Seoul (1988).

The economies of China and Japan have become closely interwoven in recent decades, as Japan began outsourcing much of its industrial production to lower-cost plants in China, while China provided the market for around 19 per cent of Japanese exports by 2011. Richard Samuels argues that while economic relations between China and Japan flourished in the new millennium, 'Japan responded to the threat of Chinese regional dominance with characteristic ambiguity and a studied ambivalence about its continued dependence on the United States' (2008: 166). Japan had sought to gain the upper hand over China through engagement in multilateral fora such as ASEAN+3 and the East Asian Community (EAC), but was consistently outflanked by more adroit Chinese diplomacy. Meanwhile, both countries were boosting their medium-range military capabilities in ways that potentially threatened one another. The Japanese Defence Ministry has engaged in extensive planning for three possible Chinese invasion scenarios (Samuels, 2008: 169). Japan has also considerably boosted maritime capabilities, partly by investing heavily in the Coast Guard, which is not technically part of the self-defence forces and so allow for 'off-budget' expenditures. China may be catching up but, for the time being, Japanese forces remain better equipped, and retain greater strike capabilities. Tensions between the two countries have emerged at various junctures. In 2005, some Japanese tourists in China were harassed by protestors objecting to Koizumi's visits to the controversial Yasukuni Shrine, a focal point of ultra-nationalist sentiments. In 2010, the Japanese detained the

**Illustration 8.1 Anti-Chinese demonstrations**

captain of a Chinese fishing boat in disputed waters; in response, Chinese government briefly suspended high-level contacts with Japan, testifying to a considerable degree of underlying tension. These tensions have the potential to make closer cooperation between the two countries more difficult, and provide a significant foreign policy challenge to a DPJ administration that has proved less than adept in handling tricky bilateral problems with both the United States and China. Anti-Chinese protests have occurred intermittently in Japan, reflecting a mixture of nationalist sentiment and fears fuelled by what some Japanese commentators see as an increasingly bellicose stance by Beijing (Illustration 8.1).

## Japan and North Korea

Japan is very close geographically to North Korea, and has a lot to lose from political instability on the Korean peninsula. From 1990 onwards, talks between Japan and North Korea began over possible normalization of relations between the two countries. A prominent supporter of a 'soft' line on North Korea was former LDP power-broker Shin Kanemaru, who was a leading figure in initiating talks with the regime. The Japan Socialist Party also had quite close connections with North Korea. In 1993, there were claims that North Korea had tested a medium-range missile in the Sea of Japan, leading to increased tension in the bilateral relationship. Since the death of Stalinist dictator Kim Il-Sung in 1994, the future of North Korea has been clouded by uncertainties. His lacklustre son Kim Jong-il failed to establish a clear sense of direction for the totalitarian 'hermit kingdom', which engaged in erratic bursts of sabre-rattling, and resisted numerous attempts at engagement by the international community. There have been persistent reports of tensions within the regime, and alarms over the country's nuclear programme have been coupled with problems of food shortages and famine. Amongst the Korean community in Japan there is evidence that loyalty to North Korea and membership of the pro-Pyongyang organization Chongryun is declining as the North Korean regime appears increasingly isolated and fossilized.

In 2002, Japanese Prime Minister Junichiro Koizumi made an historic visit to North Korea and held summit talks with Kim Jong-il, aimed at the normalization of bilateral relations. Such a step was hindered by the fact that thirteen Japanese citizens – including schoolchildren – had been mysteriously kidnapped by North Korea in the 1970s, apparently to provide information about Japanese society, and to be trained as spies. Worse still, it soon emerged that eight of the kidnap victims had since died in unexplained circumstances. This bizarre episode aroused profound anxieties about the real character of the Pyongyang regime, and its intentions towards Japan. Japan's 'soft' diplomatic approach – sending its leader to North Korea, and agreeing to an anodyne joint declaration omitting all reference to crucial issues concerning abductions, spy ships and nuclear inspections – was a risky strategy which did not play well with the Japanese public.

To a large extent, Japan has adopted a wait-and-see policy on North Korea, letting the United States take the lead, and playing little active role in the six-party talks (involving North and South Korea, the US, China, Japan and Russia) held intermittently between 2003 and 2007. The unpredictable and intermittently hostile Pyongyang regime poses the most immediate military threat faced by Japan, as evidenced by incidents such as North Korea's torpedoing a South Korean fishing boat in March 2010 – killing 46 men – and fatal artillery attacks on Yeonpyeong Island, in November 2010. However, critics assert that the Japanese defence establishment has overstated the North Korean threat as a means to justify increased military spending and to undercut the residual pacifism which remains a major element of Japanese public opinion (see Berkofsky 2010 and Hughes 2009). Hughes describes North Korea as a 'catch-all proxy threat' (2009: 303), a serviceable bogey man which can be invoked to justify greater militarization. North Korean belligerence has served to highlight tensions and contradictions in Japan's security posture and relations with the United States. In short, the supposed threat from North Korea provides useful 'cover', allowing Japan to boost defence capacities without making overt reference to the growing security challenges posed by the rise of China (Hughes, 2009: 304). Kim Jong-il himself died at the end of 2011, and the baton was duly passed to an untested successor in his late twenties, his son Kim Jong-un. The political uncertainty produced by the succession makes North Korea the continuing focus of Japanese security anxieties.

## Aid policy

Whereas many other international aid programmes target poor countries (the least among less-developed countries, or LLDCs) for the greatest support, Japan has pumped huge amounts of development aid into countries with relatively high living standards, which also happen to be major prospective or actual markets for Japanese goods and services. Japan became a significant aid donor in the 1960s, and a series of 'aid-doubling' plans which began with Fukuda in 1977 made Japan the world's largest ODA (overseas development aid) provider by 1989, a status it retained for ten years in succession. However, by 2009 Japan had slipped to fifth place globally (after the USA, France, Germany and the UK), reflecting the country's difficult economic position (Statistics Bureau, 2011). Earlier high figures partly reflected the rising value of the yen, and Söderberg notes that if Japanese aid was measured as a proportion of GNP, Japan ranked only number 17 among donor countries. (Söderberg, 1996: 35). There are also questions about the quality of Japan's aid, which involves a higher proportion of loans to grants than that of any other donor country. Around half of Japan's aid is funded by government-controlled investments such as Japanese postal savings accounts, investments that require returns (Söderberg, 1996: 40).

The Japanese government formerly used an unofficial formula of 7:1:1:1 to assign development aid to Asia, Africa, Latin America and the Middle East (Söderberg, 1996: 34), though aid to Asia had declined to below 50 per cent of the total aid budget by the time of the 1997 Asian financial crisis. Since the crisis, Asian aid briefly again surpassed 50 per cent of total ODA, reflecting a renewed concern with the stability and vitality of Japan's neighbours.

Historically, around 40 per cent of Japanese ODA has been directed into economic infrastructure (notably in the transportation and energy sectors), a much higher proportion than most other donors. Aid has regularly been used as a 'soft power' means of countering criticism of Japan – such as by the Arab world during the 1970s oil crisis – and of reducing 'Japan-bashing' in Asia and elsewhere. Compared with other donor countries, Japan is much more inclined to view ODA as an instrument of broader trade and economic policies. Certainly, there was a feeling in Japanese aid circles – based on the experience of Japan and the newly industrializing economies (NIEs) – that industrialization and better infrastructure were ultimately the keys to effective economic development. Söderberg argues that 'ODA became a tool, not only for promoting the export efforts of recipient countries, but also for restructuring Japanese industry' (1996: 72). The business community exerts significant influence over the disbursement of aid. As Cronin writes:

> The essence of the concept is the co-ordination of ODA, commercial lending and private investment to promote a division of economic labour as envisioned in the Japanese 'flock of geese' metaphor for the respective roles of Japan, the Asian NIEs and the developing countries of Asia. (Cronin, 1991: 54–5)

This scheme envisioned a three-tiered division of labour, with Japan on top, followed by the NIEs, and then ASEAN plus China. Aid is used, not simply on specific infrastructure projects, but to help create 'structural complementarities with the Japanese economy' (Pyle, 1996b: 135). However, Carol Lancaster has argued that Japanese ODA should not be simplistically typecast as the loyal sidekick of the country's economic interests. ODA policy has been extremely dynamic in recent decades, buffeted both by domestic and international pressures, and characterized by frequent changes of direction in response to current fads (Lancaster, 2009).

In 1992, Japan adopted an ODA charter emphasizing issues such as the preservation of peace, democratization, human rights and the environment as criteria for awarding aid, stipulations which have not been uniformly applied. The mixed record of the ODA charter illustrates that aid is not a one-way street, but a complex process that involves negotiations and bargaining between the Japanese agencies and recipient governments. In recent years, Japan's approach to aid has been increasingly 'two-track'. On the one hand, the long-standing emphasis on infrastructure projects has continued; on the other hand there has been a growth in 'people-centred soft' aid, often emphasizing social and environmental issues and often involving work with Japanese, international and local NGOs (Katada, 2002: 321). This dual approach reflects the two political constituencies in Japan that support high levels of ODA expenditure: the business sector represented by MITI, and the wider public represented by the Ministry of Foreign Affairs. Katada argues that the existence of this 'second track' of ODA based on humanitarian principles is now firmly embedded, and reflects a genuine change in Japan's ODA policy (Katada, 2002: 341–2).

## Trade and investment

Japan has enormous overseas investments, having shifted much of its manufacturing capacity to Asia, Europe and North America from the 1970s onwards. In areas ranging from car manufacturing to electronics, computer-related technology, and international finance, Japan has gained a powerful global position. At the same time, Japan has come under considerable criticism from trade partners – especially the United States – for creating obstacles to inward investment and trade. (A summary of Japan's exports and imports by country is shown in Figure 8.1.)

Japan has been accused of protectionist practices, and the creation of 'invisible tariff barriers' to block imports. Japanese trade negotiators frequently resorted to laughable forms of special pleading; one of the most notorious was a refusal to permit the import of American-made skis, on the grounds that they were not suitable for Japanese snow. Former US trade negotiator Clyde Prestowitz argues that: 'To some extent, Japan's success has been derived from its ability to use the international system without conforming to it or accepting its burdens' (Prestowitz, 1988: 313). Nevertheless, he insisted that viewing Japan's trade practices as 'unfair' was to miss the point: the United States could not persist in trying to change Japan's economy to a free market system. At the same time, the phenomenon of

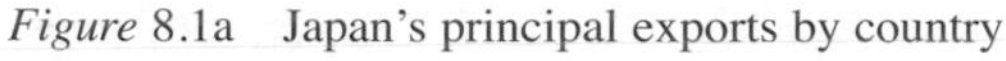

*Figure* 8.1a Japan's principal exports by country

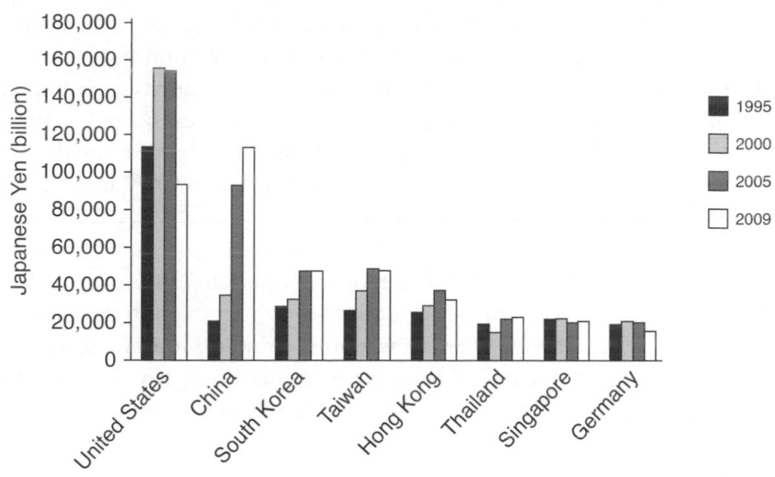


*Source*: Ministry of Finance, Japanese top 10 exports by country http://www.customs.go.jp/toukei/suii/html/data/fy4.pdf.

*Figure* 8.1b Japan's principal imports by country

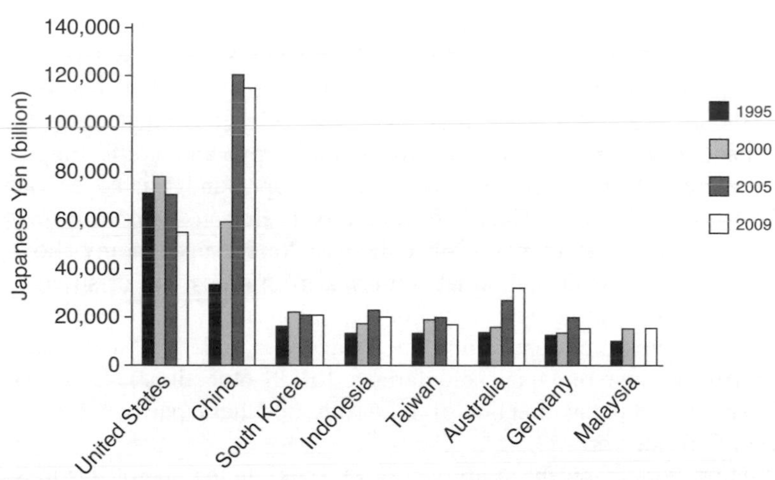


*Source*: Ministry of Finance, Japanese top 10 imports by country http://www.customs.go.jp/toukei/suii/html/data/y5.pdf.

gaiatsu, or 'foreign pressure' to alter trade and business practices, became widespread in the 1980s, when trade disputes were souring US–Japan relations. Some politicians in the USA – faced with factory closures and job losses in their home states – seized on the writings of 'revisionist' scholars with a more critical perspective on Japan (including Chalmers Johnson, Karel van Wolferen and Clyde Prestowitz), calling for tougher treatment of Japanese business. Revisionists and their self-proclaimed supporters were labelled by pro-Japan analysts as 'Japan-bashers'.

Mikanagi argues that three changes in the global political economy forced Japan to change its foreign economic policies since the 1980s: declining American tolerance for countries which exploited the open US market while closing their own markets; increasing pressures for deregulation as a means of sustaining economic growth, without replicating previous inflationary cycles; and faster pace of regional economic integration, as evidenced by developments with NAFTA and the EU (Mikanagi, 1996: 9–12).

APEC, formed in 1991, brings together Japan, the USA, Canada, Australia, South Korea, China and the ASEAN countries in a grouping of 21 members. Although it aims to promote trade between member states, it is not conceived as a protectionist regional bloc. One motive for establishing APEC was a desire by the USA and Australia to pre-empt Malaysian-backed moves for an East Asian Economic Caucus (EAEC), which would have excluded western countries. Such a bloc would have challenged NAFTA. Whereas an EAEC would have provided Japan with scope to play a leading regional role, APEC's multilateral format offered limited scope for Japanese influence. In other words, while Europe and North America have created strong regional trading blocs, Japan and Asia have much less formalized ties. The USA generally prefers to deal with trade partners on a bilateral basis, since the vast American economy allows it to negotiate with individual countries from a position of strength. Since doing nothing was an untenable option in the face of sustained external pressures, and since an Asian bloc failed to materialize (partly because of Japanese deference to US objections), Japan has been nudged in the direction of increasing openness, partly within the APEC framework.

However, in recent years the most striking feature of Japanese trade relations has been the displacement of the United States by China as a leading source of imports and destination for exports. By 2009, China topped the USA in both categories. Japan was no longer operating in a Cold War era where the US–Japan security relationship was matched by a parallel trade dependency. In economic terms at least, Japan's huge mainland Asian neighbour now loomed larger than the former conqueror across the Pacific. Following the western financial crisis that began in 2008, China and Japan became the largest holders of US treasury bonds – in other words, the main underwriters of America's debt – giving the two countries a shared interest in ensuring global economic stability. In late 2011, the two countries began discussing a possible free trade pact which would include South Korea, despite American attempts to promote the fledgling Trans-Pacific Partnership (TPP, also known as the Trans-Pacific Strategic Economic Partnership Agreement) that would include the United States in a regional economic alliance. The TPP already includes Brunei, Chile, New Zealand and Singapore, but will not be a serious player until joined by other prospective members including the USA, Australia, Malaysia, and Vietnam; Japanese membership would be a crucial step in firming up the alliance (Pilling, 2011). Washington has long feared that sooner or later the Asian powerhouse economies will gang up to create a trading bloc that excludes the USA; it seems only a matter of time before some version of this American nightmare materializes. Were Japan to sign up for the TPP, it could signal the continuing centrality of the US–Japan alliance, and stymie efforts to create an East Asian trade bloc that excludes the United States.

## Internationalization

Since the 1980s, Japan has been pursuing an overt policy of 'internationalization', making various efforts to broaden its contacts with the wider world. The internationalization strategy (perhaps most clearly articulated during the 1982–7 Nakasone governments) identified euphemistically termed deficiencies of 'mutual understanding' as a weak point in Japan's order, which might undermine the country's international standing and competitiveness. Accordingly, numerous programmes were developed to make the Japanese people more internationally minded, and to make non-Japanese more familiar with Japan.

These programmes ranged from cultural and research activities organized by bodies such as the Japan Foundation, sister-city schemes, and the establishment of 'international centres' and international student residences in cities all over Japan, to the creation of the Japan Exchange and Teaching programme (JET) to bring large numbers of language assistants (mainly young westerners) to work in Japanese schools. While many of these projects were extremely laudable, some were simply tokenistic. The political impetus behind the policy of internationalization was arguably a nationalistic one, a continuation of the Meiji-era objective of learning from foreign countries and thereby strengthening Japan. Many internationalization programmes, particularly in their early phases, focused more on the USA and other western countries than on Japan's Asian neighbours. Japan's nationalist 'internationalizers' sought to steal the thunder from the pacifist internationalists of the left, but were incompletely successful in doing so. Today, the policy of internationalization has largely run its course. The numbers of young Japanese interested in studying or even travelling abroad have declined sharply (Illustration 8.2), and while other Asian economies have been quick to buy in foreign talent to maintain their competitive edge, the upper echelons of leading Japanese companies remain composed almost entirely of middle-aged Japanese males who have been educated solely in Japan.

**Illustration 8.2 A study abroad fair**

## Other key relationships

The Asia–Europe Summit Meeting (ASEM), inaugurated in Bangkok in 1996, represented the first attempts to create a formalized framework for relations between the European Union and the countries of East and Southeast Asia. Although ASEM has yet to evolve much beyond a talking-shop, there are logical reasons for Japan to be interested in forging strong ties with Europe in order to offset its immense military, political and psychological dependence on the United States. Nuttall argues that Japan is becoming 'more like us' – in other words, more like Europe (Nuttall, 1998: 176) – and that the EU ought to consolidate strong bilateral ties with Japan in order to preserve the multilateral system from American attempts to undermine it. However, the Japanese preoccupation with their relations with the USA makes such a development difficult to implement. At the same time, substantial Japanese investments in Europe gave Japan more reasons to pursue closer economic relations, and the umbrella of the EU facilitated such developments (Hook *et al.,* 2001: 274–5). The downside of greater trade links with Europe was greater exposure of Japan to the risks associated with the 2011–12 European debt crisis; given its own high levels of government debt, Japan was not well-equipped to contend with economic meltdowns in other parts of the developed world.

Partly in an attempt to counterbalance American influence, the DPJ briefly touted the idea of a 'British model' when they assumed power in 2009 (Harris, 2009: 82–3), suggesting changes in the role of the civil service and the cabinet government system. This reflected input from leading figures in the British Labour Party who had helped the DPJ shape its agenda. But the DPJ's early flirtations with diversifying Japan's alliances and diluting ties with the United States were short-lived.

The relationship between Russia and Japan is an important one, which has long been overshadowed by a dispute concerning the 'northern territories' – including islands off the coast of Hokkaido that were seized by the former Soviet Union at the end of the war. The Japanese have long demanded the return of these territories, and since the end of the Cold War have sought to use economic aid for Russia as a bargaining tool to support this demand. To date, however, the issue – which arouses strong nationalist feelings on both sides – remains unresolved.

## Conclusion

To a large extent, Japan remains in response mode. Like Nakasone in the 1980s, prominent conservative politicians in the new millennium have called on Japan to play a more assertive international role. In the words of Ichiro Ozawa, they urge Japan to become a 'normal nation', with more conventional military forces and a seat on the UN Security Council, willing where necessary to stand up to America (a view most explicitly expressed by maverick politician Shintaro Ishihara in his 1991 book *The Japan that Can Say No*) and to take on a leading role in Asia. The end of the Cold War (followed by the end of LDP hegemony) coincided with a broader debate over the post-war Constitution (see McCormack, 1996: 202–19). In 1994, for example, Japan's leading daily newspaper, the *Yomiuri*, produced detailed and provocative proposals for revising the Constitution, including regularizing the position of the armed forces (for a full text of this and other proposals, see Hook and McCormack, 2001: 53–176). Karel van Wolferen came out in strong support of the proposal. Meanwhile, various groups on both sides of the political spectrum advocated what McCormack calls 'creative reinterpretation': preserving the Constitution in its original form, but endowing it with new meanings (McCormack, 1996: 205). For many Japanese, however, the 'peace constitution' – and the reactive international stance that it implies – remains a sacred defence against the possible resurgence of militarism. Why tinker with a formula which has brought lasting security and prosperity in the post-war period? As Hook and McCormack observe: 'It is striking that many of those calling most vociferously for a new constitution are precisely those most responsible for subverting the old one' (2001: 41).

Many of Japan's allies take an ambivalent view of this debate. The United States would like Japan to broaden its defence roles, becoming an equal rather than a subordinate partner in the 'mutual' security alliance that links the two countries. Some Asian countries (Malaysia, for example) would like to see Japan provide an alternative to US hegemony in the Pacific, yet a reactive Japan is also very useful to the West, since a passive Japan does not challenge or threaten western interests. Asian countries such as China and South Korea remain deeply wary of Japan for historical reasons. The recession in Japan since the early 1990s, compounded by the wider Asian crisis that began in 1997, raised doubts about the implicit triumphalism of some earlier Japanese views. Assumptions that Japan was inexorably 'rising', as North America and Europe entered a period of terminal decline, were not borne out by unfolding events. Japan – with its state interventionism, powerful bureaucracy, high degree of regulation and all-pervasive hierarchies – no longer looked like an ideal model for other Asian countries to emulate.

The rise of China has also posed new challenges to Japan. The remarkable rise of Japan was partly a function of the fog of Maoism that clouded China for several decades, and as this fog is lifting and economic liberalization is proceeding apace, Japan faces the prospect of a resurgent China which could undermine any residual Japanese notions of regional leadership. Events such as the first Gulf War and the Asian currency crisis provided Japan with ample opportunities to demonstrate a more active role on the international stage – opportunities that Japan has largely failed to take. In part, the failure of Japan to move beyond a reactive mode reflects Japanese weaknesses, faced with a combination of economic recession and domestic political upheaval. The more complex terrain of international relations post-September 11 is not an easy terrain for Japan to navigate, since it involves shifting alliances, quick responses, and constant uncertainty. Confronted with increasing domestic difficulties, Japan has been forced to look inwards. The three biggest challenges faced by Japan comprise how to handle relations with the United States, epitomized by the rumbling Futenma base debacle; how to handle relations with China, exemplified by tensions in disputed territorial waters; and how to manage regional relationships, symbolized by the question of the whether to join the Trans-Pacific Partnership.

Long ago, Paul Kennedy argued that without sustained political leadership that offers a clear vision for the future, serious questions remain about Japan's status as a major power (Kennedy, 1994: 199). In the intervening decades, sustained political leadership has largely failed to emerge. With the exception of the Koizumi interlude, Japan has experienced a long series of lacklustre and short-lived premierships. Nevertheless, Richard Samuels predicts the emergence of a pragmatic 'Goldilocks' leader who will ensure that Japan gets its key bilateral ties 'just right': 'a strategic posture rooted in modesty that retains options on both the economic and military fronts. Japan will position itself neither too close to nor too far from either the United States or China' (Samuels, 2008: ix). To date, however, the DPJ has failed to produce such a leader, and the short-lived premiership of Yukio Hatoyama clearly demonstrated that the United States was not above promoting regime change for one of its closest allies.

China may be rising, and has displaced the United States as Japan's top trading partner, but the Americans still literally called the shots when a Japanese prime minister adopted a strong stance on the Okinawa bases issue. The struggle between America and China to shape Japan's future will largely define the future of the Pacific in the decades to come.

# 9

# Conclusion

Evaluating, summarizing, and assessing contemporary Japan is a highly contentious business. At the beginning of the new millennium, Japan seemed to have lost the remarkable sense of purpose and direction that characterized its earlier post-war history. From the ashes of the American bombing, and the humiliations of defeat and Occupation, the Japanese successfully recreated themselves as a major nation. By the 1980s, Japan was challenging America's place in the sun, and appeared poised to become the world's 'number one' economic giant. The rest of the world looked on with awe as Japan gained a dominant economic position in the Asia-Pacific region, and began exporting productive capacity to Europe and North America as well. Yet Japan became more than simply an economic superpower. Many features of Japanese society, ranging from world-beating life expectancy to extraordinarily high levels of literacy and exceptionally low incidences of crime, attracted enormous international attention. A whole literature sprang up with a 'learn from Japan' theme, as people sought to discover what 'lessons' could be derived from the Japanese experience, and how far Japan's social and economic successes could be replicated elsewhere.

Interpretations of Japan's remarkable achievements have varied widely. Given the country's troublesome terrain and paucity of natural resources, Japan was hardly an obvious candidate for the status of economic superpower. Clearly, the answers had to lie primarily with Japan's people, rather than with the land itself. A review of modern Japanese history reveals a people not given to making a drama out of a crisis. Perhaps more than any other people in the world, the Japanese have succeeded in turning calamities into opportunities, in making the most of bad situations. Faced with seemingly disastrous predicaments in 1853 and 1945, the Japanese won through adversity to assume great power status. While it is possible to offer cultural interpretations for these responses, there was clearly a strong element of political will involved. Central political institutions were able to mould and shape national purpose, manipulating national symbols (such as the Emperor from 1931–45), forging policies which united the public and private sectors (as with MITI during the 1950s), and devising social contracts to ensure the implementation of core agendas (as with Ikeda's income-doubling policy during the early 1960s). Japanese growth was aided by a number of favourable international factors, including the onset of the Cold War, the availability of raw materials, and the existence of ready markets for industrial exports.

Whether or not one accepts the description of early post-war Japan as a 'developmental state', there is little doubt that during this period Japan saw an unusual degree of elite-level coordination which straddled the bureaucracy, the political parties and the corporate world. This elite collaboration was facilitated by the long one-party reign of the Liberal Democratic Party, from 1955 to 1993; many senior LDP figures had entered politics after bureaucratic careers, and the party was largely funded by big corporate donors. During the high-growth decades of the 1950s and 1960s, these alliances were extremely remunerative for all concerned. The LDP and its allies were highly successful in coopting and suppressing opposition and resistance: breaking up or buying off unions, riding roughshod over protest movements such as the 1960 *Anpo* rally, and pacifying the burgeoning citizens' movements with new legislation on environmental issues.

Japan's period of high growth effectively ended with the 1970s oil shocks, and the boom years of the late 1980s 'bubble economy' were based more on the rising values of Japan's currency, shares and real estate than upon any surge in productivity. Japan's economy seemed to stumble at the very point when the long-standing goal of 'catching up' with western industrialized countries had been surpassed. Having overtaken most of Europe and North America in terms of industrial efficiency, where should Japan go next? Japan had become the world's industrial economy par excellence, yet meanwhile the global economy was shifting away from manufacturing as knowledge and information-based service industries moved centre-stage. Building computers was now less important than devising the software on which they operated. Working practices which had served Japan well during the first and second industrial eras – such as seniority-based pay, reliance on in-house training, and recruiting managers from within an organization rather than bringing in specialist expertise – were less suited to the faster-changing 'third wave' industrial revolution. Japan lacked workers trained in independent thinking and problem-solving, and lacked the kind of corporate structures within which quick-witted staff could rapidly rise to positions of influence. The corporate culture of most Japanese organizations, with its emphases on hierarchism and deference to superiors, sat uneasily with the ethos of the new knowledge-based society and information economy. (See Illustration 9.1.)

Structural corruption is not new and neither is it unique to Japan. Nevertheless, the economic dynamism that characterized the bubble era generated enormous scope for the misuse of funds and resources. Problems such as bad bank debts (including huge sums owed by *yakuza* front-companies), institutionalized payoffs to politicians and the systematic subversion of financial regulators created significant weaknesses in the economy. The extent of these weaknesses was clearly revealed after the Southeast Asian economies entered a period

**Illustration 9.1 Shinjuku at night**

of crisis from 1997 onwards. Although it has been argued that corruption had some positive impacts on Japan's economic and political order during the 'catch-up' period, there is growing evidence that institutionalized corruption had begun to seriously undermine Japan's impressive achievements by the 1980s. As the full effects of the banking crisis began to bite in the late 1990s, profitable businesses began to turn in heavy losses, and bankruptcies became endemic. Although Japan did enjoy an economic revival from 2002 to 2008, this revival could not be sustained and by the second decade of the new millennium Japan has the highest levels of public debt of any developed country.

Japanese society clearly has many core strengths which helped sustain and nurture economic growth and transformation during the post-war period, and many observers have commented on the capacity of Japanese people to subordinate individual needs and wishes to the collective good. Whether this capacity derives from inherent cultural qualities (as some argue), or whether 'groupism' was actually an ideology manufactured and fostered by the state for the purposes of social control (as others insist), the end results have been extremely impressive. Divorce rates have been very low, people live longer than elsewhere in the world, and levels of popular satisfaction have been high, with most people seeing themselves as middle class.

The post-war period has seen numerous positive social developments in Japan: women have gained more independence and greater career opportunities, the position of minority groups has somewhat improved, people's outlooks have become rather more internationalized, and living standards have risen sharply. At the same time, there is a dark side to Japanese society: the falling birthrate, the low quality of family life for many people, preoccupations with futile consumerism, and the apparent alienation of some young people, especially those who are low educational achievers. Social mobility remains limited; there is a big gap between the wealth of Kanto and Kansai, and the relative deprivation of rural areas; discrimination of various kinds flourishes; and disturbing episodes such as the Aum Shinrikyo sect's murderous gas attacks in 1994 and 1995 seem to hint at darker forces stirring beneath the surface of society. The rise of 'freeters', young people with no clear career path or prospects, reflects some troubling trends. Sociologists are expressing growing dissatisfaction with traditional ways of describing and classifying Japanese society, a society which appears to contain both highly successful and acutely dysfunctional elements.

Japan's political order is also difficult to classify. On the one hand Japan has all the formal institutional prerequisites of a modern liberal democracy, yet at the same time there is little doubt that bureaucrats enjoy much greater degrees of formal and informal power in the Japanese system than in most other democracies. Japanese party politicians play an important role, but ministerial authority is weak, and the prime minister has very limited central control over the mechanisms of government. The Japanese model of elite governance is one that entails an exceptional degree of mutual back-scratching by ministers, party grandees, top civil servants and corporate leaders. Although this cosy elite collaboration may have served Japan well during the high-growth era, an unhealthy degree of collusion and cronyism had penetrated the system by the time of Tanaka's premiership in the 1970s. Despite the evident need for greater transparency and self-criticism on the part of the political elite, reforming the lumbering remnants of the 1955 system has so far proved an uphill struggle.

The most significant recent development in Japanese politics was the decisive electoral victory of the Democratic Party of Japan over the Liberal Democratic Party in 2009, the culmination of an extended political transition first evident during the LDP's brief ouster in 1993–4. The rise of the DPJ reflected growing public frustration with the complacency of LDP rule, and collusive relationships between politicians, bureaucrats and business leaders. The DPJ campaigned on a reformist platform, calling for a change in the US–Japan security relationship and for close scrutiny of budgetary appropriations favouring vested interests. Yet the new government rapidly proved a disappointment, and disillusionment quickly followed. Many Japanese voters, especially younger people and those in urban areas, no longer had any fixed party loyalties and could easily be swayed by short-term valence issues. Election manifestos and modes of campaigning have become more significant, and parties are under pressure to field a more diverse range of candidates than before. There is considerable public frustration at the emergence of a hereditary political elite – many Diet seats are now passed from father to son – which has become extremely wealthy and largely removed from the real lives of ordinary people. Japan's newfound political volatility means that future election results will be difficult to predict.

Japan's political elite does not operate in a vacuum, but has to respond to pressures from various elements of civil society. However, many features of Japanese society help to insulate the elite from vociferous public criticism and pressures. Japan's education system tends to encourage obedience and conformity, rather than an attitude of critical questioning. Policing methods and the workings of the criminal justice system, though rarely draconian, broadly privilege the power of the state over the rights of the individual. By the 1990s, the union movement was weak and internally divided, and even once powerful public-sector unions such as the teachers' union had become a shadow of their former bolshie selves. The media, despite regularly (perhaps even ritually) exposing juicy scandals, continues to enjoy highly ambiguous relationships with holders of political power. The big-five Japanese newspaper groups rarely engage in the kind of adversarial roles played by their counterparts in some Southeast Asian or western countries. Protest movements, both of the radical kind and of the milder 'citizens' variety, were widespread in Japan during the 1960s and 1970s, yet these protests appeared to decline greatly in importance during the last two decades of the twentieth century. The economic benefits of the high-growth era and the later 'bubble' period provided the Japanese state with abundant resources to buy off (or coopt) sources of dissent. Whether public protests will re-emerge in the face of sustained recession remains to be seen. Nevertheless, it could well be argued that elite mismanagement of the economic and political order in the post-catch-up era has been facilitated by a relatively tame (or tamed) civil society.

Japan's main preoccupation is now with domestic concerns, and economic and political problems at home make it difficult for opinion makers to address long-term questions about Japan's international role. Japan remains an incomplete superpower, hindered from remilitarization by constitutional limitations, and by unpleasant wartime memories. In recent decades, there were signs of a new global assertiveness as politicians such as Nakasone, Ozawa and Koizumi pushed for the 'normalization' of Japan's nationhood. There was growing talk of amending Article 9 of the constitution, and pressing for a permanent Japanese seat on the UN Security Council. Yet this assertiveness came largely from the greater confidence generated by new-found wealth. As that wealth diminished, and supposedly 'declining' competitor economies – such as those of the United States and Europe – demonstrated more resilience than Japanese nationalists had bargained for, projections of a new and more outspoken world role for Japan had to be revised downwards. Japan has thus far failed to assume a clear leadership role even in Asia, let alone globally.

Since being overtaken as the world's second largest economy in 2010, Japan has been forced to rethink its earlier regional aspirations. The terrible March 2011 triple calamity of a tsunami, earthquake and nuclear crisis in Tohoku demonstrated Japan's continuing physical vulnerabilities and, above all, Tokyo's apparent inability to muster the necessary vision and political leadership required to turn the calamity into an opportunity for restructuring and substantive reforms.

## Interpreting Japan

This book has suggested three broad (and very over-simplified) approaches to understanding Japan: a mainstream approach, a revisionist approach, and a culturalist approach. How successfully have these approaches helped answer core questions about the nature of contemporary Japan?

The mainstream approach sees Japan as a modern liberal democracy with a largely free market economy, highly comparable with other industrialized countries, and especially with Japan's old mentor, the United States. Mainstream scholars argued that Japan was outperforming the United States and many other western countries in a variety of fields by the 1970s, including industrial production, secondary education, health and nutrition, welfare and crime prevention. As social problems have risen exponentially in the West, and as traditional manufacturing has declined sharply in the 'old' industrial powers, mainstream scholars have seen these trends as vindicating their core arguments. When the LDP lost power in 2009, mainstream political scientists could rejoice. The old accusation that Japan could not be a functioning democracy since power never changed from one party to another seemed to have been decisively rebutted. Mainstream analysts argue that Japan is showing every sign of convergence with western models as markets become more open, women and minorities are improving their standing and old hierarchies are broken down.

Nevertheless, the old taunts of the revisionists remain. Revisionists see Japan as a semi-authoritarian order with a strong tendency towards centralism. Japan's loss of political direction since 2009 seems to confirm revisionist doubts about the quality and responsiveness of Japan's representative institutions, and about the capacity of leading politicians to determine the policy agenda. These large question marks tend to confirm revisionist views that something is rotten in the state of Japan. The Japanese economic recession, coupled with the 'hollowing-out' of the manufacturing base, and the difficulties encountered by Japanese firms in the information technology era, support revisionist claims that Japan's economic ascendancy was more fortuitous than miraculous. Growing domestic social problems, such as, Japan's failure to consolidate a major international role, illustrate that Japan is not an infallible giant rising inexorably to global dominance.

While mainstream and revisionist scholars can find some support for their views from recent developments in contemporary Japan, culturalist views now face serious challenges. The heyday of culturalist views of Japan was arguably in the 1970s, when cultural explanations were frequently invoked to 'explain' Japan's remarkable recovery from wartime devastation. Features of Japanese culture and society such as groupism, consensus and hierarchy were employed to account for the monumental collective efforts made by the Japanese people to reconstruct their economy and society in the post-war period. In other words, most culturalist explanations have been one-sided, setting out to describe and account for the positive features of Japan. When Japan was seen as highly successful, culturalist explanations appeared extremely persuasive. However, recent developments seem to illustrate that Japan's social, economic and political order has serious shortcomings. Can cultural readings account for the weaknesses of Japan, as well as Japan's strengths? Might hierarchy and consensus actually become obstacles to economic success, instead of positive factors? Or do we need to question whether Japanese culture was ever genuinely characterized by features such as group identity in the first place? Clearly, scholars using cultural approaches to account for Japanese society now need to ask some new questions, and probably to engage in some new research. A fine example of such research is Robin LeBlanc's book *The Art of the Gut: Manhood, Power, and Ethics in Japanese Politics* (2010), which locates a campaign to resist the construction of a nuclear power station in a Northern Japanese city – an extremely topical theme in the wake of Fukushima – in the context of Japanese gender culture and notions of masculinity. LeBlanc demonstrates that a culturally informed analysis can transcend simplistic parodies of 'Japaneseness' and offer compelling insights into political behaviour. More such work is urgently needed.

## Conclusion

Contemporary Japan is built upon the great success story of the twentieth century. The country's post-war resurgence transformed the nature of international capitalism, overturning the received wisdom about economic development in the process. In numerous social and economic fields, Japan challenged western hegemony and set world-beating standards. Japan was admired and applauded, envied and feared, both in Asia and beyond. Across the globe, people were captivated by the ingenuity of Japanese products, and by Japan's wondrous cultural artefacts. For a brief spell in the 1980s it seemed that Japan was becoming 'number one', poised to dislodge the United States from some of its global leadership positions. Three decades later, however, Japan is an ailing samurai, 'alone and palely loitering', suffering from a dual economic and political sclerosis. The fleeting mirage of a Japanese-led 'Pacific Century' has vanished. Japan is struggling to reinvent itself as a nation, and to regain its formerly vigorous sense of national purpose.

Understanding how Japan reached its present position is very difficult; and envisaging how Japan can rise above the current impasse is even harder. There is a rich and ever-expanding literature on Japan in English, but a lot of this literature is quite partisan. To make sense of it requires a familiarity with some of the main debates and disagreements among those who have produced it. This book has tried to reduce those debates to three core positions: mainstream, revisionist and culturalist. In practice, however, many Japan specialists would reject these labels. Such terms as 'revisionist' actually describe trends or tendencies in the literature, rather than offering fully accurate descriptions of the positions adopted by particular authors. Above all, though, students of Japan should understand something of the intellectual minefield they are entering when they set foot in the contested territory of contemporary Japanese studies.

# Recommended Reading

## 1 Introduction: Themes and Debates

A general overview with a mainstream perspective can be found in Reischauer (1977); for revisionist antidotes to Reischauer, read Karel van Wolferen's iconoclastic classic (1989), and the collection of articles by Johnson (1995). A good introduction to the culturalist perspective is Benedict (1989), while Dale (1986) examines the issue of Japanese uniqueness. Useful introductory books with a politics emphasis are Stockwin (2008) and Neary (2002). On Japanese culture, see Garcia (2010).

## 2 Historical Background

Two general surveys, Pyle (1996b) and Allinson (1997) offer definitive introductory accounts of modern Japanese history. Waswo (1996) is another useful book. On the Tokugawa period, see Nakane and Shinzaburo (eds) (1990); on the Meiji period, see Gluck (1985), and on Meiji himself, Keene (2002). For more detail on nineteenth-century Japanese history, see Jansen (ed.) (1989). Nakamura (1998) is a well-regarded Japanese account of the Showa period; a good overview of Showa appears in Gluck (1992), and other essays in the same volume. On the origins of constitutionalism, see Banno (1992). For discussions of the war, see Ienaga (1978) and Dower (1992). On the atomic bomb decision, read Bernstein (1995), and other articles in the same issue of *Diplomatic History*. Bix (2000) is essential reading on Hirohito, and Dower (1999) on the Occupation.

## 3 The Changing Political Economy

On Japan's economic development, see Francks (1999); for a general account of the economy, Ito (1992) is excellent, while Argy and Stein (1997) have some more recent data. For discussions of the 'developmental-state' model, and the nature of Japanese capitalism, start with Johnson (1982). On 'economism' see McCormack (1986a). Hartcher (1997) offers a gripping if rather journalistic account of the Finance Ministry. For an iconoclastic critical view, see Katz (1998); Gao (2001) is more balanced. The essays in McKinsey and Company (2011) offer a lot of recent insights into Japan's changing political economy.

## 4 Social Structure and Social Policy

A good general text is Hendry (1995, revised edn 2003); for a revisionist perspective which views Japan in a more critical light, see Sugimoto (2010). A very influential culturalist account of Japanese society can be found in Nakane (1970). An illustrated tourist manual (Japan National Tourist Organization, 1986) offers a remarkably frank account from a Japanese perspective, as does Miyamoto (1994). The best account of Japanese consumerism is Clammer (1997). Smith (1997) deals brilliantly with the urban–rural divide, while Kelly's (2002) essay on mainstream consciousness is essential reading. Hertog (2009) on illegitimacy offers considerable insights into questions of gender and class. Religion is incisively analysed by Davis (1991).

## 5 Governing Structures

A good overview of Japan's political institutions is Stockwin (2008). For local and regional government, see Reed (1986). On the political elite, see Rothacher (1993) (whose work is partly a response to van Wolferen, 1989); on the bureaucratic elite, see Koh (1989). The best account of the policy process is Nakano (1997). Rosenbluth and Thies (2010) offer a compelling and updated analysis linking recent reforms to economic and political change in Japan.

## 6 Political Society: Parties and Opposition

The end of LDP rule in 2009 means that all earlier writings on Japanese politics are now rather outdated. An excellent general text is Stockwin (2008). On political parties, the best account is Hrebenar *et al.* (2000). The classic discussion of electoral campaigning remains Curtis (1971). To get the 'feel' of Japanese politics – with its constant back-room wheeler-dealing – see the first part of Masumi (1995), whose narrative quotes extensively from the memoirs of leading political figures. More recent developments are discussed in Rosenbluth and Thies (2010) and Reed, McElwain and Shimizu (eds) (2009). For a quick overview of the 2009 election, see McCargo (2010).

## 7 Socialization and Civil Society

For discussions of the education system, see Slater (2010), Goodman (1989) and McVeigh (1997 and 2002). The Japanese media is examined in Farley (1996) and other articles in the same volume, and McCargo (2003). Issues of social control are discussed in Mouer and Sugimoto (1989), while Bayley (1991) and McCormack (1986b) offer contrasting views on policing and the criminal justice system. Adelstein (2009) offers some remarkable – and not always very academic – insights into both the media and the police. Sato (1991) is a superb study of an anti-social subculture. Avenell (2009, 2010) offers some interesting reflections on the citizens' movements. Apter and

Sawa (1984) is a classic discussion of radical protest at Sanrizuka. The best book on civil society is Pharr and Schwartz (2003). LeBlanc's (2010) work on the campaign to resist construction of a nuclear power plant in a Northern Japanese town is the best book to be published on Japanese society and politics for some years.

## 8 Japan's External Relations

For very good general accounts of Japanese international relations, see Inoguchi (1993), and more recently Hook *et al.* (2001). George (1988) provides a very thorough discussion of the US–Japan relationship, whilst Pyle (1996a) is superb on the options and dilemmas facing Japan in the international arena. Samuels (2008), however, is now by far the best study of Japan's security dilemmas. On Japan's relations with the rest of Asia, see Cronin (1991), Khamchoo (1991) and Rose (1998). For a discussion of the changing defence position, see Katahara (1998). Hughes has a must-read article (2009) on Japan's relations with North Korea. Lancaster (2009) is invaluable on Japan's development aid policy.

## 9 Conclusion

To follow unfolding developments in Japan, the three main relevant journals are the *Journal of Japanese Studies*, *Japan Forum*, and *Social Science Japan Journal*, all of which regularly carry articles on contemporary social, political and economic issues. For many years the *Japan Echo* carried excellent short translated articles summarizing current debates, though it is currently not being published. Japan coverage is poor in most UK and US daily newspapers, but much better in the *Financial Times* and *The Economist*.

# Bibliography


ABC Radio (2009) 'Bell Tolls for Japan's Hereditary Politics', 3 September, www.radioaustralia.net.au/asiapac/stories/200909/s2676097.htm, accessed 1 April 2010.

Abe, H., M. Shindo and S. Kawato (1994) *The Government and Politics of Japan*, Tokyo: University of Tokyo Press.

Abegglen, J. (1958) *The Japanese Factory,* Glencoe, IL: The Free Press.

Allinson, G. D. (1997) *Japan's Postwar History,* Ithaca, NY: Cornell University Press.

Adelstein, J. (2009) *Tokyo Vice: An American Reporter on the Police Beat in Japan*, New York, NY: Pantheon Books.

Alexy, A. (2007) 'Deferred Benefits, Romance, and the Specter of Later-Life Divorce,' in P. Backhaus (ed.) *Familienangelegenheiten*, Munich: Verlag, 169–88.

Alford, P. and D. McNeill (2010) 'Stop The Press? The Sankei and the State of Japan's Newspaper Industry,' *The Asia-Pacific Journal: Japan Focus*, March.

Allinson, G. D. (1997) *Japan's Postwar History*, Ithaca, NY: Cornell University Press.

Alvarez-Rivera, M. (2009) 'Swept Away: Japan's LDP Suffers Crushing Parliamentary Defeat', 2 September, *Global Economy Matters,* http://globaleconomydoesmatter.blogspot.com/2009/09/swept-away-japans-ldp-suffers-crushing.html, accessed 1 April 2010.

Ames, W. L. (1981) *Police and Community in Japan,* Berkeley, CA: University of California Press.

Angel, R. C. (1989) 'Prime Ministerial Leadership in Japan: Recent Changes in Personal Style and Administrative Organization', *Pacific Affairs,* 61 (4), winter, 583–602.

Apter, D. E. and N. Sawa (1984) *Against the State: Politics and Social Protest in Japan,* Cambridge, MA: Harvard University Press.

Argy, V. and L. Stein (1997) *The Japanese Economy,* Basingstoke: Macmillan – now Palgrave Macmillan.

Asher, D. (1996) 'What Became of the Japanese "Miracle"', *Orbis,* Spring, 215–34.

Avenell, S. A. (2009) 'Civil Society and the New Civic Movements in Contemporary Japan: Convergence, Collaboration, and Transformation', *Journal of Japanese Studies* 35 (2), 247–83.

Avenell, S. A. (2010) 'Facilitating Spontaneity: The State and Independent Volunteering in Contemporary Japan' *Social Science Japan Journal* 13 (1), 69–93.

Banno, J. (1992) *The Establishment of the Japanese Constitutional System,* London: Routledge.

Bayley, D. H. (1991) *Forces of Order: Policing Modern Japan,* Berkeley, CA: University of California Press.

BBC News (2007) 'How to fund Japan's ageing society', 22 November 2007, http://news.bbc.co.uk/2/hi/asia-pacific/7101663.stm.

Befu, H. (1980) 'A Critique of the Group Model of Japanese Society', *Social Analysis,* 5/6, 29–43.

Benedict, R. (1989) *The Chrysanthemum and the Sword,* Boston, MA: Houghton Mifflin.

Berkofsky, A. (2010) *Japan-North Korea Relations, Bad and Not Getting Better*, ISPI Policy Brief No 193, July, ISPI: Milan.

Bernstein, B. J. (1995) 'Understanding the Atomic Bomb and the Japanese Surrender: Missed Opportunities, Little-known Near Disasters and Modern Memory', *Diplomatic History,* 19 (2), Spring, 227–73.

Bingham, C. F. (1989) *Japanese Government Leadership and Management,* Basingstoke: Macmillan – now Palgrave Macmillan.

Bix, H. P. (1995) 'Japan's Delayed Surrender: A Reinterpretation', *Diplomatic History,* 19 (2), Spring, 197–225.

Bix, H. P. (2000) *Hirohito and the Making of Modern Japan,* London: Duckworth.

Boyd, J. P. and R. Samuels (2005) *Nine Lives: The Politics of Constitutional Reform in Japan*, Washington, DC: East-West Center.

Brenner, R. (2002) *The Boom and the Bubble: The US in the World Economy,* London: Verso Press.

Brody, B. (2002) *Opening the Door: Immigration, Ethnicity and Globalization in Japan,* New York, NY: Routledge.

Buckley, R. (2002) *The United States in the Asia-Pacific since 1945,* Cambridge: Cambridge University Press.

Butler, D. and D. Stokes (1974) *Political Change in Britain: The Evolution of Electoral Choice*. London: Macmillan.

Cabinet Office (2010) Statistics pages, http://www.esri.cao.go.jp/index-e.html, accessed 14 February 2012.

Calder, K. E. (1993) *Strategic Capitalism,* Princeton, NJ: Princeton University Press.

Callon, S. (1995) *Divided Sun: MITI and the Breakdown of Japanese High-tech Industrial Policy 1975–93,* Stanford, CA: Stanford University Press.

Campbell, A. *et al*. (1960) *The American Voter.* Chicago, IL: University of Chicago Press.

Chaplin, S (2007) *Japanese Love Hotels: A Cultural History*, Abingdon: Routledge.

Ching, L. (1996) 'Imagining in the Empires of the Sun: Japanese Mass Culture in Asia', in *Contemporary Japan and Popular Culture*, ed. John W. Treat. London: Curzon.

Christensen, R. (2000) *Ending the LDP Hegemony: Party Cooperation in Japan,* Honolulu: University of Hawaii Press.

Clammer, J. (1997) *Contemporary Urban Japan: A Sociology of Consumption,* Oxford: Blackwell.

Constantino, R. (1989) *The Second Invasion: Japan in the Philippines,* Quezon City: Karrel.

Craig, T. (ed.) (2000) *Japan Pop! Inside the World of Japanese Popular Culture,* New York: M.E. Sharpe.

Cronin, R. P. (1991) 'Changing Dynamics of Japan's Interaction with Southeast Asia', in *Southeast Asian Affairs 1991,* Singapore: Institute of Southeast Asian Studies, 49–68.

Curtis, G. (1971) *Election Campaigning Japanese Style,* New York: Columbia University Press.

Curtis, G. (1988) *The Japanese Way of Politics,* New York: Columbia University Press.

Curtis, G. (1999) *The Logic of Japanese Politics,* New York: Columbia University Press.

Curtis, G. (2001) 'The LDP in Decline: A Second JSP', *Japan Echo,* April, 25–8.

Curtis, G. (2011a), 'Creative Destruction In Japanese Politics', in McKinsey and Company, *Reimagining Japan: The Quest for a Future that Works*, San Francisco, CA: VIZ Media, 127–32.

Curtis, G. (2011b) 'Future Directions in US-Japan Relations', paper presented at New Shimoda Conference, Revitalizing Japan-US Strategic Partnership for a Changing World, February, Tokyo JCIE, at http://www.jcie.org/researchpdfs/newshimoda/CurtisFinalE.pdf, accessed 14 February 2012.

*Daily Yomiuri* (2009) 'Budget Screeners Duck Thorny Problems', 13 November.

Dale, P. (1986) *The Myth of Japanese Uniqueness,* London: Groom Helm.

Davis, W. (1991) 'Fundamentalism in Japan: Religious and Political', in M. E. Marty and R. S. Appleby (eds), *Fundamentalisms Observed,* Chicago, IL: University of Chicago Press, 782–813.

Defence Agency, Japan (1997), 'Defence of Japan 1997', Tokyo: *Japan Times*.

Dower, J. W. (1992) 'The Useful War', in C. Gluck and S. R. Graubard (eds), *Showa: The Japan of Hirohito,* New York: Norton, 49–70.

Dower, J. W. (1995) 'The Bombed: Hiroshimas and Nagasakis in Japanese Memory', Diplomatic History, 19 (2), Spring, 275–95.

Dower, J. W. (1999) *Embracing Defeat: Japan in the Aftermath of World War II,* Harmondsworth: Allen Lane.

DPJ (2011) Official Website of the Democratic Party of Japan, http://www.dpj.or.jp/english/about_us/philosophy.html

Ducke, I. (2007) *Civil Society and the Internet in Japan*, Abingdon: Routledge.

*Earthquake Report* (2011) *Japan Tohoku Earthquake and Tsunami: CATDAT 41 Report (October 2, 2011)*, http://earthquake-report.com/2011/10/02/japan-tohoku-earthquake-and-tsunami-catdat-41-report-october-2-2011/, accessed 14 February 2012.

Egami, T. (1994) 'Politics in Okinawa since the Reversion of Sovereignty', *Asian Survey,* 34 (9), 828–40.

Emmott, B. (2011) 'Shake Out of Stagnation' in J. Kingston (ed.) *Tsunami: Japan's Post-Fukushima Future, Washington: Foreign Policy*, 139–46.

Fackler, M. (2009) 'New Leaders in Japan Seek to End Cosy Ties to Press Clubs,' *New York Times*, 21 November.

Farley, M. (1996) 'Japan's Press and the Politics of Scandal', in E. Krauss and S. Pharr (eds), *Politics and Media in Japan,* Honolulu: University of Hawaii Press, 133–63.

Feldman, O. (1993) *Politics and the News Media in Japan,* Ann Arbor, MI: University of Michigan Press.

Fitzpatrick, M. (2011) 'Galapagos Syndrome: Japan's Gaze Turns Inward', *Times Higher*, 27 January.

Flanagan, S. C. (1991a) 'Mechanisms of Social Network Influence in Japanese Voting Behavior', in S. C. Flanagan *et al., The Japanese Voter,* New Haven, CT: Yale University Press, 143–97.

Flanagan, S. C. (1991b) 'The Changing Japanese Voter and the 1989 and 1990 Elections', in S. C. Flanagan *et al., The Japanese Voter,* New Haven, CT: Yale University Press, 431–68.

Foreign Press Center (1995) *The Diet, Elections and Political Parties,* Tokyo: Foreign Press Center (supplement, 1997).

Francks, P. (1999) *Japanese Economic Development: Theory and Practice,* 2nd edn, London: Routledge.

Freeman, L. (2000) *Closing the Shop: Information Cartels and Japan's Mass Media,* Princeton, NJ: Princeton University Press.

Friman, H. R. (1996) 'Gaijinhanzai: Immigrants and Drugs in Contemporary Japan', *Asian Survey,* 36 (10), 964–77.

Fukatsu, M. (1995) 'Whither Goes the 1955 System?' *Japan Quarterly,* April–June, 163–9.

Funabashi, Y. (2011) 'March 11 – Japan's Zero Hour', in McKinsey and Company, *Reimagining Japan: The Quest for a Future that Works*, San Francisco, CA: VIZ Media, 8–14.

Furnham, A. and K. Saito (2009) 'Cross-cultural Study of Attitudes Toward and Beliefs About, Male Homosexuality,' *Journal of Homosexuality*, 56 (3), 299–318.

Gao, Bai (2001) *Japan's Economic Dilemma,* New York: Cambridge University Press.

Garcia, H. (2010) *A Geek in Japan: Discovering the Land of Manga, Anime, Zen, and the Tea Ceremony*, Tokyo: Tuttle.

Garon, S. (1997) *Molding Japanese Minds: The State in Everyday Life,* Princeton, NJ: Princeton University Press.

George, A. (1988) 'Japan and the United States: Dependent Ally or Equal Partner?' in J. A. A. Stockwin *et al., Dynamic and Immobilist Politics in Japan,* Basingstoke: Macmillan – now Palgrave Macmillan, 237–98.

Gibney, F. (1998) 'Politics and Governance in Japan', in R. Maidment, D. Goldblatt and J. Mitchell (eds), *Governance in the Asia-Pacific,* London: Routledge, 51–78.

Gluck, C. (1985) *Japan's Modern Myths,* Princeton, NJ: Princeton University Press.

Gluck, C. (1992) 'The Idea of Showa', in C. Gluck and S. R. Graubard (eds), *Showa: The Japan of Hirohito,* New York: Norton, 1–26.

Gluck, C. (2009) '*Seninkin*/Responsibility in Modern Japan', in C. Gluck and A. Lowenhaupt Tsing (eds), *Words in Motion: Towards a Global Lexicon*, Durham, NC: Duke University Press, 83–106.

Goodman, R. (1989) 'Japanese Education: A Model to Emulate?', *The Pacific Review,* 2 (1), 24–37.

Goodman, R. (1998) 'The "Japanese-Style Welfare State" and the Delivery of Personal Social Services', in R. Goodman *et al.* (eds), *The East Asian Welfare Model,* London: Routledge, 139–58.

Goold, B. (2004) 'Idealizing The Other? Western Images of the Japanese Criminal Justice System,' *Criminal Justice Ethics*, 23 (2) 14–24.

Haley, J. O. (1987) 'Governance by Negotiation: A Reappraisal of Bureaucratic Power in Japan', *Journal of Japanese Studies,* 13, Summer, 343–57.

Haley, J. O. (2006) *The Spirit of Japanese Law*, Athens, GA: University of Georgia Press, 90–122.

Hall, I. (1998) *Cartels of the Mind: Japan's Intellectual Closed Shop,* New York: Norton.

Hanami, A. K. (1993) 'The Emerging Military–Industrial Relationship in Japan and the US Connection', *Asian Survey,* 33 (6), 592–609.

Hane, Mikiso (1996) *Eastern Phoenix: Japan Since 1945,* Boulder, CO: Westview Press.

Harada, M. (2002) 'Japanese Male Gay and Bisexual Identity', *Journal of Homosexuality*, 42 (2), 77–100

Harris, T. (2009) 'How Will the DPJ Change Japan?' *Naval War College Review,* (63), 1.

Hartcher, P. (1997) *The Ministry: The Inside Story of Japan's Ministry of Finance,* London: HarperCollins.

Hastings, M. (2007) *Nemesis: The Battle for Japan, 1944–45*, London: HarperPress.

Hatoyama, Y. (2002) 'My Scenario for Defeating the Liberal Democrats', *Japan Echo,* 37–40.

Hatoyama, Y. (2009) Press Conference, 16 September, available at www.kantei.go.jp/foreign/hatoyama/statement/200909/16kaiken_e.html, accessed 1 April 2010.

Hayashi, S. and A. McKnight (2005) 'Good-bye Kitty, Hello War: The Tactics of Spectacle and New Youth Movements in Urban Japan' *Positions: East Asia Cultures Critique*, 13 (1), 87–113.

Hayes, L. (1995) *Introduction to Japanese Politics,* 2nd edn, New York: Marlowe.

Helton, W. (1966) 'Political Prospects of Soka Gakkai', *Pacific Affairs,* 37: 231–44.

Hendry. J. (1995) *Understanding Japanese Society,* London: Routledge.

Hertog, E. (2009) *Tough Choices: Bearing an Illegitimate Child in Japan*, Stanford, CA: Stanford University Press.

Herzog, P. J. (1993) *Japan's Pseudo-democracy,* Folkestone: Japan Library.

Hester, J. T. (2008), 'Datsu Zainichi-ron: An Emerging Discourse on Belonging Among Ethnic Koreans in Japan,' in Graburn, N. H. H., Ertl, J. and Tierney, R. K. (eds) *Multiculturalism in The New Japan: Crossing The Boundaries Within*, New York: Berghahn Books.

Higuchi, Y. (1997) 'Trends in Japanese Labour Markets', in Mari Sako and Hiroki Sato (eds), *Japanese Labour and Management in Transition: Diversity, Flexibility and Participation,* London: Routledge, 27–52.

Hill, P. B. E. (2003) *The Japanese Mafia: Yakuza, Law, and the State,* Oxford: Oxford University Press.

Hirata, K. (2002) *Civil Society in Japan,* New York: Palgrave.

Hoffman, D. M. (1992) 'Changing Faces, Changing Places: The New Koreans in Japan', *Japan Quarterly,* October–December, 479–89.

Hondro, M. (2010) 'Smoking Rates Falls in Japan as Tobacco Companies Seek New Markets', *Suite101.com* (online).

Hook, G. and G. McCormack (2001) *Japan's Contested Constitution: Documents and Analysis,* London: Routledge.

Hook, G. *et al*. (2001) *Japan's International Relations: Politics, Economics and Security,* London: Routledge.

Horiuchi, A. (2000) 'Japan's Bank Crisis and the Issue of Governance' in P. Drysdale (ed.), *Reform and Recovery in East Asia,* London: Routledge, 28–58.

Horsley, W. and R. Buckley (1990) *Nippon, New Superpower: Japan Since 1945,* London: BBC Books.

Hoshi, T. and A. Kashyap (2001) *Corporate Financing and Governance in Japan,* Cambridge, MA: MIT Press.

Hrebenar, R. and A. Nakamura (2000) The Liberal Democratic Party', in R. Hrebenar *et al., Japan's New Party System,* Boulder, CO: Westview Press, 85–147.

Hrebenar, R. *et al*. (2000), *Japan's New Party System,* Boulder, CO: Westview Press.

Hughes, C. W. (2009) '"Super-Sizing" the DPRK Threat: Japan's Evolving Military Posture and North Korea,' *Asian Survey*, 49 (2), 291–311.

Hunziker, S. and I. Kamimura (1996) *Kakuei Tanaka: A Political Biography of Modern Japan,* Singapore: Times.

Ienaga, S. (1978) *The Pacific War, 1931–1945: A Critical Perspective on Japan's Role in World War II,* New York: Random House.

Iida, Y. (2005) 'Beyond the 'Feminization of Masculinity': Transforming Patriarchy With the "Feminine" in Contemporary Japanese Youth Culture', *Inter-Asia Cultural Studies*, 6 (1), 56–74.

Ijiri, H. (1996) 'Sino-Japanese Controversy since the 1972 Diplomatic Normalization', in C. Howe (ed.), *China and Japan: History, Trends, and Prospects,* Oxford: Oxford University Press.

Ikeda, K. *et al*. (2007) *A Comparative Survey of Democracy and Development. Japan Country Report, Second Wave of Asian Barometer Survey,* Working Paper No. 32, Taipei, Asian Barometer Project Office, National Taiwan University and Academia Sinica, available at www.asianbarometer.org/newenglish/publications/workingpapers/no.32.pdf.

Inoguchi, T. (1993) *Japan's International Relations,* London: Pinter.

Ishida, H. (1993) *Social Mobility in Contemporary Japan,* Basingstoke: Macmillan – now Palgrave Macmillan.

Ishihara, S. (1991) *The Japan That Can Say No,* New York: Simon & Schuster.

Ishii-Kuntz, M. (2008) 'Sharing of Housework and Childcare in Contemporary Japan', Paper for UN Division for the Advancement of Women, available at http://www.un.org/womenwatch/daw/egm/equalsharing/EGM-ESOR-2008-EP4Masako%20Ishii%20Kuntz.pdf.

ISS (2011) *The Military Balance*, London: Institute of Strategic Studies.

Ito, T. (1992) *The Japanese Economy,* Cambridge, MA: MIT Press.

Ito, M. (2009) 'Tying The Knot: Marriage Ever Changing Institution', *Japan Times*, 3 November.

Iwao N. (1998) 'Reforming the Catch-up Economy', in F. Gibney (ed.), *Unlocking the Bureaucrat's Kingdom: Deregulation and the Japanese Economy,* Washington, DC: Brookings Institution, 30 10.

Jain, P. C. (1991) 'Green Politics and Citizen Power in Japan: the Zushi Movement', *Asian Survey,* 31 (6), 559–75.

Jansen, M. B. (ed.) (1989) *The Cambridge History of Japan, Vol. 5, The Nineteenth Century,* Cambridge: Cambridge University Press.

Japan Institute of Labour (1997), *Japanese Working Life Profile 1996–97: Labor Statistics,* Tokyo: JIL.

Japan National Tourist Organization (1986) *Salaryman in Japan,* Tokyo: JNTO.

*Japan Times* (2008) 'Random Attack Claims Okayama Official: Teen Held In Deadly Train Platform Push,' 27 March.

Johnson, C. (1982) *MITI and the Japanese Miracle: The Growth of Industrial Policy, 1925–1975,* Stanford, CA: Stanford University Press.

Johnson, C. (1986) 'Tanaka Kakuei, Structural Corruption and the Advent of Machine Politics in Japan', *Journal of Japanese Studies,* 12 (1), 1–28.

Johnson, C. (1987) 'Political Institutions and Economic Performance: The Government–Business Relationship in Japan, South Korea and Taiwan', in F. C. Deyo (ed.), *The Political Economy of the New Asian Industrialism,* Ithaca, NY: Cornell University Press.

Johnson, C. (1995) *Japan: Who Governs? The Rise of the Developmental State,* New York: Norton.

Johnson, C. (1998) 'Economic Crisis in East Asia: the Clash of Capitalisms', *Cambridge Journal of Economics,* 22, 653–61.

Johnson, D. M. (2009), 'Early Returns from Japan's New Criminal Trials', *The Asia-Pacific Journal*: *Japan Focus*, September.

Johnson, D. T. (2002) *The Japanese Way of Justice: Prosecuting Crime in Japan*, New York: Oxford University Press.

Johnson, S. (1994) 'Continuity and Change in Japanese Electoral Patterns: the 1993 General Election in Yamanashi', *Japan Forum,* 6 (1), 8–20.

Jolivet, M. (1997) *Japan: The Childless Society?* London: Routledge.

Jones, R. S. (1988), 'The Economic Implications of Japan's Aging Population', *Asian Survey,* 28 (9), 958–69.

Kabashima, I. (2000) 'The LDP'S "Kingdom of the Regions" and the Revolt of the Cities', *Japan Echo,* October, 22–8.

Kabashima, I. (2001) 'The Rise of the Anti-LDP Independents', *Japan Echo,* June, 9–15.

Kakehashi, K. (2007) *Letters from Iwo Jima*, London: Weidenfeld and Nicolson.

Kamata, S. (1982) *Japan in the Passing Lane: An Insider's Account of Life in a Japanese Auto Factory,* London: Counterpoint.

Kaplan, D. E. and A. Marshall (1996) *The Cult at the End of the World: The Incredible Story of Aum,* London: Hutchinson.

Katada. S. (2002) 'Japan's Two-Track Aid Approach', *Asian Survey,* 42 (2), 320–42.

Katahara, E. (1998) 'Japan', in C. E. Morrison (ed.), *Asia Pacific Security Outlook 1998,* Tokyo: Japan Center for International Exchange, 65–76.

Katz, R. (1998) *Japan: The System That Soured,* New York: M.E. Sharpe.

Kawai, K. (1960) *Japan's American Interlude,* Chicago, IL: University of Chicago Press.

Kawanishi, H. (1986) 'The Reality of Enterprise Unionism', in G. McCormack and Y. Sugimoto (eds), *Democracy in Contemporary Japan,* New York: M.E. Sharpe, 138–56.

Keehn, E. B. (1990) 'Managing Interests in the Japanese Bureaucracy: Informality and Discretion', *Asian Survey,* 30 (11), 1021–37.

Keene, D. (2002) *Emperor of Japan: Meiji and His World 1852-1912,* New York: Columbia University Press.

Kelly, B. (1998) 'Japan's Empty Orchestras: Echoes of Japanese Culture in the Performance of Karaoke', in D. Martines (ed.), *The Worlds of Japanese Popular Culture,* Melbourne: Cambridge University Press, 75–87.

Kelly, W. (2002) 'At the Limits of New Middle Class Japan: Beyond Mainstream Consciousness,' in L. S. O. Zunz and N. Hiwatari (eds), *Social Contracts Under Stress: The Middle Classes of America, Europe and Japan at the Turn of the Century*, New York: Russell Sage Foundation.

Kennedy, P. (1994) 'Conclusion - Japan: A Twenty-First-Century Power?', in C. C. Garby and M. Brown Bullock (eds), *Japan: A New Kind of Superpower?* Washington, DC: Woodrow Wilson Center Press, 193–9.

Khamchoo, C. (1991) 'Japan's Role in Southeast Asian Security: Plus ca Change . . .', *Pacific Affairs,* 64 (1), 7–22.

Knight, J. (1994) 'Rural Revitalization in Japan: Spirit of the Village and Taste of the Country', *Asian Survey,* 34 (7), 34–46.

Kobayashi, Y. (2000) 'Reading the Election Results', *Japan Echo,* October, 29–32.

Koh, B. C. (1989) *Japan's Administrative Elite,* Berkeley, CA: University of California Press.

Kohno, M. (1997) *Japan's Postwar Party Politics,* Princeton, NJ: Princeton University Press.

Koll, J. (2011) 'Poised for Prosperity' in McKinsey & Company (eds), *Reimagining Japan: The Quest for a Future that Works,* San Francisco, CA: VIZ Media, 114–20.

Kosugi, R. (2006) 'Youth Employment in Japan's Economic Recovery: "Freeters" and "NEETs", *The Asia Pacific Journal: Japan Focus.*

Krauss, E. S. (1988) 'The 1960's Japanese Student Movement in Retrospect', in G. Bernstein and H. Fukui (eds), *Japan and the World,* London: Macmillan – now Palgrave Macmillan, 95–115.

Krauss, E. S. and B. L. Simcock (1980) 'Citizens' Movements: The Growth and Impact of Environmental Protests in Japan', in K. Steiner, E. S. Krauss and S. C. Flanagan (eds), *Political Opposition and Local Politics in Japan,* Princeton, NJ: Princeton University Press, 187–227.

Krauss, E. S. and M. Muramatsu (1988) 'The Japanese Political Economy Today: The Patterned Pluralist Model', in D. I. Okimoto and T. P. Rohlen (eds), *Inside the Japanese System,* Stanford, CA: Stanford University Press, 208–10.

Krugman, P. (1999) 'The Return of Depression Economics', *Foreign Affairs,* 78 (1), 56–74.

Kume, I. (1998) *Disparaged Success: Labor Politics in Postwar Japan,* Ithaca, NY: Cornell University Press.

Lancaster, C. (2009) 'Japan's ODA: Naiatsu and Gaiatsu,' in D. Leheny and K. Warren (eds), *Japanese Aid and The Construction of Global Development: Inescapable Solutions*, New York: Routledge, 29–53.

Large, S. S. (1992) *Emperor Hirohito and Showa Japan: A Political Biography,* London: Routledge.

LeBlanc, R. (2010) *The Art of the Gut: Manhood, Power, and Ethics in Japanese Politics*, Berkeley, CA: University of California Press.

Liddle, J. and S. Nakajima (2000) *Rising Suns, Rising Daughters: Gender, Class and Power in Japan,* London: Zed.

Liddy, J. (2002) 'Brandname Beauties On Sale', Freezerbox.com, 14 March, http://www.freezerbox.com/archive/article.php?id=188, accessed 14 February 2012.

Lincoln, E. J. (1988) *Japan: Facing Economic Maturity,* Washington, DC: Brookings Institution.

Lincoln, E. J. (2001) *Arthritic Japan: The Slow Pace of Economic Reform,* Washington, DC: Brookings Institution.

Liu, X. (2005) 'The Hip Hop Impact on Japanese Youth Culture', *Southeast Review of Asian Studies*, 27.

Lock, M. (1996) 'Centering the Household: The Remaking of Female Maturity in Japan', in A. E. Imamura (ed.), *Re-imaging Japanese Women,* Berkeley, CA: University of California Press, 73–103.

MacDougall, T. (1988) 'The Lockheed Scandal and the High Cost of Politics in Japan', in A. Markovits and M. Silverstein (eds), *The Politics of Scandal,* New York: Holmes & Meier, 193–229.

Maclachlan, P. (2006) 'Storming the Castle: The Battle for Postal Reform in Japan.' *Social Science Japan Journal*, 9 (1), 1–18.

*Mainichi Daily News* (2010) 'No. of Crime Cases in Japan in 2010 Likely To Hit 23-Yr Low', 17 December.

Mansfield, M. (1989) 'Japan and the US: Sharing the Destinies', *Foreign Affairs,* 38 (2), 3–15.

Martin, S. L. (2011) *Popular Democracy in Japan: How Gender and Community are Changing Modern Electoral Politics*, Ithaca, NY: Cornell University Press.

Masumi, J. (1995) *Contemporary Politics in Japan,* Berkeley, CA: University of California Press.

Matsui, S. (2011) *The Constitution of Japan: A Contextual Analysis*, Oxford: Hart.

Matsumoto, K. and J. Shoji (2002) 'Critiquing Herbert Bix's "Hirohito"', *Japan Echo,* December: 64–8.

Matsutani, M. (2010) 'Shedding Light On Death Penalty: Japan Part of a Shrinking Roster of Nations With Capital Punishment,' *Japan Times*, 28 August.

McCargo, D. (1998) 'Elite Governance: Business, Bureaucrats and the Military', in R. Maidment, D. Goldblatt and J. Mitchell (eds), *Governance in the Asia-Pacific,* London: Routledge, 126–49.

McCargo, D. (2003) *Media and Politics in Pacific Asia,* London: Routledge.

McCargo, D. (2010) 'An Incomplete Change of Course: Japan's Landmark 2009 Lower-House Elections and Their Aftermath', *Representation*, 46 (4), 471–9.

McCargo, D. and Lee Hyon-suk (2010) 'Japan's Political Tsunami: What's Media Got To Do With It?' *International Journal of Press/Politics* 15(2), 236–45.

McCormack, G. (1986a) 'Beyond Economism: Japan in a State of Transition', in G. McCormack and Y. Sugimoto (eds), *Democracy in Contemporary Japan,* New York: M.E. Sharpe, 39–64.

McCormack, G. (1986b) 'Crime, Confession and Control in Contemporary Japan', in G. McCormack and Y. Sugimoto (eds), *Democracy in Contemporary Japan,* New York: M.E. Sharpe, 186–94.

McCormack, G. (1996) *The Emptiness of Japanese Affluence,* New York: M.E. Sharpe.

McCormack, G., S. Kunitoshi and U. Etsuko (2012) 'Okinawa, New Year 2012: Tokyo's Year End Surprise Attack', *The Asia-Pacific Journal* 10 (2), January.

McCurry, J. (2010) 'Japan's Women Toast Their Own Health As Life Expectancy Rises Again'. *The Guardian,* 1 August, available: http://www.guardian.co.uk/world/2010/aug/01/japan-women-life-expectancy-rises, accessed 14 February 2012.

McCurry, J. (2007) 'Japan enters the age of silver divorces', *The Guardian,* 18 October, available: http://www.guardian.co.uk/news/2007/oct/18/internationalnews, accessed 17 November 2010.

McCurry, J. (2010) 'Centenarians "missing" ahead of Japanese day honouring elderly', *The Guardian*, 12 August 2010, http://www.guardian.co.uk/world/2010/aug/12/japan-missing-elderly-centenarians.

McGregor, R. (1996) *Japan Swings,* St Leonards: Allen & Unwin.

McKean, M. A. (1980) 'Political Socialization Through Citizens' Movements', in K. Steiner, E. S. Krauss and S. C. Flanagan (eds), *Political Opposition and Local Politics in Japan,* Princeton, NJ: Princeton University Press, 228–73.

McKean, M. A. (1981) *Environmental Protest and Citizen Politics in Japan,* Berkeley, CA: University of California Press.

McKinsey and Company (2011) *Reimagining Japan: The Quest for a Future that Works*, San Francisco, CA: VIZ Media.

McLelland, M. (2000) *Male Homosexuality in Japan,* Richmond: Curzon.

McVeigh, B. J. (1997) *Life in a Japanese Women's College: Learning to be Ladylike,* London: Routledge.

McVeigh, B. J. (1998) *The Nature of the Japanese State: Rationality and Rituality,* London: Routledge.

McVeigh, B. J. (2002) *Japanese Higher Education as Myth,* New York: M.E. Sharpe.

Mendl, W. (1995) *Japan's Asia Policy,* London: Routledge.

Messmer, P. (2010) 'Drop in Number of Japan's Foreign Workers Amid Economic Crisis,' *The Guardian*, 3 August.

Metraux, D. A. (1995), 'Religious Terrorism in Japan: The Fatal Appeal of Aum Shinrikyo', *Asian Survey,* 35 (12), 1,140–54.

Midford, P. (2003) 'Japan's Response to Terror', *Asian Survey*, 43 (2), 329–51.
Mikanagi, Y. (1996) *Japan's Trade Policy: Action or Reaction?* London: Routledge.
Miyamoto, M. (1994) *Straightjacket Society: An Insider's Irreverent View of Bureaucratic Japan*, Tokyo: Kodansha.
Mouer, R. and Y. Sugimoto (1989) *Images of Japanese Society*, London: Kegan Paul International.
Murakami, H. (2001) *Underground: The Tokyo Gas Attack and the Japanese Psyche*, London: Panther.
Murphy, R. T. (1996) *The Weight of the Yen*, New York: Norton.
Nagata, K. (2009) 'Hereditary Politicians A Fact of Life: Some in LDP Call for Curbs on Bluebloods', *The Japan Times*, 27 April.
Nakamura, T. (1998) *A History of Showa Japan, 1926–1989*, Tokyo: University of Tokyo Press.
Nakane, C. (1970) *Japanese Society*, Berkeley, CA: University of California Press.
Nakane, C. and O. Shinzaburo (eds) (1990) *Tokugawa Japan*, Tokyo: University of Tokyo Press.
Nakano, M. (1997) *The Policy-making Process in Contemporary Japan*, Basingstoke: Macmillan – now Palgrave Macmillan.
Neary, I. (1997) 'Burakumin in Contemporary Japan', in M. Weiner (ed.), *Japan's Minorities: The Illusion of Homogeneity*, London: Routledge: 50–78.
Neary, I. (2002) *The State and Politics in Japan*, Cambridge: Polity Press.
Neill, M. (2009) 'Japan's "Herbivore Men" – Less Interested in Sex, Money,' CNN World, 5 June, available at http://articles.cnn.com/2009-06-05/world/japan.herbivore.men_1_japanese-men-men-and-women-girl-friend?_s=PM:WORLD, accessed 14 February 2012.
Noguchi, H. and Takahashi, K. (2012) 'Hurdles still high for foreign care-givers / Govt measures help, but exam success rates still lag far behind those for Japanese', Yomiuri Online 30 March 2012, http://www.yomiuri.co.jp/dy/national/T120329005997.htm.
Nuttall, S. (1998) 'Europe and Northeast Asia', in H. Maull, G. Segal and J. Wanandi (eds), *Europe and the Asia Pacific*, London: Routledge, 174–83.
O'Brien, D. M. and Y. Ohkoshi (2001) 'Stifling Judicial Independence From Within: The Japanese Judiciary', in P. H. Russell and D. M. O'Brien (eds) *Judicial Independence in the Age of Democracy: Critical Perspectives From Around the World*, University Press of Virginia, 37–61.
OECD (Organisation for Economic Co-operation and Development) (2010) 'Share of Births Outside of Marriage and Teenage Births', *OECD Family Database* [Online] available: www.oecd.org/els/social/family/database, accessed 17 November, 2010.
Oka, T. (1994) *Prying Open the Door: Foreign Workers in Japan*, Washington, DC: Carnegie Endowment for International Peace.
Okabe, M. (2001) *Cross Shareholdings in Japan*, Cheltenham: Edward Elgar.
Okano, K. and M. Tsuchiya (1999) *Education in Contemporary Japan*, Melbourne: Cambridge University Press.

Okimoto, D. I. (1989) *Between MITI and the Market,* Stanford, CA: Stanford University Press.

Osaki, T. (2011) 'Japanese Teens Not Interested in Sex', CNN GO, http://www.cnngo.com/tokyo/life/no-sex-japanese-teens-boys-increasingly-show-no-interest-521163, accessed 14 February 2012.

Ozawa, I. (1994) *Blueprint for a New Japan: The Rethinking of a Nation,* New York: Kodansha.

Parker Jr, L. C. (1984) *The Japanese Police System Today: An American Perspective,* Tokyo: Kodansha.

Passin, H. (1982) *Society and Education in Japan,* Tokyo: Kodansha.

Pekkanen, R. (2006) *Japan's Dual Civil Society: Members Without Advocates*, Stanford, CA: Stanford University Press.

Pempel, T. J. (1987) 'The Tar Baby Target: "Reform" of the Japanese Bureaucracy', in R. E. Ward and S. Yoshikazu (eds), *Democratizing Japan: The Allied Occupation,* Honolulu: University of Hawaii Press.

Pempel, T. J. (1998) *Regime Shift: Comparative Dynamics of the Japanese Political Economy,* Ithaca, NY: Cornell University Press.

Pharr, S. J. (1990) *Losing Face: Status Politics in Japan,* Berkeley, CA: University of California Press.

Pharr, S. J. and F. Schwartz (2003) *The State of Civil Society in Japan,* Cambridge: Cambridge University Press.

Pilling, D. (2011) 'Trans-Pacific Partnership: far-reaching agreement could form powerful new trade bloc, *Financial Times*, 8 November.

Police Policy Research Center (ed.) (2005) 'Japanese Community Police and Police Box System', *National Police Agency (NPA)* [Online] Available: http://www.npa.go.jp/english/index.htm, accessed 14 February 2012.

Posen, A. (1998) *Restoring Japan's Economic Growth,* Washington, DC: Institute for International Economics.

Posen, A. (2011) 'Send in the *Samurai*' *in McKinsey and Company (eds), Reimagining Japan: The Quest for a Future that Works,* San Francisco, CA: VIZ Media, *102–7*.

Potter, D. M. (1996), *Japan's Foreign Aid to Thailand and the Philippines,* Basingstoke: Macmillan – now Palgrave Macmillan.

Prestowitz, C. V. (1988) *Trading Places: How America Allowed Japan to Take the Lead,* Tokyo: Tuttle.

Pyle, K. B. (1996a) *The Japanese Question: Purpose and Power in a New Era,* 2nd edn, Washington, DC: AEI Press.

Pyle, K. B. (1996b) *The Making of Modern Japan,* 2nd edn, Lexington, MA: D.C. Heath.

Ramseyer, J. M. and N. Nakazato (1999), *Japanese Law: An Economic Approach,* Chicago, IL: University of Chicago Press.

Raymo, J. *et al*. (2009) 'Cohabitation and Family Formation in Japan', *Demography*, 46 (4), 785–803.

Reed, S. R. (1981) 'Environmental Politics: Some Reflections Based on the Japanese Case', *Comparative Politics,* April, 235–70.

Reed, S. R. (1986) *Japanese Prefectures and Policymaking,* Pittsburgh, PA: University of Pittsburgh Press.

Reed, S. R., K. M. McElwain and K. Shimizu (eds) (2009) *Political Change in Japan: Electoral Behavior, Party Realignment and the Koizumi*

*Reforms*, Stanford, CA: The Walter H. Shorenstein Asia-Pacific Research Center

Reed, S. R., and K. Shimizu (2009) 'Avoiding a Two-Party System: The Liberal Democratic Party versus Duverger's Law' in S. R. Reed, K. M. McElwain and K. Shimizu, *Political Change in Japan: Electoral Behavior, Party Realignment and the Koizumi Reforms*, Stanford CA: The Walter H. Shorenstein Asia-Pacific Research Center, 29–46.

Reischauer, E. O. (1977) *The Japanese,* Cambridge, MA: Harvard University Press.

*Religion in Japan Today* (1992) Tokyo: Foreign Press Center, Japan.

Rohlen, T. (1983) *Japan's High Schools,* Berkeley, CA: University of California Press.

Rose, C. (1998) *Interpreting History in Sino-Japanese Relations: A Case Study in Political Decision-making,* London: Routledge.

Rosenberger, N. (2001) *Gambling with Virtue: Japanese Women and the Search for Self in a Changing Nation,* Honolulu: University of Hawaii Press.

Rosenbluth, F. M. and M. F. Thies (2010) *Japan Transformed: Political Change and Economic Restructuring*, Princeton, NJ: Princeton University Press.

Rothacher, A. (1993) *The Japanese Power Elite,* Basingstoke: Macmillan – now Palgrave Macmillan.

Rowley, A. and L. do Rosario (1991) 'Japan's View of Asia: Empire of the Sun', in N. Holloway (ed.), *Japan in Asia,* Hong Kong: Far Eastern Economic Review, 7–20.

Ruoff, K. J. (1993) 'Mr Tomino goes to City Hall: Grassroots Democracy in Zushi City, Japan', *Bulletin of Concerned Asian Scholars,* 25 (3), July–September, 22–32.

Ryang, S. (1997) *North Koreans in Japan: Language, Ideology and Identity,* Boulder, CO: Westview Press.

Sako, M. (1997) 'Introduction', in M. Sako and H. Sato (eds), *Japanese Labour and Management in Transition: Diversity, Flexibility and Participation,* London: Routledge, 1–24.

Samuels, R. J. (2008) *Securing Japan: Tokyo's Grand Strategy and the Future of East Asia*, Ithaca, NY: Cornell University Press.

Samuels, R. J. (2011) 'Japan After Kan: Implications For The DPJ's Political Future', Interview with Chris Acheson, National Bureau for Asian Research, 19 August, http://www.nbr.org/research/activity.aspx?id=168, accessed 14 February 2012.

Sato, I. (1991) *Kamikaze Biker: Parody and Anomy in Affluent Japan,* Chicago, IL: University of Chicago Press.

Sato, T. (1990) 'Tokugawa Villages and Agriculture', in Chie Nakane and Shinzaburo Oishi (eds), *Tokugawa Japan,* Tokyo: University of Tokyo Press, 37–80.

Scalise, P. (2011) 'Can TEPCO Survive?' in Jeff Kingston (ed.) *Tsunami: Japan's Post-Fukushima Future,* Washington: Foreign Policy, 204–10.

Schaller, M. (1989) *Douglas MacArthur: The Far Eastern General,* New York: Oxford University Press.

Schlesinger, J. M. (1997) *Shadow Shoguns: The Rise of Fall of Japan's Postwar Political Machine,* New York: Simon & Schuster.

Schoppa, L. J. (1991) *Education Reform in Japan: Case of Immobilist Politics,* London: Routledge.

Schwab, K. (2011) 'Is Japan Past Its Creative P*rime?' in McKinsey and Company (eds), Reimagining Japan: The Quest for a Future that Works,* San Francisco, CA: VIZ Media, *121–6.*

Shibusawa, M. (1984) *Japan and the Asian Pacific Region,* London: Croom Helm and Royal Institute of International Affairs.

Shigenori M. (2011) *The Constitution of Japan: A Contextual Analysis*, London: Hart.

Siddle, R. (1996) *Race, Resistance and the Ainu of Japan,* London: Routledge.

Skov, L. (1996) 'Fashion Trends, Japonisme and Postmodernism, or "What is so Japanese about Comme des Garçons?"', *Theory, Culture and Society*, 13:3, 129–51.

Slater, D. H. (2010) 'The Making of Japan's New Working Class: "Freeters" and the Progression From Middle School to the Labor Market', *The Asia-Pacific Journal*, January.

Slove, L. (1996) 'Fashion Trends, Japonisme and Postmodernism' in J. W. Treat (ed.), *Contemporary Japan and Popular Culture,* Richmond: Curzon, 137–68.

Smith, B. (1986) 'Democracy Derailed: Citizens' Movements in Historical Perspective', in G. McCormack and Y. Sugimoto (eds), *Democracy in Contemporary Japan,* New York: M.E. Sharpe, 157–72.

Smith, P. (1997) *Japan: A Reinterpretation,* New York: Random House.

Smith, R. J. (1987) 'Gender Inequality in Contemporary Japan', *Journal of Japanese Studies,* 13 (1), 1–25.

Söderberg, M. (ed.) (1996) *The Business of Japanese Foreign Aid,* London: Routledge.

Son, M. (2011) 'Beyond Nuts and Bolts', in McKinsey & Company (eds), *Reimagining Japan: The Quest for a Future that Works,* San Francisco, CA: VIZ Media, 57–8.

Statistics Bureau, Ministry of Internal Affairs and Communication (2011), http://www.stat.go.jp/english/data/handbook/c11cont.htm, chapter 11, accessed 14 February 2012.

Steiner, K. (1965) *Local Government in Japan,* Stanford, CA: Stanford University Press.

Steinhoff, P. G. (1989) 'Protest and Democracy', in Takeshi Ishida and Ellis S. Krauss (eds), *Democracy in Japan,* Pittsburgh. PA: University of Pittsburgh Press, 171–98.

Stockwin, J. A. A. (1992) 'The Japan Socialist Party: Resurgence After Long Decline', in R. Hrebenar *et al., The Japanese Party System,* Boulder, CO: Westview Press, 81–115.

Stockwin, J. A. A. (1996) 'New Directions in Japanese Politics', in I. Neary (ed.), *Leaders and Leadership in Japan,* Richmond: Japan Library, 265–75.

Stockwin, J.A.A. (2008) *Governing Japan: Divided Politics in a Resurgent Economy*, Oxford: Blackwell.

Sugimoto, Y. (1986) 'The Manipulative Basis of "Consensus" in Contemporary Japan', in G. McCormack and Y. Sugimoto (eds), *Democracy in Contemporary Japan,* New York: M.E. Sharpe, 65–75.

Sugimoto, Y. (1997) *An Introduction to Japanese Society*, Cambridge: Cambridge University Press.

Sugimoto, Y. (2010a) *An Introduction to Japanese Society*, Melbourne: Cambridge University Press.

Sugimoto, Y. (2010b) 'Class and Work in Cultural Capitalism: Japanese Trends' *The Asia-Pacific Journal: Japan Focus 2010*, http://japanfocus.org/-Yoshio-Sugimoto/3419.

Suzuki, K. (1995) 'Women Rebuff the Call for More Babies', *Japan Quarterly,* January–March, 14–20.

Suzuki, T. (2002) 'Koizumi vs Hatoyama', *Japan Echo,* December, 31–6.

Taira, K. (1997) 'Troubled National Identity: The Ryukuans/Okinawans', in M. Weiner (ed.), *Japan's Minorities: The Illusion of Homogeneity,* London: Routledge, 140–77.

Takagi, M. (1991) 'A Living Legacy of Discrimination', *Japan Quarterly,* July–September, 283–90.

Takayama, K. (2008) 'The Politics of International League Tables: PISA in Japan's Achievement Crisis Debate,' *Comparative Education,* 44(4), 387–407.

Takenaka, H. (2002) 'Introducing Junior Ministers and Reforming the Diet in Japan', *Asian Survey,* 42 (6), 928–39.

Tanaka. N. (2000) 'Does the LDP Have a Future', *Japan Echo,* December, 20–5.

Tanaka, Y. (1996) *Hidden Horrors: Japanese War Crimes in World War II,* Boulder, CO: Westview Press.

Taoka. S. (1997) *The Japanese-American Security Treaty without a US Military Presence,* Japan Policy Research Institute, Working Paper no. 31, March.

Taro, Y. (1990) 'The Recruit Scandal: Learning from the Causes of Corruption', *Journal of Japanese Studies,* 93–114.

*The Guardian* (2010) 'Centenarians "Missing" Ahead of Japanese Day Honouring Elderly', 12 August.

Thurston, D. (1973) *Teachers and Politics in Japan,* Princeton, NJ: Princeton University Press.

Thurston, D. R. (1989) 'The Decline of the Japan Teachers Union', *Journal of Contemporary Asia,* 19 (2), 186–205.

Tomita, N. *et al*. (1992) 'The Liberal Democratic Party: The Ruling Party of Japan', in R. Hrebenar *et al., The Japanese Party System,* Boulder, CO: Westview Press, 237–84.

Totani, Y. (2009) *Tokyo War Crimes: the Pursuit of Justice in the Wake of World War II*, Cambridge, MA: Harvard University Asia Center.

Treat, J. W. (ed.) (1996) *Contemporary Japan and Popular Culture,* Richmond: Curzon Press.

Tsunoda, T. (1985) *The Japanese Brain: Uniqueness and Universality,* Tokyo: Taishukan.

Tsutsui, W. M. (2010) *Japanese Popular Culture and Globalization*, Ann Arbor, MI: Association for Asian Studies.

Uesugi, T. (2008) *Journalism hokai* [The collapse of journalism], Tokyo: Gentosha.

Ui, J. (1992) 'Minamata Disease', in Jun Ui (ed.), *Industrial Pollution in Japan,* Tokyo: United Nations University Press.

UNODC (United Nations Office on Drugs and Crime) (2001) 'The Seventh United Nations Survey of Crime Trends and Operations of Criminal Justice Systems' [Online] Available: http://www.unodc.org/pdf/crime/seventh_survey/7sc.pdf, accessed 14 February 2012.

Upham, F. K. (1987) *Law and Social Change in Postwar Japan,* Cambridge, MA: Harvard University Press.

van Wolferen, K. (1989) *The Enigma of Japanese Power,* London: Papermac.

van Wolferen, K. (1993) 'Japan's Non-revolution', *Foreign Affairs,* 72 (4), 54–65.

Vogel, E. F. (1979) *Japan as Number One: Lessons for America,* Cambridge, MA: Harvard University Press.

Wade, R. (1999) 'The Coming Fight Over Capital Flows', *Foreign Policy,* 113,41–54.

Waswo, A. (1996) *Modern Japanese Society, 1868–1994,* Oxford: Oxford University Press.

Watanuki, J. (1991) 'Social Structure and Voting Behavior', in S. C. Flanagan *et al., The Japanese Voter,* New Haven, CT: Yale University Press, 49–83.

Weiner, M. (1997) 'Introduction', in M. Weiner (ed.), *Japan's Minorities: The Illusion of Homogeneity,* London: Routledge, x–xviii.

Westney, D. E. (1996) 'Mass Media as Business Organisations: A U.S.–Japanese Comparison', in S. J. Pharr and E. S. Krauss (eds), *Media and Politics in Japan,* Honolulu: University of Hawaii Press, 47–88.

Whittaker, D. H. (1997) *Small Firms in the Japanese Economy,* Cambridge: Cambridge University Press.

Whittaker, D. H. and Y. Kurosawa (1998) 'Japan's Crisis: Evolution and Implications', *Cambridge Journal of Economics,* 22, 761–71.

Williams, D. (1996) 'Ozawa Ichiro: The Making of a Japanese Kingmaker', in I. Neary (ed.), *Leaders and Leadership in Japan,* Richmond: Japan Library, 276–97.

Woodall, B. (1996) *Japan Under Construction: Corruption, Politics and Public Works,* Berkeley, CA: University of California Press.

World Bank (1993) *The East Asian Miracle: Economic Growth and Public Policy,* New York: Oxford University Press.

Wright, D. (2010) 'Impasse at MCAS Futenma,' *Critical Asian Studies*, 42 (3), 457–68.

Wright, M. (2002) *Japan's Fiscal Crisis,* Oxford: Oxford University Press.

Yamamoto, H. (1993) 'The Lifetime Employment System Unravels', *Japan Quarterly,* October–December, 381–94.

Yayama, T. (1998) 'Who Has Obstructed Reform?', in F. Gibney (ed.), *Unlocking the Bureaucrat's Kingdom: Deregulation and the Japanese Economy,* Washington, DC: Brookings Institution, 91–115.

Yoneyama, S. (1999) *The Japanese High School: Silence and Resistance,* London: Routledge.

Young, L. (1998) *Japan's Total Empire: Manchuria and the Culture of Wartime Imperialism*, Berkeley, CA: University of California Press.

Zielenziger, M. (2006) *Shutting Out the Sun: How Japan Created Its Lost Generation*, New York: Nan. A. Talese.

# Index

**Notes: bold** = extended discussion or term highlighted in text;
B = box, f = figure, n = footnote, t = table, * = illustration.